GOD ON TRIAL

PAUL K. MOSER

GOD ON TRIAL

Testing for the Divine

FORTRESS PRESS
Minneapolis

GOD ON TRIAL
Testing for the Divine

30 29 28 27 26 25 1 2 3 4 5 6 7 8 9

Library of Congress Control Number: 2025933814 (print)

Cover image: Dramatic sky and clouds watercolor painting background, from kampee patisena/Getty Images
Cover design: Ashley Muehlbauer

Print ISBN: 979-8-8898-3185-3
eBook ISBN: 979-8-8898-3186-0

Let us go to trial.

—Isaiah 43:26

CONTENTS

PREFACE

Can people reasonably trust God, in the face of their suffering, grief, and other kinds of loss? Can they, with good reason, consider God to be trustworthy in bringing about what is ultimately good for them? Inquirers about God typically ask, and some even seek for durable answers. This book seeks. God, according to many biblical writers, seeks *self-vindication* regarding divine goodness. As perfectly righteous, God aims to vindicate or exonerate to humans God's ways of relating to them. This book focuses on the God of traditional monotheism as found in mainline versions of Judaism, Christianity, and Islam. This God is characterized as being worthy of worship and morally perfect, free of moral defect. So, the standard for God is high, even perfectionist.

This book distinguishes the authority of God and the authority of scripture. God's character and authority determine what has derived authority in scripture and what does not. So, the Bible is not self-authoritative or self-authenticating. God, in contrast, is self-authoritative and self-authenticating on the basis of God's perfect character, morally and otherwise. Some parts of scripture can earn their keep, as reliable, by reflecting God's perfect character; other parts fail by this divine standard. For instance, scriptural claims that God hates evil people fail by the standard of God's morally perfect character. They also fail by the standard for God set by Jesus in his Sermon on the Mount. As the book explains, God is not limited to scripture for manifesting God's character. God can self-manifest in human experience and can guide cooperative people to learn who God truly is. Much of the history in scripture testifies to this reality. Responsible human discernment is indispensable in this area, and this fits with the uncoercive character of a morally perfect God toward inquiring humans.

Many people consider how God could vindicate or justify wayward humans, but a prior issue is whether God can vindicate *God* as perfectly righteous in relating to humans. If God cannot, humans should not trust God to be perfectly good. In that case, even if people believe that God exists, their alleged God will fail to be uniformly trustworthy for goodness in human life. This deficiency will hinder people from willingly being guided by God. They then will be rightly suspicious of where, or even whether, God will lead them.

This book develops and defends a widely neglected view: Divine self-vindication includes a vital role for human cooperation with God as represented in human moral experience. God thus relies on cooperative humans for divine vindication. In particular, God seeks vital, practical vindication that brings humans into a righteous relationship of life with God in their thoughts, feelings, attitudes, and actions. Their voluntarily sharing in divine moral power presented to them—a presentation I call a *moral theophany*—enables God to vindicate God as righteous in actual human life. It also enables God to build a righteous society on God's vision and schedule, thus reflecting God's righteous character and will. So, the desired vindication is life-forming and society-forming, and not just belief-forming, for cooperative humans.

The divine project of vindication is not just a human self-help program. Divine moral power enables humans to contribute to the desired righteous relationship and society. We thus need to consider divine *cooperative* vindication, involving voluntary human sharing in divine moral power and corresponding values of perfect righteousness. Even so, it is divine self-vindication in that God initiates and guides the process while enabling human freedom in response. God holds both factors together in vindicating God and cooperative humans. The initiator is a moral theophany whereby God self-manifests God's unique moral character to receptive people. A human response to a theophany stems from a person's voluntary, free agency without divine manipulation or coercion.

Human fear of being misguided by God obstructs a good, trustworthy response to God and divine moral powers. The opening story of the book of Genesis indicates a devastating effect of fear, suspicion, and distrust toward God. It also suggests how God puts God on trial for the vindication of divine righteousness to humans, thus inviting human trust in God. God adopts the task of being a rectifier for righteousness, seeking to renew humans in a cooperative and voluntary righteous relationship with God and other humans. The divine aim is to show God to be righteous in and through human life as humans voluntarily become co-rectifiers with God. As perfectly good, God is morally obligated to rectify what can be made right or good in a world created by God. God, then, has a moral duty regarding humans, and they are to share in it cooperatively, enabling it to be life-forming and society-forming for them. This book does not develop a theology of society or community, but it lays the foundations for doing so.

Can God self-vindicate in a way that attracts and guides humans in a righteous manner without coercing their wills? Although seldom asked, this question lurks behind any robust theology and theological ethics. This book faces this question directly and defends an answer on the basis of relevant evidence available to humans. It contends that God self-manifests and self-vindicates in a way that challenges people to coordinate and cooperate with God in welcoming, sharing in, and practicing divine righteousness. The challenge allows people to be genuine moral agents with voluntary actions.

God self-vindicates through self-manifestation in perfect goodness in theophany and in a cooperative human response to divine renewal in moral character formation. God thus rectifies for righteousness by renewing cooperative humans in righteous relating to God and others as they share in manifested divine moral power and corresponding values. God thus initiates the needed renewal, and humans are to choose cooperation.

The divine effort toward human cooperation includes a divine self-manifesting interruption in human awareness and a divine voucher in the renewal of humans toward divine righteousness. This challenging effort works through self-presented but uncoercive character traits of God in what the apostle Paul calls "the fruit of the Spirit": love, joy, peace, patience, kindness, generosity, faithfulness, gentleness, and self-control. We can add divine forgiveness to the list as part of love in intended divine-human reconciliation, and we can think of the fruit as constitutive of divine righteousness in general.

The presented fruit amounts to a moral theophany, as it manifests God's self-revealing value traits, showing who God truly is. Although closely associated with what Paul calls "Christ formed in you," this fruit has been widely neglected in accounts of divine self-evidence and self-vindication. Even so, it points those accounts to an experienced reality in the lives of many humans. This reality is God self-disclosed to humans.

The book identifies the unsurpassed value of the fruit of the Spirit in illuminating divine evidence and divine vindication. It also highlights the importance of voluntary human sharing in the perfect divine righteousness found in the fruit of God's intervening Spirit. Knowing God and cooperating with God include human value-coordinating with God. Our failure to value-coordinate with God leaves us out of interpersonal harmony with God and blocks our recognition of the divine vindication and evidence on offer in our lives. Humans thus have the power to blunt God's intended self-evidence and moral influence, including moral power, toward them.

We can and should put God on trial, but we must ask what standpoint is informing our assessment of God in the trial. If our standpoint is at odds with divine perfect righteousness, distortion will arise. Where we start thus can doom our inquiry. This book offers a trustworthy, God's-eye standpoint in the shared righteousness characteristic of God. It also explains how this standpoint favors re-creative prayer that remakes people to receive exceptional goodness by a gift of grace in resurrection life.

The book's chapters cover a range of topics bearing on a trial for God, who rectifies in righteousness without coercing humans to comply. They present an intentional God, who is far morally better than we are but seeks nonetheless to befriend and improve us while often puzzling us. We can know God and God's moral character without knowing all of the divine purposes at work in our lives, including in suffering and evil. Faith in God is our struggle to cooperate with the divine friendship on offer. Our ongoing question is: To struggle with trust or to abandon with despair? Our response forms our lives. Job knew.

Academic readers often wonder about the main influences on a book from previous writers. I recognize the apostle Paul, P. T. Forsyth, John Oman, H. R. Mackintosh, H. H. Farmer, John Baillie, and Helmut Thielicke. I also have benefited from the comments of various anonymous referees and my students at Loyola University Chicago. In addition, I have benefited from exchanges with many academic colleagues over the years, including Tom Carson, Harry Gensler, Todd Long, Chad Meister, Ben Nasmith, and Tom Wren. I also have received much good advice from J. Michael West, editor-at-large, and Marissa Wold Uhrina, production editor, at Fortress Press. Finally, Doreen Michleski did outstanding work in the copyediting of the book's manuscript. I thank all of them for their good help.

Parts of the book develop ideas from some of my recent essays: "Experiential Dissonance and Divine Hiddenness," *Roczniki Filozofiozne (Annals of Philosophy)* 69 (2021), 29–42; "We Have the Mind of Christ: Religious Epistemology Transformed," *Philosophia Christi* 25 (2023), 261–80; "God Has Something to Prove: Vindication in Biblical Theology," *Theology Today* 80 (2023), 250–60; "Being Commanded by God: Katharsis for Righteousness," *Journal of Philosophical Theological Research* 25 (2023), 1–21; and "From Glory to Glory: Divine Perfection Shared," *Expository Times* 135 (2024), 134–44.

P.K.M.
Chicago, Illinois

INTRODUCTION

God's Self-Vindication in Voluntary Human Renewal

I am again in the pain of childbirth until Christ is formed in you.
—Galatians 4:19

The present world, mixed with remarkable good and horrifying evil, often leaves us without adequate explanation. God would be responsible somehow for a world created by God, at least for allowing its moral or psychological troubles. A perfectly good God, however, would find a way to vindicate or exonerate, as uniformly good, God's involvement with the created world. We may think of God's self-vindication as God's current theodicy for humans, even if we are left with a partial theodicy for now. We also may think of this divine effort as God putting God on trial to show divine goodness on God's terms and times. This goodness shows God to be a rectifier who seeks to make things right and good while eventually perfecting all amenable things in accordance with God's self-manifested perfect character and will.

Talk of "vindicating" God in relation to the world is talk of "justifying" or "exonerating" God to some extent as good or righteous. It prompts the question of *how* God would self-vindicate as blamelessly good, divine involvement with the world. Without our having at least a sketch of an answer, God would be not only deeply puzzling but also morally suspect to us. God, then, is not exempt from moral accountability, and our evidence for God nowhere suggests otherwise. Even so, a major issue concerns how we should expect God to be morally accountable and self-vindicating toward humans. The book uses "moral" to concern righteousness mainly in values, actions, personal characters, and interpersonal relationships.

A widely neglected theme is that God self-vindicates through the divine renewal of humans in righteous moral character formation with their cooperation. This book offers an account of cooperative vindication and vital renewal through voluntary human sharing in the self-manifested fruit of God's Spirit in a moral theophany. It thus contends that cooperative humans have a vital role in God's self-vindication as righteous, owing to their cooperation as a way to receive and manifest life-giving righteousness. They voluntarily decide to become, through their righteousness from God, witnesses to God's goodness and co-rectifiers with God, sharing in the divine task of vindication through righteousness. Such vindication is divine self-vindication because God initiates and guides the effort while safeguarding free human agency in response. It aims to be life-forming and society-forming, and not just belief-forming, for cooperative humans.

Our world, on its surface, does not appear to be the product or the possession of a uniformly good God. It also is an open question whether the world's appearance significantly changes with our looking more carefully. In any case, God would have a moral burden regarding self-vindication in relation to our troubled world, even if a full explanation would be unavailable now for humans. It would be morally negligent of God to offer nothing by way of explanation. Human well-being is at stake and depends on our having some understanding of our general situation in the world. Humans need, in particular, some plausible way to consider God as favorable to the world's moral goodness and opposed to its evil.

Interruption by God with Value

A perfectly good God would be in a better position than humans to decide what kind of self-vindication is appropriate for God. God would be ideally positioned to decide what is most effective for meeting divine aims, particularly the self-avowed divine aim to build a righteous society among humans. Cognitive modesty for humans is fitting here, relative to God's superior perspective.

Perhaps we have our own preferences for how to put God on trial and for divine self-vindication. Such preferences, however, may or may not match what God favors for a suitable trial and for vindication. We can distort our inquiry with a perspective at odds with a standpoint of divine perfect righteousness, thus leaving us with an inquiry about a false god, or at least a misleading vindication. So, there is room for humans to be surprised and even corrected about what God does for self-vindication. We shall identify some features of such surprise and correction and their bearing on God's self-vindication as righteous in human renewal.

As caring toward people, God would seek to interrupt their attention or awareness in order to indicate to them who God is, including what God is like. Otherwise, they would be in the dark about God and perhaps confused too. God could interrupt in many ways, some indirect and others direct, but not all coherent ways would indicate with any specificity who God is. The needed indication of who God is would come by way of God's self-presentation, in a moral theophany, of God's distinctive moral character or personality to humans. Such a presentation would bear on whether God is worthy of worship and thus on whether God is morally perfect and truly divine. A mere show of power would fall short on this front. So, we should consider the prospect of a morally relevant self-presentation by God involving *divine values* that represent who God is.

A self-presentation of God's moral character would include a manifestation of moral features, or values, indicating God's worthiness of worship and moral perfection. Such features include perfect righteousness, love, forgiveness, peace, patience, kindness, faithfulness, gentleness, and joy. The apostle Paul calls such features "the fruit of the Spirit" and he thinks of this Spirit as "the Spirit of God's Son" sent to humans, thus giving the moral character of Jesus a central role in this Spirit and in human conformity to God's moral character (Gal 4:6; cf. Rom 8:9–10, 29). Indeed, the character of Jesus is so central in the divine spirit and its fruit, according to Paul, that he states the relevant divine goal as "Christ formed in you" (Gal 4:19, NRSV updated edition, here and in subsequent biblical translations, unless otherwise noted).

The fruit of the Spirit indicates the reality and goodness of God's Spirit and hence of God. It presents in human experience God's self-revealing value traits that show who God truly is. Its virtuous features thus are not moral norms or virtues as ordinarily characterized. They are God's interpersonal ways of relating directly and actively to humans in a moral theophany, courtesy of God's unique moral character in action toward humans. They thus reveal what God truly cares about in relating to humans, as God tries to make humans fit for, and thus worthy of, a life of perfect righteousness with God.

God could relate to people in various ways on the basis of a variety of divine purposes. Some ways could have merely impersonal causal influence from God, say, with sensations of various sorts for recipients. Other ways could have interpersonal causal influence, say, with a direct representation of God's moral and thus personal character. An important question concerns how inquirers should expect God to relate to them, if at all. Our answer will depend on what we take to be God's purposes in relating to people.

If we assume that God aims merely to stimulate human sensation, we should be prepared for a morally thin manner of divine relating. Suppose, however, that we consider divine relating to seek the interpersonal moral renewal of humans for building a righteous society. In that case, we should expect challenges from some morally robust divine features in our experience. More generally, if God is morally perfect, we should expect God to relate to humans through some morally significant features. Moral indifference would not fit with a God who is worthy of worship and thus morally perfect. Even so, we humans would not be in charge, even as advisers, of how a morally perfect God relates to us as our rectifier in righteousness.

Our world of experience might have lacked the fruit of the Spirit, and the world would be morally inferior for that. We can ask, in any case, what accounts for the emergence of such fruit in our experience. We ourselves, as individuals or groups, evidently do not create that fruit, even if we experience it and share in it at times. The manifestation of the fruit apparently comes to us with an interruption of our awareness, without our creating it or often without our asking for it. It can come to us even if we prefer, at least initially, that it not come to us at all. God does not always look for our permission in the self-disclosure of a moral theophany.

The manifestation of the fruit of the Spirit to humans interrupts their ordinary awareness of some visible features. Such an interruption attracts their attention, perhaps in conscience, and shows a contrast with their tendencies of selfishness, impatience, rudeness, and meanness. It thus manifests a difference between divine righteousness and human unrighteousness, including when a recipient chooses not to cooperate with the righteousness on offer. Even so, the difference can seem to be meager to some humans, especially if they cloud it with inattention or opposition to divine righteousness. Its *seeming* to be meager, however, does not mean that it is meager or that the fruit is meager. The problem of apparent meagerness can arise from the interfering attitudes of intended recipients, that is, from us as inquirers.

The divine self-manifestation of righteous features does not coerce humans as if they were pawns to be forcefully moved by God. Instead, going beyond mere manifestation, it is often coupled with a divine challenging nudge in the experience of some people. This nudge encourages, invites, or calls them freely to consider, to value, and to conform to the righteous features offered. So the divine nudge of such people does not coerce their wills. They thus need to allow God to interrupt and challenge them with divine self-manifestation instead of blocking God from doing so, say, by turning their attention away. We often have the power to ignore prospective input to our awareness, and this bears on our reception of divine input in many cases.

A human response to divine input as a self-manifestation with a challenging nudge can be either cooperative or uncooperative. The latter option will include either neglect or rejection of the divine intervention. A cooperative response, in contrast, will accommodate the features offered by incorporating them, to some extent, in attitude and action. In this regard, cooperation would be practical and not merely intellectual. It thus would figure in the chosen direction of a human life and not just in human thought. It would be, then, life-forming and not just belief-forming. The response from humans sought by a perfectly righteous God would be practical in that way and not simply intellectual. It would move toward the divine renewal of humans in conformity to the righteousness presented and offered. It would aim for people to coordinate with God—intellectually, emotionally, and practically—by their choosing to live in full harmony with the fruit of God's Spirit.

People do not always recognize divine interruption in human experience as divine. They sometimes interpret it as nothing special, perhaps (following Freud) as just a lingering effect of parental influence in childhood. In any case, we need to ask how an interruption in human experience can reasonably be taken to be from God, even if the relevant evidence is fallible and potentially misleading. Some interpersonal evidence for the reality and goodness of God's role is in guided character formation for people that stems from a moral theophany of divine self-manifestation. Such evidence represents who God is with regard to God's unique moral character as worthy of worship and hence morally perfect. It also represents the divine guidance of a human toward righteousness of the kind characteristic of God. We thus shall see the importance of understanding the title "God" in terms of worthiness of worship and moral perfection.

As suggested, neither a divine interruption nor a divine challenge toward righteousness coerces a human will or human recognition toward God. Each allows for divine failure to attract humans, given a voluntary role of humans in an uncooperative response. People therefore can be an obstacle to their realization and recognition of divine moral power and corresponding evidence offered to them. So, character formation of humans resulting from their cooperation with a divine interruption has no guarantee. (We cannot digress to cases of psychological or moral injury in people.) God's intentional challenge can fail as long as it comes to autonomous human agents with an option to ignore or resist. We shall examine the bearing of this consideration on divine trustworthiness and vindication in the moral renewal of humans. This consideration complicates the divine effort to build a righteous society of people conformed to God's self-manifested moral character.

Character Formation by God

Biblical writers from Isaiah to Paul have suggested that a divine interruption can include affliction and even judgment for humans, for their benefit. The book of (second) Isaiah talks of "woe" (not to be confused with evil) created by God in human lives (Isa 45:7), and Paul speaks of God subjecting some things to the frustration of futility (Rom 8:20). In such cases, not to be confused with divine condemnation, God's interruption of human awareness can bring affliction and judgment to people in order to (seek to) rectify their moral character in relation to God. The latter goal of actual rectifying, as we know, is not always reached, given human shortcomings, but it still can be an ongoing divine goal.

Paul suggests a constructive role for some affliction in relation to what "produces character": "We boast in our afflictions, knowing that affliction produces endurance, and endurance produces character, and character produces hope, and hope does not put us to shame, because God's love has been poured into our hearts through the Holy Spirit that has been given to us" (Rom 5:3–5). In this perspective, we can gain some understanding of God's self-vindication among humans through a divine goal of renewing them by their voluntary sharing in God's manifested righteous love. Given the life and death of Jesus, this is suffering, compassionate love (to which chapter 7 returns).

If divine self-vindication emerges through the moral renewal of humans and their lives, it can have guiding motivational value for them. It can guide them to live in a way representative of God, in coordination with the manifested Christlike fruit of God's Spirit. As our moral character is willingly renewed in conformity to God's self-manifested moral character, we can apprehend, appropriate, and reflect its distinctive features captured in the guiding fruit of God's Spirit. We thus can encounter God firsthand, including God's perfectly righteous moral will, in that fruit. We also can allow the fruit to come to salient maturity or fruition as we cooperate with its guiding intention and power for our moral renewal. Our own guided moral character under renewal becomes, in cooperating with the manifested fruit of the Spirit, our motivating evidence for God's reality and goodness. Inquirers about God have widely overlooked this consideration.

As we humans receive and cooperate with divine evidence from the fruit in question, we become like God, owing to our moral character being renewed in conformity to God's character. Our renewed moral character then serves as salient evidence for us of God's reality and goodness. Such evidence is significant for current lives but is also directed toward their future and thus is eschatological. We need to consider whether we humans sincerely allow God to interrupt our experience with divine self-manifestation and guidance, including when the latter go against some of our own priorities and projects. In allowing such manifestation and guidance in our lives, we allow for divine self-vindication in our lives, as God self-presents divine righteousness to us. The divine goal is for humans to coordinate with God in a way that includes cooperation with the divine fruit of righteousness on offer to them.

The challenge of renewal in human character formation by God includes a divine goal of inward, or inner, change in humans. Following the grand promise from Jeremiah and Ezekiel for a new divine covenant, God's people are to allow God to renew them morally from within. The divine promise from Jeremiah is for God's law to be "within" people, "written on their hearts," as a way for them to "know the Lord" (Jer 31:31–34). The corresponding promise from Ezekiel is for God to "put my spirit within you and make you follow my statutes," along with a "new heart" (Ezek 36:26–27). People then "shall know that I am the Lord" (Ezek 36:38; cf. 37:14).

Following Jeremiah and Ezekiel, Paul values the role of inward renewal in relation to God. This renewal includes "delight in the law of God in my inmost self" in order to serve in "the newness of the Spirit [of God]" rather than in "the oldness of the written code" (Rom 7:21, 6; cf. Gal 2:20). Drawing also from the book of (second) Isaiah, Paul portrays God to aim to deliver God's people from godlessness: "Out of Zion will come the Deliverer; he will banish ungodliness from Jacob" (Rom 11:26; cf. Isa 59:20, LXX). As righteous, in Paul's perspective, God seeks such deliverance, or salvation, and it extends to divine renewal to rectify inward ungodliness among humans. The same holds for the perspective of Jesus before him (Mark 7:14–23).

The "written code" of the Mosaic law fails in the inward renewal of humans toward righteousness. It cannot personally challenge, attract, or guide humans to an inward change of heart toward God. The law is not an intentional, goal-directed agent able uncoercively to woo and nudge people toward moral change in relation to God. God thus will be unable to self-vindicate with just the Mosaic law as long as a guided renewal of a human heart is required. Somehow the intentional Spirit of God must be directly involved in changing humans toward what God primarily values. This book explores such involvement and its role in human discernment of God's moral will and in divine self-vindication through human renewal.

James D. G. Dunn has clarified Paul's understanding, in Galatians 5, of the role of God's Spirit in human character formation: "Paul is deliberately posing an alternative understanding of how the people of God should conduct themselves—not by constant reference to laws and statutes, but by constant reference . . . to the Spirit; and not to the Spirit as norm, but to the spirit as a [divine responsive] resource. . . . This means that he is putting considerable weight on what they had experienced—as an experience of acceptance by God (Gal 3:14), of sonship to God (Gal 4:6), of liberty (Gal 5:1, 13), and now of guidance for daily living."[1] In this perspective, God takes the initiative in renewing character formation of humans, and this initiative is part of divine grace toward humans. Such renewing and grace are primarily interpersonal rather than primarily legal.

Divine grace, including mercy, looms large in divine self-vindication. Its unearned gift of renewal in cooperative character formation among humans seeks to overcome their alienation, distrust, and sin toward

God. Aiming for human salvation as lasting divine-human reconciliation, God morally challenges wayward humans, including with judgment of human recalcitrance and complacency toward cooperation with God. So, divine self-vindication includes judgment (not to be confused with condemnation) of humans that manifests divine righteousness favoring their salvation. It stems from a divine aim to rectify wayward humans, including wayward tendencies and actions, through cooperation with God.

Paul brings together themes of unsurpassed importance when he describes the gospel as "the power of God for salvation to every one who has faith, to the Jew first and also to the Greek. For in it the righteousness of God is revealed through faith for faith" (Rom 1:16). He extends this summary with a statement on forthcoming divine "righteous judgment" against human unrighteousness (Rom 2:5), connecting this judgment to divine self-vindication (Rom 3:4). This process of righteous vindication is ongoing and progressive, not yet complete. It rests for its effectiveness toward righteousness on a divine voucher, with a future orientation, from God's Spirit.

Divine Voucher in Hope

Jesus's frequent talk of the kingdom of God has its parallel in Paul's central notion of the righteousness of God. Paul thus remarks that the kingdom of God consists in "righteousness and peace and joy in the Holy Spirit" (Rom 14:17). The righteousness of the kingdom for humans, according to Paul, comes from divine grace as a gift (Rom 5:17), and this grace "reigns through righteousness" (Rom 5:21). We need to clarify how such righteous grace contributes to divine self-vindication in the renewal of human character formation. Part of our problem is that we have difficulty finding a consistent triumph of divine righteousness in the world, including in us. Instead, we find a world, including humans, burdened by extensive unrighteousness, even if there are occurrences of righteousness at times.

Suppose that divine righteous grace includes God's moral character in action toward humans. It thus offers and promotes to humans the active fruit of the Spirit constitutive of that character: love, joy, peace, and so on. A divine goal for humans is their cooperative reconciliation to God's character in its unique fruit (Rom 5:11, 2 Cor 5:18–21), with sincere human resolve. Such reconciliation goes beyond justification as the divine approval of humans to ever-deepening human renewal in cooperation with, and conformity to, God's righteous character.

The desired reconciliation with God takes time for humans. It does not occur in an instant because humans have deep-seated tendencies at odds with God's perfect moral character. So God works over a period of time for the renewal of humans as uncoerced, voluntary "works in progress." The results now, we easily observe, are mixed, but we await a final verdict on the divine effort. We do well not to presume to bring about God's future now.

A process of divine self-vindication among humans who cooperate with God has the following typical steps:

1. a divine interruption, as a moral theophany, in human awareness from self-presented active fruit of the Spirit
2. a divine challenging nudge, in conscience, toward human renewal in conformity to this fruit
3. voluntary human cooperation with the convicting challenge to conform, permitting the divine leading of the fruit to character formation toward itself
4. the fruit as a divine promising voucher, or down payment, of its eventual fulfillment in full realization
5. an eventual divine eschatological fulfillment of the fruit at God's preferred time

The voucher offered is the down payment, or installment, for the future from the intervening reality of God's guiding fruit now in cooperative human lives. It underwrites current human hope in God's ultimate future triumph in righteousness, despite the moral turmoil of the present world.

Paul calls God's voucher for humans "the first fruits of the Spirit" (Rom 8:23), adding that it underwrites "hope that the creation itself will be set free from its enslavement to decay and will obtain the freedom of the glory of the children of God" (Rom 8:20–21). This voucher grounds, with experiential evidence, God's self-vindication to humans, leading Paul to remark: "It is God who justifies. Who is to condemn? In all these things we are more than victorious through him who loved us" (Rom 8:33–34, 37). We may paraphrase: "It is God who vindicates, including self-vindicates. Who can condemn God? God vindicates through divine righteous love." This book develops and defends this perspective, with special attention to the renewal of human character formation in divine self-vindication that includes moral theophany.

Paul has in mind the prospect of a divine theodicy that vindicates God's righteousness to humans. Drawing from Psalm 51, he remarks, "Although every human is a liar, let God be [proved] true, as it is written, 'So that you may be justified in your words and you will prevail when you go to trial [literally, in your being judged]'" (Rom 3:4). His appeal to "let God be true" is clarified by his hope that God will be justified as vindicated in his righteous purpose. Paul adds:, "It is not as though the word of God has failed" (Rom 9:6). He reiterates, "What shall we say then? Is there unrighteousness with God? God forbid" (Rom 9:14, KJV).

In explaining how God vindicates divine righteousness in the renewal of humans, this book incorporates Paul's message that God demonstrates and vindicates divine righteousness in the sending of his Son, Jesus Christ (Rom 3:21–26). Jesus serves as God's vice rectifier for righteousness among humans, in his earthy life, self-giving death, and resurrected life. The divine sending for righteousness also includes the sending of God's Spirit and the Spirit's distinctive fruit, both portrayed by the moral character of Jesus (Gal 4:6,19, 5:24; Phil 1:11). We should join these two modes of divine sending, of the Son and the Spirit, for the vindication of divine righteousness, even though the key role of the active fruit of the Spirit as a moral theophany has been widely neglected in this area.

The divine voucher in the fruit of the Spirit includes the self-presentation of God's moral character now, with full realization of its fruit in the future, at God's appointed time. So cooperative humans have a felt reality of "now (in part) but not yet (fully)" in the realization of righteousness from the Spirit's fruit. The divine goal of full character formation by the fruit of the Spirit accommodates the time needed by humans for such voluntary formation. It recognizes their deep-seated tendencies at odds with divine righteousness in a human life. As a result, we should expect the divine voucher to allow for considerable temporal delay in its fulfillment. No quick fix, in any case, is at hand.

Divine righteousness seeks human renewal in a right interpersonal relationship with God, beyond mere righteous actions by humans. It acknowledges human unrighteousness, in character and action, as an impediment to a fully righteous relationship with God. The divine-human relationship of righteousness thus aims to build human hope in God and God's ultimate triumph in righteousness, with patience now toward this outcome (Rom 8:25). Paul thus remarks, "Through the Spirit, by faith, we wait for the hope of righteousness" (Gal 5:5). God, in this perspective, seeks hopeful waiting among humans for the fulfillment of the divine voucher in the manifested fruit of the Spirit. In such waiting, humans undergo renewal in character formation that enables them to share in and manifest God's righteousness for the sake of building a righteous society under God.

The divine voucher and the corresponding hope make sense only if God highly values human renewal and salvation as lasting reconciliation with God in righteous life together. Various biblical texts talk interchangeably of divine righteousness and divine salvation (see, e.g., Isa 51:4–5; Ps 98:2–3, NIV). In representing divine righteousness (Phil 1:11), the active fruit of the Spirit has a central role in the divine renewal and salvation of humans. This fruit not only manifests God directly to humans but also sets the standard for a positive human response in cooperation and conformity with divine righteousness. Such a response will enable divine righteousness to be fulfilled in humans, as they are renewed and empowered by God's Spirit to live according to the fruit of the Spirit (Rom 8:3–4; 2 Cor 5:21).

The renewal and the resulting vindication in question proceed in a context of struggle and opposition: God's Spirit of righteousness clashes with a human tendency to unrighteousness (the "flesh" [σὰρξ], in Paul's language). Such a context can include human moral distress and dissonance, owing to felt moral disharmony, perhaps in conscience. Paul remarks, "The flesh desires what is contrary to the Spirit, and the Spirit what is contrary to the flesh. They are in conflict with each other, so that you are not to do whatever you want" (Gal 5:17). The Spirit, then, is not yet victorious in the divine renewal of humans in righteousness. The desired renewal is now in part, but not yet fully, realized. This feature of incompleteness fits with the nature of a voucher for the eventual fulfillment of divine righteousness in human lives.

God's self-vindication to humans is not restricted to the past, the present, or the future. It occupies all three temporal domains, given that God is Lord of all three. So it would be a mistake to limit this vindication, for instance, to the historical crucifixion of Jesus as God's unique Son. That past event is a central part of the divine vindication, as Paul states (Rom 3:21–26) but does not exhaust it. Similarly, the future resurrection of the people of God (like the past resurrection of Jesus) does not fully represent God's self-vindication, nor does God's present activity among humans.

Divine vindication depends on God's rectifying for righteousness in the past, the present, and the future among humans. The past includes God's righteous offer of salvation (i.e., redemption as reconciliation) to humans, including through Christ's crucifixion and resurrection. The present includes, for some people, interruption of their awareness with potentially character-forming fruit of God's Spirit experienced now. The future, in contrast, is represented by a voucher in experience from fruit aiming to guide people into a promised future of full righteousness with God. We need to consider the importance of voluntary and intentional human sharing in divine righteousness.

Sharing in Perfect Righteousness

Divine vindication for perfect righteousness has two objects: God and humans. God seeks vindication of God and humans, aiming to have humans cooperate fully in their becoming worthy of divine vindication of them. Such full cooperation requires that humans coordinate with divine righteousness by adjusting and harmonizing themselves toward God's perfect moral character, intellectually, emotionally, and practically, including volitionally. Such cooperation thus includes human value-coordinating with God. In its absence, humans are out of harmony with God and tend to overlook the reality of divine vindication in righteousness. They also then lack a practical means to become worthy of, or fit for, God's vindication.

Having commanded his followers to practice unselfish love toward people, even enemies, Jesus tells them, "Be perfect, therefore, as your heavenly Father is perfect" (Matt 5:48). The author of Matthew's Gospel uses the term *τέλειός* to capture God's moral perfection, with the sense of morally "perfect," "complete," or "fulfilled." Jesus thus commands his followers to coordinate, conform, and cooperate fully with God's morally perfect character and purposes.

Divine moral perfection, when realized in cooperative humans at a future time, will fully image God's moral character and will—intellectually, emotionally, and practically. This goal takes us back to Leviticus, "You shall be holy, for I the Lord your God am holy" (Lev 19:2), and Deuteronomy: "You must remain completely loyal to the Lord your God" (Deut 18:13). We may think of the relevant perfection to include complete loyalty to and cooperation with the God of complete goodness.

Paul, in agreement with Jesus, thinks of God and God's will as "perfect": "Do not be conformed to this age, but be transformed by the renewing of the mind, so that you may discern what is the will of God—what is good and acceptable and perfect [τέλειον]" (Rom 12:2; cf. 1 Cor 13:10). Paul also recognizes that we humans have not been fully conformed to that perfection: "Not that I have already obtained this [the perfection of divine full resurrection] or have already reached the goal, but I press on to lay hold of that for which Christ has laid hold of me. . . . I press on toward the goal, toward the prize of the heavenly [upward] call of God in Christ Jesus" (Phil 3:12, 14). Jesus and Paul acknowledge a standard of divine perfection for humans. It calls for complete human loyalty to God and full conformity to God's moral character and will, on the ground that God bears and represents perfect moral goodness.

Paul offers the following injunction in response to God's goodness: "Since we have these promises [of God being with God's people], beloved, let us cleanse ourselves from every defilement of flesh and of spirit, making holiness perfect [ἐπιτελοῦντεςἁγιωσύνην] in the fear of God" (2 Cor 7:1). Since perfect holiness includes perfect righteousness, in Paul's thought, his charge includes perfecting righteousness in cooperative relation to God. So Paul assumes that human righteousness can be improved by humans in their agreeably moving toward perfect righteousness, with help from God's presence and power in moral theophany among them.

Many people seem either indifferent or opposed to their perfecting righteousness in cooperative relation to a perfectly good God. They seem indifferent or opposed to the God whom Isaiah declares to be "Holy, Holy, Holy" in moral contrast to people of morally "unclean lips" (Isa 6:3, 5). Perhaps human fear of such a morally superior God is often an impediment, grounded in being afraid of judgment from God on moral grounds.

Selfish fear, in contrast with reverential fear, causes some people to prefer to avoid God and even indicators of God's reality and goodness. They prefer not to wait patiently for God to self-reveal to them over time or to self-vindicate on God's schedule. This attitude of impatience neglects not only a fruit of the Spirit, namely patience, but also God's chosen pace of moral renewal. It proceeds with a human expectation of a different pace. A danger thus arises here from assuming authority over God in matters of timing for the moral renewal of all things in righteousness.

Going beyond waiting, human cooperating with divine righteousness requires conforming to it, and this includes coordinating with the presented fruit of the Spirit. Coordinating here requires co-ordering, and thus calibrating and harmonizing, one's life with the divine fruit of righteousness. It is, then, coordinating with God, thereby letting God be Lord of one's life in all matters of righteousness, intellectually, emotionally, and practically.

Failure to coordinate with the presented fruit of righteousness will leave people out of harmony with God's moral character and thus with God. As a result, it can leave people with a failure to recognize God's desired self-vindication in their own experience. If they ignore or oppose the desired value coordination and cooperation with God, they should expect not to recognize the divine vindication working through such coordination and cooperation.

The fruit of God's Spirit sets a standard not only for divine righteousness in general but also for what such righteousness requires in a particular situation we experience. So, our current situation, whatever it appears to be, is an opportunity for cooperation with the fruit of the Spirit. Full cooperation with that fruit yields full harmony with God, including full peace with God. Paul indicates that "since we are justified by faith, we have peace with God through our Lord Jesus Christ" (Rom 5:1). Such justification depends on divine vindication of humans through their cooperative faith in God, given that God is the one who justifies (Rom 8:33) by a divine standard of grace through righteousness (Rom 5:21).

Some human standards, as suggested, distort our assessing God's reality and goodness. For instance, some standards omit a role for divine corrective judgment on human unrighteousness. Paul, like Jesus, assumes that God will judge the world with divine righteousness (Rom 3:6). Here we can benefit by asking why, in terms of our motivating grounds, we settle on our own preferred standards for assessing divine reality and goodness. We face many ways of going wrong in this area. A key issue is whether we and our preferred standards are suitably accommodating toward God's unique moral character. If not, we may be distorting our inquiry about God, hindering its accuracy or reliability.

A danger arises from either of two extremes: denying any role for divine judgment of human unrighteousness and affirming excessive divine condemnation of unrighteous humans. The first extreme would have us not consider judgment in conscience of our unrighteousness as an indicator of God. It would block us from seeing divine presence to us in such judgment. The second extreme would incline us to regard a sense of condemnation in conscience as an indicator of God when its source lies elsewhere. This extreme can contribute to undue fear of and alienation from God. It can obstruct human coordination and cooperation with divine corrective judgment that seeks repentance. An antidote to the two extremes is found in righteous divine love that is creative in its judgment toward renewing people in a cooperative relationship with God.

Our standards for assessing God's reality and goodness need to cover a range of phenomena. The following objects of assessment (and thus objects of standards of assessment) are relevant to this book's inquiry:

1. humans experiencing (or being aware of) God's self-revealing value traits in a moral theophany (i.e., God's fruit of the Spirit; hereafter "value traits")
2. humans ignoring or opposing God's value traits and thereby God
3. humans taking a standpoint for assessing God's value traits and thereby God
4. humans explaining or elucidating God's value traits and thereby God
5. humans valuing (appreciating) God's value traits and thereby God
6. humans coordinating and cooperating with, and thereby intentionally sharing in, God's value traits
7. humans loving God's value traits and thereby God

These objects of potential assessment merit our attention in an effort to understand and assess divine self-vindication. We shall attend to them as our inquiry develops.

Corresponding to God's self-revealing traits, we humans have our own self-revealing value traits. An important question is whether our value traits conform to God's. Are they, and we, God-accommodating regarding the divine character traits presented to us? We humans can "play God" (presume to be God) regarding who decides the suitable kind of evidence and assessment of divine reality, goodness, and vindication.

When we do so, we typically distort the fitting standards for evidence and assessment of God. We thereby can be misled, by our own doing, regarding divine reality, goodness, and vindication.

Perhaps we humans, at least at times, do not want to honor the role of the fruit of the Spirit as divine evidence, on the ground that we do not want that fruit to characterize God. We may not want God to be like that fruit, for instance, in having love for enemies as a divine value. We may prefer to find God elsewhere, in something more convenient for us from a moral point of view. A problem, however, is that our preferring, whatever it actually involves, would not override God's own superior preference. We humans lack the kind of authority needed to override God's moral superiority or authority, and that may be for our benefit.

If we are God-accommodating, we and our settled standards for assessing divine reality and vindication will be God-conformable. That is, we and they will be amenable to honoring and sharing in God's self-revealing value traits, such as those involved in the aforementioned subjects 1–7. We humans thus have a voluntary role in settling whether we ourselves are God-accommodating, if only by seeking divine aid for us to cooperate.

We are not considering just a self-help program because we humans respond to divine moral powers in the values of righteousness manifested by God in our experience. We humans have a moral-power deficit from the standpoint of the powers of divine righteousness. The latter powers, however, are supplied in the manifested fruit of the Spirit on offer, and they invite our cooperation without coercion. We face an option of cooperative vindication by God through our voluntary sharing in moral values of divine righteousness. This sharing ideally includes our thoughts, feelings, attitudes, and actions.

We often exercise our voluntary role through considering whether God is trustworthy for a good or righteous future for us. Our considering this issue can benefit from attending to what God has done through God's people, including Jesus. If God is not trustworthy for a righteous future, at God's preferred time, we should consider God to be a failed redeemer. A key issue for divine vindication is thus whether

God is ultimately self-vindicating rather than a failure in supplying and sustaining righteous life with God for cooperative humans. The correct answer depends on what God has actually done and will do; so, it is important for us to get the latter matters right.

Our suitably apprehending what God has done and will do toward righteous life, according to this book, depends on our moral attitude toward God's moral character and will. Such apprehending needs to join with our valuing God's moral purpose in revealing divine intentions and corresponding evidence of God to humans. If we are indifferent or opposed to God's moral character and will, we will lack due valuing and welcoming of divine righteousness in our experience. We then will neglect a central divine purpose in revealing divine righteousness to us through moral values in our experience. This purpose is to elicit our full cooperation with divine righteousness coming to fruition in our lives, for our moral benefit and relationship with God.

Given our indifference or opposition to God, our evidence of God will lack salience for us. This lack would be part of God's purpose in self-manifestation and self-hiding because this purpose seeks to attract cooperative reception by humans. We then will not be hospitable to the relevant moral powers in the values on offer from God. As a result, we will not suitably experience firsthand a divine vindication at work in our moral experience and life, even if our experience includes some initial glimmers of divine values. Initial glimmers do not supply a stable indication of God, even though they can lead to salient evidence, with our cooperation. A suitable firsthand awareness of divine values at work includes a direct awareness of their coming to maturity or fruition in relatively stable moral powers for us as we voluntarily share in them. Omitting this voluntary sharing will omit our suitably apprehending their coming to such maturity in our lives. It thus will omit our firsthand experience of their effective divine power for our experiencing moral renewal.

The intended divine vindication, as suggested, includes God's bringing life-giving righteousness to us through our voluntary sharing in manifested divine values as evidence of God. God has no need to be promiscuous with this moral self-evidence, as God would seek not to trivialize its vital significance for humans. God would uphold the unsurpassed value of God and divine values for the sake of all concerned, even when humans fail to do so. To that end, God would seek voluntary human sharing in those values for the benefit of humans relating to God, in thoughts, feelings, attitudes, and actions.

A rough analogy to divine vindication appeals to character witnesses in a court of law. Such witnesses can testify, on the basis of influence on their words and actions, to the moral integrity of someone charged with wrongdoing. They thus can contribute to the vindication of the person charged. The good influence of the latter person on the character witnesses enables them to represent and commend the person in question. The supporting testimony of the witnesses therefore can persuade, at least in principle, some other people to consider the goodness of the person charged. God could use character witnesses in a similar manner for an expanding contribution to divine vindication among humans.

Human shortcomings toward cooperation with divine self-evidence and self-vindication come in various forms. One common factor is human fear or at least suspicion that God will fail to benefit humans and will even bring harm to them. This fear sometimes stems from the divine delay in banishing human evil and extreme suffering. Another familiar factor is doubt about a genuine option of humans cooperating with an invisible God, given an apparent absence of tangible measures of cooperation. These two shortcomings are widespread, but an important consideration tempers their threat, as this book will argue.

The tempering factor is that many people actually experience the divine values in question. They are morally challenged by those values to become morally better, even if they do not cooperate. As we cooperate with the value traits in God's self-manifested fruit and conform to God's moral character, we gain salient evidence of God in our moral experience. We then become like God in moral character, to some extent, through our sharing in divine values. We thereby learn not only to tolerate but also to appreciate and value God, as we value what God values.

We then begin to love as God loves, including what God loves. This can be something strikingly new in human life.

Co-valuing with God redirects cooperative human lives to moral flourishing in life with God as a righteous guide. How we humans respond to experienced moral values from God, then, matters for a good life for us. It also bears on our recognition of the reality of divine vindication through human sharing in divine values. We are thus voluntary agents and not coerced pawns in the divine moral renewal among humans.

God seeks to remove misplaced human fear, doubt, and suspicion by building human trust in God through our sharing in divine values. As we allow these values to come to fruition, we see divine power at work in us and for us. We then can reasonably begin to let go of misplaced fear, doubt, and suspicion toward God. We can come to experience divine moral power and recognize God through our sharing in divine values.

The relevant divine values are not mere talk or belief but instead are an expression of divine moral power on our behalf. In welcoming this power cooperatively, we allow it to become salient as morally renewing for us, in our own lives, thereby accommodating God's plan for voluntary righteous lives among humans. Divine vindication emerges from such voluntary moral renewal in response to a moral theophany of divine self-manifestation in values to humans.

We should ask why God favors cooperative self-vindication with humans rather than an "easier" way. We might think that God alone could offer exclusive self-vindication to humans without their cooperation. This option seems to avoid the considerable delays and other complications arising from human resistance or indifference to cooperating with divine righteousness. A problem with this option, however, is that God aims to bring divine self-vindication into the center of human lives. At this center, humans become self-identified with the divine values of righteousness that characterize who God truly is. God does not settle for the periphery of a human life.

Divine self-vindication in righteousness is not a mere theoretical or explanatory reality for humans. It goes deeper to their voluntarily renewed moral character as intentional moral agents, that is, as morally responsible agents. So if divine self-vindication is to involve humans as morally responsible agents, it will rely on their voluntary cooperation. It will nurture such cooperation for the sake of divine self-vindication. An "easier" approach will neglect this morally important opportunity and value.

We now can ask why God wants to connect divine self-vindication with human agency in the morally challenging way indicated. The answer is that God aims to build a morally responsible society of righteous lives among voluntary human agents. God does not settle for just "the true" or "the beautiful," given a divine concern for "the good," including what is morally good, or righteous, in human lives, individually and socially. This book does not develop a theology of a righteous society or community, but it pursues foundations for such a theology. It identifies the kind of divine action and evidence grounding social or communal practices that embody and manifest divine righteousness. Divine righteous love commands that people be socially engaged with such love, and this requires goodness in community. We shall see how God's moral character sets guidelines in this area, particularly with the "fruit" of God's Spirit.

If we ask why God values righteous lives, we approach the rock bottom of God's moral character and will. God is, with divine commitment, a God of perfect righteousness, and this righteousness is central to God's worthiness of worship, that is, to God's being *God*. From the standpoint of God's moral character and will, nothing goes deeper than perfect righteousness, including perfect love. A fundamental explanation of God comes to its suitable foundation here, but we humans still must decide whether—and if so, how—we value divine righteousness and love. This book's chapters identify the main factors in this vital decision. They show that God's self-appointed trial becomes ours, for better or worse. This trial will settle whether we voluntarily share in God's self-vindication and righteous life.

We shall see that divine self-vindication ultimately depends on renewal in divine, full resurrection for humans. God's modus operandi seems clear to this extent: We must go through, and not around, this world's troubles for ultimate relief in the gift of resurrection by God. So, any full theodicy will be by grace in divine resurrection and not in any human explanation of purposes for evil. The divine strategy of resurrection shows where the needed power of life is—in God and divine grace, not in us or our achievements. This strategy often comes as difficult news for us, in the absence of a full explanation, but it includes preliminary resurrection as divine renewal in present human life (see Rom 6:11, 13). Given unexplained suffering, we cannot adequately explain our way into trusting God. Our explaining must be subsidiary to something that can adequately ground our trusting God. God's perfect moral character figures in this ground (as chapter 7 explains).

We shall explore a primary role for moral theophany that favors resurrection life now with God. Such life is anchored in the self-giving cross of Jesus as a demonstration of divine love. Anthony J. Kelly remarks, "The resurrection of the crucified Jesus means that [God's] love is not [ultimately] frustrated. It is not diminished or changed into something else in its lethal encounter with evil. Despite its exposure to rejection, betrayal, condemnation, torture, and death, [God's] love keeps on being love, to the end (John 1:5, 13:1)."[2]

We need to regard divine resurrection and love to extend from Calvary into the present, if they are to figure in divine self-vindication now in cooperative human lives. God's question for us is whether we are willing to represent and cooperate with such divine love in our own lives, given that it is suffering love. As part of divine self-vindication, God aims to show in human lives that such compassionate love, characteristic of God, is stronger than any suffering, death, or evil opposing it. God thus allows the latter three to exist in various forms for this purpose at least. They provide a context for manifesting that God is worthy of human love. (Chapter 7 returns to this topic.)

The good news of divine resurrection calls for humans, in receiving divine love, forgiveness, adoption, and reconciliation, to begin dying into new life now with God. As we taste the divine gift of renewed life, we must die to our old wayward person and life.

We must begin to kill our unrighteous deeds now, with aid from the powerful and active fruit of God's Spirit. This killing is central to dying into renewed life now with God. Divine self-vindication relies on our voluntarily dying in order to live with God now, as we undergo co-dying and co-rising with Jesus. God's Spirit confirms our filial adoption by God as we cry in prayer to God, "Abba, Father," just as Jesus did (Rom 8:13–15). This book develops the vital theme of resurrection life now, accompanied by Gethsemane prayer in response to moral theophany.

Apart from resurrection life for humans, it seems, God now would be a moral failure. Divine resurrection is the only viable avenue to divine reparation for pained humans. It is needed to save divine moral integrity in relation to humans. Without the active power of divine righteous love in resurrection life now, we lack a needed basis for not only hope in God's future goodness but also trust in God's full goodness now. We shall return to this crucial topic in due course.

Chapter Overviews

The book's chapters aim to clarify divine self-vindication through God's self-manifestation in moral theophany to humans. This vindication relies on humans who cooperate with God's self-revealing value traits, that is, the fruit of God's Spirit. The chapters explain how God expects humans to cooperate and empowers them to do so.

Chapter 1, "Vindication Through Revealing and Hiding," clarifies how God aims to attract the attention of humans. The goal is to lead them to cooperative reconciliation with God in righteousness. A central thesis is that God self-manifests in moral theophany with the value traits found in the fruit of the Spirit. These traits show who God truly is, without human distortion. The chapter acknowledges, contrary to a view of revelation as static, that divine self-revealing to cooperative humans at times is accompanied with divine self-hiding from them at other times. One goal is to improve human motives in inquiring about God and relating to God.

An important lesson is that human attitudes uncooperative with divine righteousness can cloud available evidence of God's reality, goodness, and vindication. A result can be distortion in human inquiry about God. So, human moral attitudes bear on whether people suitably receive evidence from God. The evidence can be available but not suitably received owing to people being at odds with it in their moral attitudes. As a result, people can interfere with a divine purpose of the evidence in how it is to emerge and develop toward righteousness in reconciliation with God.

Chapter 2, "Vindication from a God's-Eye Standpoint," asks what perspective we should adopt in assessing God's self-vindication in righteousness. We could formulate our own perspective with special concern for our own aims or interests. Such a perspective, however, could mislead us about how and why God seeks to self-vindicate among us. An important issue is whether we have an available alternative to our own potentially distorting perspective for assessing God. A live option, widely neglected among inquirers, is that God provides the needed perspective to receptive humans.

Many biblical writers, as the chapter documents, report that God provides a perspective for humans, given their otherwise inadequate access to God. They claim that God comes to humans with a divine standpoint offered as a gift to them, without their earning it. In particular, the intervening Spirit of God (God in action) offers to humans a perspective shared by God, a God's-eye standpoint. According to the chapter, the fruit of the Spirit on offer provides the need perspective for assessing God's reality and goodness. By sharing in this fruit, humans share in God's standpoint for assessing the world and its activities, including human activities. They also gain a standpoint for assessing God in terms of divine love, joy, peace, patience, and so on. Wielding such value traits, we co-value with God in a way that lets God's true character intervene in our otherwise troubled lives and even vindicate God.

Chapter 3, "Vindication Through Interpersonal Showing," elucidates the divine plan to attract humans to be co-vindicators and co-rectifiers with God toward righteousness. They conform to the plan as they cooperatively receive and share in God's self-revealing value traits in the fruit of the Spirit. The chapter portrays God as the ultimate moral-character-builder who aims to cultivate the divine fruit of the Spirit within and among cooperative humans. A serious problem arises from human distrust and alienation in relation to God. They hinder the divine goal of having humans become worthy of receiving God's Spirit and its fruit.

Paul puts the divine goal as "Christ formed in you" (Gal 4:19), where he understands this to include the fruit of the Spirit as the moral character of Christ being formed in you. God has something to show to humans: divine righteousness that vindicates God's faithful righteousness toward them. To this end, God offers reconciliation in Christ (Rom 5:10–11) as a gift of grace. In addition, God aims to attract humans as co-rectifiers who receive and bear divine righteousness through the obedience of faith in God. The chapter explains how the fruit of the Spirit figures in a renewed life in righteousness, joined with dying to a wayward will.

Chapter 4, "Vindication with Moral Direction," examines the role of divine commands in divine self-vindication among humans. Such commands, in Paul's perspective, have the goal of humans being "conformed to the image of God's son" (Rom 8:29). This goal does not assume moralism that depends only on human moral power. Instead, it looks to divine power to be received by humans as they obey God's will. This power is courtesy of the Spirit of God, who is active in human experience with the fruit of the Spirit.

God uses commands to overcome human alienation from God, but humans can frustrate the effort. Their voluntary response can be uncooperative with God. Even so, God's commands are genuine and well-intended. As a context for divine commands, God's manifested fruit of the Spirit aims to guide people in reconciliation with God. The reality and goodness of divine commands offer a moral gift and a moral challenge for people cooperative with God. They also offer interpersonal evidence of God's righteous reality for the same people. As a result, divine commands can contribute to the self-vindication of God in the lives of cooperative humans.

Chapter 5, "Vindication for Righteous Splendor," considers the role of divine glory in God's self-vindication in righteousness. Such glory is irreducible to righteousness but includes it. Divine glory is perfectly righteous glory and thus is morally perfect splendor. God's self-vindication shares divine glory with cooperative humans for their benefit in relation to God. The shared splendor serves to attract cooperative humans to God and deepen interpersonal relationships between God and humans.

The chapter reconciles its claim of shared divine glory with a biblical claim that God does not share divine glory with humans. Its reconciliation assumes a biblical conception of divine glory as inexhaustible perfect goodness. Divine glory could be shared either with human controlling ownership over it or without such ownership. The sharing in question, according to the chapter, does not supply controlling human ownership, but it still seeks voluntary human cooperation with God in sharing divine glory. Divine perfect goodness, as a result, inhabits a context of moral imperfection among humans. This context, according to the chapter, does not preclude divine glory among humans. Instead, it can highlight the vital importance of sharing in God's "gospel of the glory of Christ" (2 Cor 4:4) and "boasting in our hope of sharing the glory of God" (Rom 5:2).

Chapter 6, "Frustrating Divine Vindication," acknowledges that some people report having an experience of God, including rapport with God, whereas others disavow any such experience or rapport. It considers what figures in bringing about this difference, which includes an obstacle for divine self-vindication among humans. The causes of the difference, in any case, vary and resist a simple explanation. God, according to Jesus and Paul, allows humans to block or obscure divine self-manifestation and, thus, divine evidence in their experience. As a result, God does not coerce or otherwise force people to apprehend a moral theophany or divine self-vindication.

Humans have a certain amount of control, courtesy of God, over the extent of their evidence of God's reality and goodness. The chapter elucidates the purpose of this control granted to humans. Ideally, we would exercise our control to let God be God, and this would let God's Spirit be God's Spirit active in our moral and spiritual lives. God aims for humans to allow God to bring divine intervention to maturity, through the fruit of the Spirit, in their character formation. This consideration enables us to explain, given the resistance by some humans, some variability in evidence of God's reality and goodness among humans. It also accounts for some variation in opportunities for divine self-vindication among humans.

Chapter 7, "Higher Ways in Vindication: Beyond Divine Neglect," considers that God's putting God on trial before humans leads to a familiar charge of neglect. The charge is that God is guilty of neglecting many humans in not rescuing them from extreme suffering and evil, at least without undue delay. The chapter asks how this charge bears on God's moral character. It finds a lack of care or concern for good in typical cases of neglect, but it raises doubt that God has been shown to be guilty of neglect by this standard.

The chapter suggests that many people alleging divine neglect have failed to consider a distinction between character-knowing and occurrence-knowing regarding God and the purposes for human suffering and evil. It contends that God will not be shown to be guilty of neglect, as long as we know God's righteous moral character without our knowing all of the divine purposes for allowing the occurrence of suffering and evil. Character-knowing of God yields knowledge of God's goodness in a way that allows for our being unable to explain why God allows various occurrences of suffering and evil. Given our limitations on knowledge of divine purposes, we should expect our occurrence-knowing regarding God to have significant gaps but not in a way that precludes our having character-knowing of God. This consideration bears on how we should approach God on trial, with due attention to the difference between character-knowing and occurrence-knowing.

Chapter 8, "Concluding Postscript: Vindication Through Divine Cooperative Prayer," assesses the role of prayer in divine self-vindication.

It introduces divine cooperative prayer as including the co-praying of both God and humans, with God as initiator and guide. Such prayer has a divine pathos in God's giving an uncoercive volitional nudge toward righteousness to a human will. This pathos enables prayer to be motivational, courtesy of divine power, toward the renewal of humans in righteousness. With human cooperation, such renewal is re-creative of people in their receiving divine goodness beyond the human domain.

The chapter portrays divine cooperative prayer to be based in divine grace rather than human earning. As a result, there is no room for human self-credit in such prayer. The chapter also finds divine resurrection power to come to humans in divine cooperative prayer. This power works with divine giving of the fruit of the Spirit to empower voluntary human character transformation in righteous renewal. It brings to humans the same kind of divine power that motivated Jesus in his ministry and underwrote his resurrection. Such power includes divine righteous love that can overcome evil, suffering, and death with God's guidance. In such overcoming, God is self-vindicated as righteous among humans. The timing is God's, and not ours, but this is no deficiency. God's delay is for the sake of mercy, allowing due time for many humans to join in resurrection life when presented to them. Patience is thus an important fruit of the Spirit, in service of divine mercy for all concerned.

CHAPTER ONE

Vindication Through Revealing and Hiding

I thank you, Father, Lord of heaven and earth, because you have hidden these things from the wise and the intelligent and have revealed them to infants.

—Luke 10:21

OUR EXPECTATIONS FOR human experience of God and for divine self-vindication can obscure the reality and goodness of such experience and vindication for us. They can lead us to look in the wrong places for God's experienced presence and vindication, and they can lead us not to look at all. This chapter counters the threat of misleading expectations regarding God while acknowledging a role for not only divine self-manifesting in theophany but also divine hiding from humans on occasion.

Given God's perfect moral character, according to the chapter, we should expect typical human experience of God to have *moral dissonance*, that is, experiential conflict in our moral life. We shall identify the evidential or cognitive importance of how humans respond to such dissonance. Our failing to respond cooperatively with God can result either in our obscuring direct evidence of divine reality from a theophany or in God's hiding divine self-manifestation for redemptive purposes aimed at improving our response.

God and Interpretive Norms

Talk of God tends to be easy for humans. Historically, we have used the term *god* for a wide range of beings, covering such differing figures as Apollo, Baal, Brahma, Krishna, Marduk, Osiris, Vishnu, Yahweh, and Zeus. The list is much longer than this sample, of course, but the point is clear: People have meant very different things with the term *god*, with incompatibility at various points. Human talk of God yields an abundance of supposed gods, but they cannot all be God if consistency of character matters. For instance, some gods call for child sacrifice and genocide by humans, whereas other gods deplore such evils. This kind of conflict prompts a simple question: What would it take *to be God* rather than to be just an alleged god? As expected, the answer is complicated.

According to an important strand within the monotheism of Judaism, Christianity, and Islam, the term (or at least the notion of) *God* is a perfectionist title: It requires worthiness of worship and hence perfect moral goodness of any titleholder. Being or doing evil thus excludes an agent from being God. The perfectionist title sets the standard as high as possible for being God and is a helpful place to start. We can lower the standard later if problems emerge for the maximally exalted title. For now, we start at the top, inquiring about a morally perfect God.

Worthiness of worship entails worthiness of full commitment from humans, even if they have various difficulties with full commitment to God. The required full commitment demands full love, trust, and obedience toward God, come what may. God's moral character thus results in God's being morally demanding toward humans in this regard. Being perfectly good entails being perfectly loving toward humans, and being perfectly loving entails being perfectly caring toward humans regarding what is best for them, all things considered. God's character thus sets high expectations for humans.

God seeks to be *redemptive* toward wayward humans by attracting and leading them to (ever-deepening) reconciliation with God. Such reconciliation calls for God's self-presenting divine goodness in a theophany to humans and for humans' responding by agreeably cooperating with God above all else. We need to consider how this kind of interpersonal reconciliation figures in human experience of God and in divine hiddenness. We also need to consider a viable standard for an assessment of competing positions on divine reality and goodness.

We humans face countless decisions about what to believe, typically in settings of conflicting claims, inside and outside theology. The various claims complicate our decisions as we try to test or assess them for truth and relative credibility. We thus look for a basis to help us separate the good, well-grounded claims from the bad, groundless claims presented to us. Our concern now fits with the following advice from Paul: "Do not despise prophecies, but test everything; hold fast to what is good" (1 Thess 5:20–21). Testing everything includes testing claims regarding God and divine purposes.

Sometimes we consider a basis for testing or assessing in a general claim, such as "The Bible is the Word of God." We then settle, typically with input from others, on which writings are included in "the Bible" and on whether these writings adequately serve as a norm to separate well-grounded from groundless claims in some areas of theology. A question then arises: What basis have we for supposing that the Bible adequately serves as such a norm? In other words, what supporting evidence, if any, gives it this special status?

An obvious problem is that the Bible itself, as widely acknowledged, offers conflicting statements that do not support a uniform norm for assessing various theological and historical claims. God, for instance, is portrayed both as hating evil people (Ps 5:6, 11:5) and as loving God's enemies (Matt 5:43–48). Such a norm will yield contradictory results and therefore will fail to serve as a trustworthy or reliable standard for assessment regarding God. We thus need an alternative or at least some special story about the Bible.

A general problem is that any set of claims offered as the desired norm must face the issue of what, if anything, grounds those claims with regard to their trustworthiness in supplying truth rather than falsehood. If nothing grounds a proposed set of claims, it will suffer a kind of arbitrariness from the standpoint of supplying truth rather than falsehood. Some sets of claims, such as those that are merely bias or prejudice, clearly will not serve here, and therefore a ground is needed to separate good candidates from nonstarters for the desired norm. This ground cannot be a mere belief, given the potential arbitrariness of mere belief from the standpoint of supplying truth rather than falsehood. So, we shall look elsewhere.

Trustworthy Theophany

Some inquirers propose human faith or trust as not only a standard for the divine justification of humans but also a norm, or hermeneutic, for interpreting scriptures and experience of God. They also attribute such a position to the apostle Paul. Richard B. Hays, for instance, claims that Paul has a "hermeneutic of trust."[1] We shall see, however, that Hays fails to distinguish adequately between a basis in trust for a hermeneutic and a basis in a needed ground for trust itself.

Hays sums up his position on Paul's hermeneutic as follows: "Paul's understanding of *trust* not only characterized his view of atonement but also shapes his hermeneutical theory and practice." Israel, he says, failed to trust the oracles of God (Rom 3:2–3), but he is determined that this error not be repeated in the interpretative practices of the new community of faith that is constituted by the trust of Jesus. "With his mind remade by the gospel, Paul goes back to Scripture and reads it anew through a hermeneutic of trust."[2] Hays proposes, then, that trust in God and Jesus figures centrally in Paul's hermeneutic for scripture as well as his understanding of atonement. We need to clarify this proposal in our consideration of how God self-manifests for divine vindication among humans.

Hays offers some features characteristic of Paul's hermeneutic of trust, two of which are germane to our discerning God's self-manifestation. First, "to read Scripture rightly we must *trust the God who speaks through Scripture*" (italics his).[3] Apart from how God might speak "through Scripture," this claim calls for some explanation of which (parts of) scripture God actually speaks through and the ground for the explanation offered. An interpreter of scripture might balk, for instance, at the claim that God speaks through parts of scripture that call for genocide, slavery, or torture. The Joshua saga of extreme violence in Canaan serves as a potential obstacle to an unqualified appeal to "scripture" as God's voice, given divine goodness.

Interpreters should face the larger issue of the boundaries of a canon (or normative collection) of scripture. For instance, should we include the Apocrypha, and should we favor the Hebrew Bible over the Septuagint? An appeal to "scripture" should face such complex matters, sooner rather than later. It should clarify, in addition, whether and, if so, how "God speaking" can provide an independent standard for what qualifies as "scripture." The latter issue calls for a norm for "God speaking" in contrast to its being merely apparent that we have God speaking.

Second, according to Hays, "Reading [Scripture] receptively and trustingly does not mean accepting everything in the text at face value. . . . Cases may arise in which we must acknowledge internal tensions within Scripture that require us to choose guidance from one biblical witness and to reject another."[4] A pressing issue concerns our norm for making such a choice between conflicting parts of scripture. On what ground, for instance, do we rightly balk at the alleged divine command to commit genocide in the Joshua saga? This question bears on what kind of divine action is included in God's self-vindication in righteousness among humans.

Hays remarks, "If our critical readings lead us away from trusting the grace of God in Jesus Christ, then something is amiss."[5] He understands this trust and his hermeneutic of trust in relation to "a hermeneutics of death and resurrection." The latter hermeneutics is "a way of seeing the whole world through the lens of the *kerygma*. Our reliance on God entails a death to common sense, and our trust is validated only by the resurrection."[6] As a result, he proposes that "God's oracles and promises are interpreted anew, in ways no one could have foreseen, in light of the *experience* of grace through the death and resurrection of Jesus, and the *experience* of the conversion of many gentiles."[7] In this manner, the proposed hermeneutic of trust assigned to Paul is "a hermeneutics of death and resurrection," which includes "the ability to discern in Scripture a witness of God's life-giving power."[8]

We now face the question of what the reported "witness" of God's power is. What, in particular, is this "witness" in connection with the actual experience had by inquirers about God, scripture, and divine vindication? A related question concerns how the demanded "trust" is connected with the aforementioned experience of grace through the death and resurrection of Jesus and the experience of gentile conversion. Trust, of course, can be misplaced, and thus it calls for an evidential basis that indicates it to be *trustworthy*. This evidential basis will bear on the trust had by individual inquirers, including contemporary inquirers about God, scripture, and divine vindication. A proposed hermeneutic of trust needs to face such matters with clear answers. Paul has definite answers, but they are typically overlooked or underdeveloped by his interpreters, including Hays.

Paul relies on a divine action mentioned in the book of Isaiah: divine self-manifestation to humans. He portrays God to announce, "I have shown myself [ἐμφανὴς ἐγενόμην] to those who did not ask for me" (Rom 10:20; cf. Isa 65:1). This self-manifestation, according to Paul, shows the center of God's moral character directly to receptive humans: "Hope [in God] does not put us to shame [or disappointment; καταισχύνει], because God's love [ἀγάπη] has been poured into our hearts through the Holy Spirit that has been given to us" (Rom 5:5). Paul makes this claim in the context of remarking about faith (or trust [πίστεως]) in God (Rom 5:1). It concerns not being put to shame or disappointment about such faith or trust with regard to its evidential basis.

Our "not being put to shame" comes from our having an adequate evidential basis for hope and trust in God from God's unique self-manifestation. God's Spirit supplies this basis by directly presenting God's moral character of righteous love to us, indeed pouring it out in our hearts, or moral centers, including our consciences. This moral character is thus living and active and no static abstraction. It impinges on the experience of some humans in a way that gives them divine evidence inviting a response of faith and hope in God. We shall see that some humans voluntarily avoid or reject the vital evidence in question.

The divine character of love heads Paul's list of the Spirit's fruit that shows God's unique living and active moral character to receptive humans: "The fruit of the Spirit is love, joy, peace, patience, kindness, generosity, faithfulness, gentleness, and self-control" (Gal 5:22–23). God's self-identifying manifestation to humans, according to Paul, presents such fruit to indicate to receptive humans the active presence and good character of God. It saves their hope and trust in God from being disappointing or shameful because it serves as the needed basis for trustworthiness, in contrast with arbitrariness. Such hope and trust are trustworthy for righteousness when they are based in the trustworthy theophany given by the self-identifying fruit of God's Spirit. Paul, we shall see, thinks of Jesus as the image of God whose character exhibits and promotes this active fruit.

The direct fruit of God's Spirit manifests divine personality traits that give humans needed contours, boundaries, and constraints for trust in God. This fruit saves such trust from either incongruity with or irrelevance to needed evidence of God in our experience. Trust, in the end, is only as good or trustworthy as its object, and humans need corresponding evidence for such an object. Paul's hermeneutic accommodates this lesson by grounding trust in God in a trustworthy God and this God's theophany of moral constraints of righteousness in human experience. God's being trustworthy, at its center, is God's being a guarantor of righteousness, not only for God but also for cooperative humans. Even when health and wealth are not on trustworthy offer to humans, divine righteousness is, as the divine hallmark available to humans.

Paul remarks that "the love of [from] Christ constraineth [συνέχει] us" (2 Cor 5:14, KJV), and this uncoercive constraining is central to the basis of his hermeneutic and epistemology. Paul takes the moral character presented to humans by the Spirit of God to match the Spirit and moral character of Christ (Rom 8:9–10; Gal 4:6, 19, 5:22–24). He acknowledges a theophany, at times through a Christophany, that is no mere spectacle or sensory disturbance but is morally challenging for humans toward righteousness in relationship with God.

Commenting on the veil worn by Moses after a theophany at Sinai (Exod 34:33–34), Paul remarks, "In Christ it [the veil] is set aside. Indeed, to this very day whenever Moses is read, a veil lies over their minds, but when one turns to the Lord, the veil is removed. Now the Lord is the Spirit, and where the Spirit of the Lord is, there is freedom. And all of us, with unveiled faces, seeing the glory [δόξαν] of the Lord as though reflected in a mirror, are being transformed into the same image from one degree of glory to another, for this comes from the Lord, the Spirit" (2 Cor 3:14–18).[9] Paul connects this theophany to knowledge of God: "It is the God who said, 'Light will shine out of darkness,' who has shone in our hearts to give the light of the knowledge of the glory of God in the face of Christ" (2 Cor 4:6). This is knowledge of God's glory through the manifestation of the (unique moral character of the) risen Christ to receptive humans.

Adequately perceiving and knowing God's glory in Christ, according to Paul, depend on "one's turning to the Lord" (2 Cor 3:16), thus relying on a kind of voluntary human repentance. The perceiving and the knowing, then, do not come to humans as if they are pawns under divine manipulation. The seeing and the knowing include intentional human responses to God's direct intervention with manifested "glory" in their lives. The initial manifestation may be but a glimmer, but in "turning" to it, humans can allow it to gain salience for them.

Divine glory resists easy description, as we should expect, but Paul takes it to include the splendor of God's supreme goodness. He thus identifies, in a question, what prompts some people to "turn to" God in repentance: "Do you despise the riches of [God's] goodness, forbearance, and longsuffering, not knowing that the goodness [χρηστὸν] of God leads you to repentance?" (Rom 2:4, NKJV). Such goodness fits with the kind of theophany reported in Exodus 33–34 and 2 Corinthians 3, manifesting the splendor of God's unique goodness.

The idea of a theophany manifesting God's goodness, including moral goodness, was known to Paul from the book of Exodus. One well-known theophany at Sinai begins, "The Lord will come down upon Mount Sinai in the sight of all the people. . . . Moses would speak and

God would answer him in thunder" (Exod 19:11, 19). The Israelites responded by withdrawing from God and falling into disobedience (Exod 20:18–20). They "acted perversely" by making and worshipping a golden calf instead of obeying the supreme God calling for their worship (Exod 32:7–8).

Enduring the conflict at Sinai, Moses requests of God, "'Show me your glory.' And [the Lord] said, 'I will make all my goodness pass before you and will proclaim before you the name, "The Lord"'" (Exod 33:18–19). The divine reply in the Jewish Bible introduces "goodness" that includes moral features characteristic of God. Such goodness self-manifests God, and not just divine effects, by portraying God's unique moral character. It actively shows God's moral character to humans and is thus a *moral* theophany, even in the absence of extraordinary sensory accompaniments (see also Exod 34:6–8). Saying that a theophany is moral, however, is not to say that it is merely moral; its splendor or glory includes and exceeds perfect moral goodness.

A moral theophany seeks not the coercion of humans but a cooperative human response toward its motivational moral power. It thus seeks to come to fruition, or maturity, and thereby to attract fitting recognition and appreciation by humans. Merely visual theophanies typically fall short of something desirable from a moral point of view, namely, human cooperation with the splendid goodness characteristic of God.

At Sinai, God initially self-manifests and receives a response of sensory astonishment by the Israelites. They are amazed by the sheer power manifested. God's people come to disregard, however, the moral expectations of the divine goodness involved. Humans thus can be astonished by a supremely powerful being without obeying that being. In such a case, they will be at odds with a moral theophany that calls for human honoring of divine goodness. This honoring includes cooperating with the manifested divine goodness as worthy to lead humans in a good life.

The Christophany invoked by Paul in chapter 3 of 2 Corinthians is a moral theophany. It is loaded with righteous content and power from a living and active moral character, courtesy of God's intervening Spirit and the risen Christ. Paul does not digress to the metaphysics of the relation between the Spirit, Christ, and God. Such digressing would not serve his main purpose to motivate his audience to cooperate with God's good-news intervention for divine-human reconciliation. He focuses instead on divine moral influence through self-manifestation that is uncoercive but challenging for wayward human wills. This influence serves what Paul calls his "ministry of righteousness [διακονία τῆς δικαιοσύνης]" (2 Cor 3:9, NASB) and offers what he calls "freedom [ἐλευθερία]" (2 Cor 3:17).

Paul thinks of the relevant freedom as moral freedom to fulfill the divine law with righteous *agapē*. This fits with his remark in a different context: "You were called to freedom [ἐλευθερίᾳ], . . . only do not use your freedom as an opportunity for self-indulgence, but through love become enslaved to one another. For the whole law is summed up in a single commandment, 'You shall love your neighbor as yourself'" (Gal 5:13–14). Given this understanding, Paul's mention of freedom in connection with theophany points to the relevance of vital moral considerations. It thus suggests a moral theophany, which is to culminate in "the freedom of the glory of the children of God" (Rom 8:21).

Paul holds that a Christophany as theophany grounds his good-news message and his status (including his trust) regarding God. Speaking of the "confidence we have toward God through Christ," Paul states, "Not that we are adequate in ourselves *so as* to consider anything as *having come* from ourselves, but our adequacy is from God, who also made us adequate *as* servants of a new covenant" (2 Cor 3:5–6, NASB; cf. 1:21–22, 10:17–18). This is a statement about trustworthiness regarding his message about God, including his interpretation of the Jewish scriptures.

Facing criticism at Corinth, Paul claims that the adequacy of his trustworthiness comes "from God." This provision is grounded in the theophany he describes, the moral Christophany that transforms receptive inquirers with divine glory (2 Cor 3:18). This glory yields "knowledge of the glory of God in the face of Christ," thereby setting needed normative constraints on human trust, belief, and interpretation regarding God. This consideration is widely neglected by interpreters but is central to Paul's hermeneutic and epistemology of God.

Regarding his proposed hermeneutic of trust for Paul, Hays claims that "our trust is validated only by the resurrection."[10] I have argued, instead, that Paul takes the validation to be something more directly interpersonal between God and cooperative humans: a moral theophany toward them. The resurrection, as God's objectively raising Christ can omit the actual experience of contemporary inquirers. The risen Christ is a key figure here, but the main ground for human trust and hope in God, according to Paul, is in God's self-manifesting to humans, including contemporary inquirers, in righteous love in their moral experience (as Rom 5:5 confirms, in keeping with 2 Cor 3–4). Paul invokes the latter ground when he faces questions about the "adequacy" of his message and of his hope and trust in God. Contemporary advocates of Paul's message can, and should, appeal to the same ground, thus going deeper than human trust to the trustworthy God who intervenes with theophany to underwrite trust in God and to save it from evidential disappointment.

Scripture and Experience

Some interpreters favor scripture over experience as a basis for a hermeneutic and an epistemology of God. They claim that experience is too subjective and thus too variable to serve. People have significantly different experiences, and this consideration prompts the view that scripture is needed as a unifying and stabilizing norm for experience. The plausibility of the latter view, however, depends on the kind of experience at issue.

A moral theophany of divine glory is not altogether subjective in human experience where it intervenes. It includes divine self-manifestation with moral power that is irreducible to subjective human factors. This manifestation also can recur in human experience, at God's discretion; it need not occur just once for a person. It also can be shared by people in a way that leads them in a common moral direction.

The common direction, according to Paul, is for people to become Christlike, to become "conformed to the image of God's Son" (Rom 8:29), who is "the image of God" (2 Cor 4:4). This direction is morally robust, owing to its central role for the fruit of God's Spirit as presenting God's unique moral character of perfect righteousness. This fruit can mature in humans as it comes to fruition with human cooperation in divine guidance toward Christlike character formation. Such a process, according to Paul, is human transformation toward God's glory, courtesy of God's guiding Spirit in relation to voluntary humans.

Divine glory from the Spirit's fruit can inform, ground, and motivate human trust in God, but it does not depend for its reality on such trust. Such glory thus can be a needed norm or check on this trust for its trustworthiness toward God. It can also be a needed constraint on a hermeneutic for the interpretation of scripture. In doing so, it can be an indicator of what in scripture is genuinely characteristic of God and what is not. For instance, the priority of loving others, including enemies, can invite interpreters to have doubts about the alleged divine role in the Joshua saga of the genocide of Canaanites, including their children. In this perspective, we need not treat the Jewish Bible, or the New Testament for that matter, as uniformly the word of God. Instead, we should sift its contents for God's role with the norm of the moral theophany, including the fruit of the Spirit, described by Paul.

Paul's hermeneutic enables us to moderate a sharp, unqualified contrast between scripture and experience in all cases. Some parts of scripture represent the kind of moral theophany and fruit of the Spirit Paul finds in normative Christian experience that includes experiences of God. In these cases, we can award scripture a derived normative status, owing to its integrating the needed norm in experience that preserves God's self-presented character worthy of worship. The experience of the moral theophany in such cases is the foundation for a hermeneutic and an epistemology of God, as it includes God in interpersonal action toward humans. Even so, it informs parts of scripture in a way that gives derived authority and reliability to those parts, courtesy of God's direct role. For instance, parts of the book of Exodus are informed by a moral theophany, and they thus demand serious consideration by interpreters (as seen by Paul and the author of John's Gospel, for instance). The Joshua saga stands in sharp contrast here and therefore merits our suspicion regarding God's role.

We should not identify the relevant experience here with physical visual experience, as God is not a physical visual object. In the context of identifying theophany conveying divine glory, Paul remarks, "We look not at what can be seen but at what cannot be seen, for what can be seen is temporary, but what cannot be seen is eternal" (2 Cor 4:18; cf. Rom 8:24–25). This fits with his follow-up comment that "we walk by faith [trust], not by sight" (2 Cor 5:7). Such faith or trust is the human manner of cooperatively receiving the divine goodness in the glory on offer.[11]

Faith or trust in God, as noted, has its needed epistemic and causal ground in a moral theophany. Given the inherently moral character of the theophany in question, it would be a mistake to value a physical visual theophany over a moral one. The fruit of the Spirit is not physically visual, and therefore it calls for a special kind of "looking at" with the "eyes" of faith, that is, with the spiritual heart. An analogy comes from our perceiving humility in a person. We can perceive such a valued feature but not with our physical eyes. Moral theophany, then, calls for human spiritual vision, akin to our perceiving moral reality. When we see someone as humble, for instance, this seeing is irreducible to physical vision; it is likewise for divine realities.

The special vision fits with a divine concern for human inwardness as deep cooperative commitment in response—not to be confused with complete subjectivity. Paul has such inwardness in mind with his remark "A person is not a Jew who is one outwardly, nor is circumcision something external and physical. Rather, a person is a Jew who is one inwardly, and circumcision is a matter of the heart, by the Spirit, not the written code. Such a person receives praise not from humans but from God" (Rom 2:28–29; cf. Phil 3:3). Paul's concern for inwardness agrees with a theme from the book of Jeremiah indicating what God desires for people. Regarding human inward status and knowledge, God announces, "I will give them a heart to know that I am the Lord; and they shall be my people and I will be their God, for they shall return to me with their whole heart" (Jer 24:7; cf. Ezek 11:19–20, 36:26–27).

God desires people to have "a heart to know that I am the Lord," and this heart is to be given to them by God. Paul echoes this theme in his message of a new standpoint of knowing from "new creation" by God (2 Cor 5:16–17). This standpoint is now available in part to humans, according to Paul, and is a gift of God's Spirit seeking human reconciliation with God through moral theophany and human cooperation.[12]

The divine glory of a theophany is the splendor of a divine personal character, including a divine moral character. Its intentional and active bearing on humans concerns their full personal character, including their moral character (cf. Rom 12:1–2). A personal character has inward and outward features: more specifically, outward features that include actions toward other persons and inward features that can motivate such actions. Respect for temporal voluntary factors in the formation of human character calls for allowing needed time for human maturation of character. Humans thus can be works in progress in this area (Phil 3:12–14), courtesy of the patient influence of moral theophany over time. We should not assume a quick fix here.

Probing Moral Theophany

The nature of a theophany as inherently moral stems from what God aims to reveal and accomplish with it. Paul suggests that God wants divine-human reconciliation where "in him [Christ] we might become the righteousness of God" (2 Cor 5:21; cf. Rom 8:4). We do so by our cooperative response of yielding and conforming to the manifested fruit of the Spirit in a theophany of righteousness, such as that in the Christophany of chapters 3–4 of 2 Corinthians. Paul contends of the Spirit involved that "the Spirit is life because of righteousness" (Rom 8:10) and that this Spirit is in service of the aforementioned "ministry of righteousness." Given that righteousness is inherently moral, the same holds for the purposes of the theophany in question.

Theophanies come in degrees of clarity. Some are more transparently revealing of God than others, even though all reveal God to some extent. God self-reveals with varying degrees of clarity, and even hides from humans at times, for redemptive purposes sometimes known only to God. In Paul's understanding, we humans now live in a time of cognitive and revelatory partiality as incompleteness toward God: "For now we see only a reflection, as in a mirror, but then we will see face to face. Now I know only in part; then I will know fully, even as I have been fully known" (1 Cor 13:12). God self-manifests at God's discretion and time, and God guides the level of clarity in a manifestation. We should expect as much, given God's supremacy over humans.

The time of "knowing fully" by humans is set by God, according to Paul, and humans should expect this as part of God's rightful authority. Humans thus will "know fully" divine glory (as they have been known) only at a future time set by God, whose knowledge surpasses current human knowledge. So, human experience and knowledge of divine glory in theophany can be "now here but not yet fully." They thus share a central feature of God's kingdom preached by Jesus: It is now here but not yet fully. This feature arises from patient divine waiting for cooperative human responses to invitations from moral theophany. Humans' full realization of the divine kingdom or glory will be postponed as long as God seeks to include future recipients or current outsiders. God provides the time needed by humans while seeing fit to wait for them to decide freely to cooperate.

If God uses a temporal process to build human hope in God through moral theophany, we should not expect a full theodicy now that reveals all divine purposes in allowing evil. Such hope assumes that humans, in their relative limitations, do not see all of God's ways and means now (Rom 8:24–25). A theophany, however, can occur for humans in the absence of a full theodicy for them. So, familiar problems of evil do not undermine the reality of a moral theophany.[13] In addition, God's using a temporal process does not make God such a process. God is a personal, intentional agent irreducible to a mere process, temporal or otherwise.

Some people hold that our evidence for a theophany is too mixed to justify an endorsement. They thus recommend withholding judgment on the matter. A decision is complicated, however, by an important role for our moral attitude toward the moral character of the God of theophany. To the extent that we value the fruit of God's Spirit, including righteous *agapē*, we value God; to the extent that we do not value it, we do not value God. God does not coerce humans here.

In not cooperatively valuing the divine fruit, we do not let it come to fruition or result in transparency in our lives. We thus fail to honor it aright, given God's purpose for it to come to fruition as we cooperatively value it. In not allowing it to come to fruition, we hinder and miss its unique power of moral transformation, and we easily fail to recognize its distinctive reality and goodness. It may be left as just a glimmer in our experience, owing to our neglect. So, our moral attitude toward God and divine self-manifesting fruit matters here.

A moral theophany and its presented fruit of the Spirit show divine authenticity in their goal-directed probing, or testing, of humans regarding righteousness. This probing is not an abstract idea; it is intentional divine action, if subtle at times, aimed at leading or guiding people to a righteous relationship with God, perhaps through human conscience. Paul thus remarks, "All who are led by the Spirit of God are children of God" (Rom 8:14; cf. Gal 5:18). Being led toward a moral goal of righteousness figures in the best evidence of God's reality and goodness.[14] It indicates that the experience in question is not merely imaginary or simply physical. It is more powerful for motivating and upholding good in human lives than is mere imagination or a wholly physical process.

The process of moral transformation by God's Spirit calls for mutual probing: We are to probe God while God probes us. God first probes us, but we are expected to follow suit in probing, or testing, who God truly is in order agreeably and obediently to relate to God. In any context of life, we can raise and face the question of what divine righteousness expects of us. In doing so, we put ourselves under moral scrutiny before God, for the sake of enhancing our righteousness in relation to God and thereby in relation to other humans. Such moral scrutiny is interpersonal and thus irreducible to a moral law.

Under moral scrutiny, we find a struggle in human life that Paul characterizes as follows: "What the flesh [σὰρξ] desires is opposed to the Spirit, and what the Spirit desires is opposed to the flesh, for these are opposed to each other, to prevent you from doing what you want" (Gal 5:17). Our "flesh" is what has a tendency within us to neglect or oppose divine righteousness and thus God. What God desires, namely righteous relationships, opposes this tendency. As a result, our lives face moral conflict from within, even if we try to ignore or oppose the ongoing conflict.

The moral conflict resulting from moral probing endures in human life and bears on our question of the basis of hermeneutics and epistemology as well as divine vindication. We are not neutral observers from God's standpoint of perfect righteousness. We are people needing moral correction and renewal toward divine righteousness, and we cannot satisfy this need on our own. We need moral power that can attract us away from our unrighteousness, including our selfishness, toward genuine righteousness in interpersonal relationship with God. That power is God's, and it works inwardly and uncoercively for us as we cooperate with it.

God's moral power moves first, before we do, to foster righteousness, but it expects us to respond in kind, in favor of righteousness. This is the modus operandi of the divine kingdom. As Paul remarks, "The kingdom of God is not food and drink but righteousness and peace and joy in the Holy Spirit" (Rom 14:17). Such righteousness, when appropriated by trust in God, gives us a perspective, including the basis of a hermeneutic and an epistemology, to see God at work redemptively in our lives, despite surrounding evils. Without appropriating this perspective, we suffer the distortions from our own unrighteousness for our perception of things divine. Our perspective then obscures God, given its incongruity with God's perspective of perfect righteousness.

Paul's response to our being at odds with God is to urge us to focus cooperatively, and without hostility, on the righteous traits of God's

Spirit. He comments, "Those who live according to the flesh set their minds on the things of the flesh, but those who live according to the Spirit set their minds on the things of the Spirit. To set the mind on the flesh is death, but to set the mind on the Spirit is life and peace. For this reason the mind that is set on the flesh is hostile to God" (Rom 8:5–7). This is not a call to set our minds on our trust or faith or our other own efforts. It is, instead, a call to set our minds on the divine object of our trust or faith.

Paul amplifies his advice in a different context: "Whatever is true, whatever is honorable, whatever is just, whatever is pure, whatever is pleasing, whatever is commendable, if there is any excellence and if there is anything worthy of praise, think about these things" (Phil 4:8). He suggests that this kind of focus figures in God being "with [μεθ']" us (Phil. 4:9). This consideration fits with a role for moral theophany, particularly its offering divine attraction of humans by their attending cooperatively to God's moral splendor given as a gift of grace in human experience.[15]

Paul thinks of the God of moral theophany as not just a revealer but also a moral rescuer for humans. He sums up his shared moral struggle with the following exclamation: "Wretched person that I am! Who will rescue me from this body of death? Thanks be to God through Jesus Christ our Lord!" (Rom 7:24–25).[16] Paul does not expect a full rescue now, but he offers it as a hope through Jesus Christ, the risen Lord. A present moral theophany, then, is not itself the full rescue, but it can point to that rescue through resurrection, partly now and fully in the future (Rom 6:11, 13; 8:11).[17]

The promised full rescue is a delivery by God, at God's appointed time, from our unrighteousness and consequent death. So, the basis of Paul's hermeneutic and epistemology, and of divine vindication in moral theophany, includes a promise of eventual full rescue and thus exceeds cognitive matters. This is fitting for a hermeneutic and an epistemology in service of the good news of God's lasting kingdom for us. It is also fitting for divine self-vindication that gives ultimate authority to a God of perfect righteousness in the present and the future.

Paul's recommended response to theophany via Christophany is: "Put on the Lord Jesus Christ, and make no provision for the flesh, to gratify its desires" (Rom 13:14). We now can recast this: Appropriate for yourself the presented fruit of God's Spirit emerging from the Christophany in your experience and thereby counter any dissonance from the flesh. The glory of such theophany comes with an invitation for renewed life in new creation that is unsurpassed in splendor. This reality indicates that moral theophany now merits our cooperative attention as a basis for not only our trust and hope in God but also our hermeneutic and epistemology of God that illuminate divine self-vindication. Such theophany, joined with human cooperation, can endure in the face of moral dissonance, as we shall see.

Divine Goodness and Dissonance

The God of monotheism, as the perfectionist title "God" requires, is uniquely worthy of worship. So, God's self-presentation of perfect moral goodness in a theophany is unique and thus differs from the mixed moral goodness typical of humans. It indicates *God's* reality and presence, thus differing from lesser manifestations of goodness in human experience, such as the goodness arising just from a typical human.

The divine self-manifestation of perfect goodness in a moral theophany does not come to humans for their entertainment or amusement. Instead, it brings God's perfectly redemptive aim to humans in need: the aim to attract them to divine-human reconciliation as agreeable cooperation with God. So, the self-manifestation arises from an unfulfilled divine goal for humans, even if they are initially unclear about the goal and oppose or neglect it.

A conflict between God's self-manifested moral character or will and a typical human moral character or will includes an internal dissonance or discord in human experience. *The Oxford English Dictionary* offers the following definition of *dissonance*: "want of concord or harmony (between things); disagreement, incongruity." It also offers this as a definition: "an inharmonious sound." Using auditory language, we might think of God's perfect character as yielding "an inharmonious sound" in the experience of wayward humans, stemming from its conflict with "the sound" of a morally inferior human character.

A central part of God's perfect moral character would be the perfect divine *will* regarding humans, that is, God's intentional resolve and plan for them. The divine will, in its moral perfection, is incongruous with a morally wayward human will, and this yields moral dissonance in human experience. We then have a moral conflict between two wills, one perfect and the other imperfect. From a moral point of view, God's will has priority, of course, with no serious moral challenge from an inferior human will.

Suppose that I intend to defraud my next-door neighbor. He has come to me for investing advice, and I have agreed to invest a large sum of his money in an account under my name. My plan is to skim from his investment money for my own gain, even though I have told him that my service is free. In the quiet of the night, however, I am struck with a guilty conscience regarding my plan. My conscience delivers, without coercion, volitional pressure against my intention to defraud. It gives me a sense of an alternative attitude to my neighbor that attracts me and creates dissonance with my initial intention. It presents a moral character and will to me that conflict with my own character and will regarding my neighbor. I am left with dissonance in my moral experience. This experiential dissonance is part of my awareness, in attracting my attention, whatever interpretation or resolution I bring to it in the end.

I have a decision to make regarding my conflicted experience in conscience. I could (1) ignore the dissonance and divert my attention away from it, (2) resist or oppose the volitional pressure to refrain from defrauding my neighbor, or (3) cooperate with the challenge to refrain from the defrauding. Options (1) and (2) would amount to my failing to cooperate with the goodness manifested in my conscience. They are not the same decision, but from the standpoint of my favoring the presented goodness in my experience, they entail my being uncooperative. They amount to my deciding against God and the divine goodness presented in my experience.

The dissonance in my experience is not just cognitive, as a matter of conflicting pieces of knowledge, or even just doxastic, as a matter of conflicting beliefs. It goes deeper, to my experiences that underlie my beliefs or knowledge. So, talk of either doxastic dissonance or cognitive dissonance does not capture the reality of my situation. An adequate phenomenology of my experience must attend to the features of my actual experience, regardless of what I know or believe about my experience. If God's will shows up in my experience, I will do well to consider my experience of it, even if my relevant knowledge or belief lags behind.

In my guilty conscience at night, I confront volitional pressure as part of my felt moral experience. It disturbs my sleep, but it does not force my particular decision in response. It challenges me, in the experienced dissonance, not to defraud my neighbor, but I am left to respond freely. On reflection, I consider the volitional pressure in conscience to be part of God's will toward me. I have been presented with moral goodness that manifests God's character, and it goes against my devious will to defraud my neighbor. God's self-manifested will in my conscience challenges me to care for my neighbor rather than defraud him. It thus aims to frustrate my morally inferior will and character, for the sake of realizing God's better will. Morally, the latter will calls me up short, seeking to attract me to cooperate with it instead of my inferior will.

The presentation of a good will from a morally superior agent in my moral experience, including in conscience, has a distinctive feature. It nudges me toward cooperative conviction in a way best described, given my overall experience, as *seeking to lead* me to cooperate with divine goodness. Its uncoercive nudging comes to me as goal-directed toward righteousness and thus as intentional toward that moral end. So, it does not simply present content to be described by me. Instead, it presents a morally relevant volition that conflicts with my intention to defraud. It also aims to attract me, for the sake of righteousness, to replace my decision to defraud. Its intentional feature of goal-directedness indicates a superior person, as an intentional agent, at work in the dissonance of my moral experience.

Only a personal agent, individually or in a group of agents, would aim to lead me in the case at hand. A mere object or idea would not be intentional in that goal-directed way. In addition, the personal agent in question differs from me, with a better will than mine, and this agent challenges for the sake of good my will. Of course, I can contradict myself, but I am not doing so in the present case. I am causally responsible for the inferior will, at least initially, but not for the morally better will. The better will is not mine; it meets my will with dissonance, seeking to frustrate my lesser will to defraud, for the purpose of my moral improvement.

My basic, foundational evidence for God's reality and presence comes from the divine self-manifestation of God's good character and will in a moral theophany in my conscience. This evidence is experiential; it is not a belief or an argument. It is qualitatively featured in a morally relevant way, even if I disregard it. I meet it in my moral experience, and it goes against some of my familiar selfish or indifferent ways. When this evidence is undefeated, relative to my total evidence, it can contribute to epistemic justification for my belief that God exists and is morally good.

Going beyond my experience itself, I can reason and formulate arguments about my experiential evidence. In particular, I can present my belief that God exists as central to a best available explanation of my overall experience. This belief about God is my best available answer to the following explanation-seeking question: Why am I having my present experience of moral dissonance rather than some other experience or no experience at all? A role for God's moral intervention figures in the best available explanation, given my overall evidence. Even so, my basic evidence of God's reality is experiential and not a belief or an argument.[18]

With perfect redemptive caring, God would seek, at God's preferred time, to frustrate and subject to futility anything contrary to the intended redemption of humans, including wayward human aims. Paul thus remarks, "The creation was subjected to futility, not of its own will but by the will of the one who subjected it, in hope that the creation itself will be set free from its bondage to decay and will obtain the freedom of the glory of the children of God" (Rom 8:20–21). The divine subjection of creation to futility would include the subjecting of an opposing human will to frustration and futility when God deems suitable.

God would use dissonance in moral experience, including in conscience, to challenge human wills in conflict with God's will. The challenge would be directed toward their conformity with God's better, perfectly righteous will. So, the kind of moral dissonance in experience we have noted would have a divine purpose: the rectifying of wayward humans in reconciliation with God. We need to clarify how such dissonance figures in this conciliatory purpose, including in the self-vindication of God in righteousness.

Integration or Disintegration

Dissonance in moral experience yields a conflict within people that threatens their moral integration or unity. It results in moral disintegration, at least for a time. A natural response by the prophet Isaiah to dissonance from God is: "Woe is me! I am lost, for I am a man of unclean lips, and I live among a people of unclean lips; yet my eyes have seen the King, the Lord of hosts!" (Isa 6:5). A similar response comes from the apostle Peter: "Simon Peter . . . fell down at Jesus's knees, saying, 'Go away from me, Lord, for I am a sinful man!'" (Luke 5:8). The pain of the moral dissonance can prompt a desire for escape from its moral challenge.

An escape can come either from (1) ignoring or rejecting the moral challenge from God or (2) agreeably cooperating with it. As long as the challenge persists in my experience, I will suffer a kind of moral disintegration. I will have an unresolved moral conflict in my moral experience and conscience that hinders the unity or integration of my moral life. I then will face moral division within. It will threaten my acting as a consistent moral agent by giving nudges in opposing directions.

I have, as suggested, two main options available for my voluntary decision: On the one hand, I can ignore or reject God's better will and, on the other hand, I can cooperate with it. Either option would remove the dissonance, at least from my awareness. If I ignore or reject God's better will for the sake of my inferior will, I choose the moral low road. I then persist, for instance, in my intention to defraud my neighbor, and my moral life will tend to go from bad to worse. This will be a moral life at odds with God, but I will have silenced my conscience, at least for a time, by ignoring or rejecting God's better will. This is an ongoing risk for moral agents inclined to choose their own ways over God's will. We can suppress the divine attraction through conscience toward righteousness, even when God is directly at work there.

We have a voluntary option not to cooperate with God's moral will and thus not to share in God's moral character as willing participants. Likewise, on the doorstep of a striking cathedral, we can choose not to enter but to view its stained glass windows only from outside. We then will see at most only dark shades on the windows, from their protective coverings, and not the bright colors seen from inside the cathedral. We will miss out on the attractive power of the beautiful windows because we have not put ourselves in a position to behold their attractive power in its fruition.

Our choosing to enter the cathedral can make a big difference for us. It can acquaint us with the uplifting power of the windows' colorful beauty. Entering the cathedral is analogous to sharing in God's moral character by cooperating with God's will. Using moral dissonance, God invites people to enter the cathedral with appreciation of the beauty and depth within. It is then their moral move, as free agents, to accept the invitation or not. Divine coercion of humans is not a live option here because God seeks morally responsible commitment from persons. So people can stay outside in relative color deprivation. In doing so, they can seek to integrate their moral lives without divine involvement. God, however, may have other plans for their lives.

My sharing in God's moral character, with my due cooperation, would bring integration to my moral life around divine goodness. It would put God's will first in my life and take me beyond the dissonance that threatens to leave me with moral disintegration. My cooperation, however, would not need to be perfect; it would be enough that it be *on balance for* directing my life toward God's will. The ideal is perfect cooperation, but this ideal may be realized only in the fullness of time.

For now, my overarching decision is to conform to God's will, accompanied by a struggle to follow through in particular cases. My overarching decision, in addition, leaves me struggling against my initial intention to defraud my neighbor. It contributes, as it happens, to my finally saying no to defrauding my neighbor. God's will is thus realized here in my cooperation. I have shared in God's moral character as a willing participant, and that character differs from my self-made moral character. It has an interpersonal feature that leaves me with profoundly good moral challenges, beyond the challenges from myself or other humans.

Paul thought of a suitable human response to God in terms of people *being led* by God upon, and in keeping with, divine intervention in their experience. He commented, "It is God who is at work in you, enabling you both to will and to work for his good pleasure" (Phil 2:13). This perspective acknowledges the importance of God's enabling, but not coercing, people to will in a certain way.

The divine enabling involves an experience of God's moral character and will of righteous love as evidence that sets a moral standard for a person: "Hope [in God] does not disappoint us, because God's love has been poured into our hearts through the Holy Spirit that has been given to us" (Rom 5:5). This love is a divine self-manifestation of God's moral character and love, and Paul thought of it as not only experienced but also motivating for a cooperative person. He thus remarks, "The love of Christ urges us on," on the assumption that this is *God's* love *from* Christ (2 Cor 5:14). This kind of divine motivating *guidance* for cooperative people figures in his understanding of being a child of God: "All who are led by the Spirit of God are children of God" (Rom 8:14).

Being led by God includes being attracted by God's perfect goodness to cooperate with God's will self-manifested in experience. This kind of "being led" guides a person, without coercion, to conform to God's moral character in reconciliation with God. In being thus led, a human moral character is integrated with divine goodness, thereby bringing considerable unity to one's moral experience and conscience. It also receives salient experiential evidence of God's presence and goodness in a human life while undergoing moral renewal in human cooperation with God. The evidential domain and the moral domain work together in a transformative manner as humans cooperate with God.

Owing to redemptive cooperation, a significant transformation occurs in human moral character, and this bears on evidence of God for cooperative humans. Rufus Jones has remarked, "The monumental evidence of God is, I believe, the fact of spiritual personality through which divine traits of character are revealed. Stars and mountains and ordered processes of nature reveal law and mathematics and beauty, but they reveal and can reveal no traits of character, no qualities of personality, no warmth and intimacy of heart and mind. If we are ever to be convinced that self-giving love is a reality of God's nature, we shall be convinced by seeing this love break through some human organ of [God's] Spirit."[19] This love will "break through" as people cooperate with it. Human personality transformation toward God's character or personality stems from divine leading as people cooperate in their experience with the self-manifestation of God's moral character and will. The fruit of God's Spirit is at the center of this self-manifestation.

Viewed from the inside, with a person's cooperating with God's will, the relevant transformation can give a person firsthand evidence in experience of divine intervention and presence. Viewed from the outside, apart from a person's cooperating with, or sharing in, God's moral character, the evidence will tend to be ambiguous at best for that person, given a lack of firsthand experience of God's moral character and leading. So, we should not expect the relevant evidence to be universally compelling. Its interpersonal volitional nature accounts for the variability in its salience and cogency.

Divine character transformation of a human goes beyond the following of moral rules. It rests on the interpersonal cooperation of a human with God as self-presented in moral experience. Morality thus takes on new depth and power in this interpersonal perspective, courtesy of God's empowering purposive role. The newness will be apprehended by people "inside the cathedral," who join in cooperation with God. They will be like the people who see the bright colors of the stained glass windows from inside. They will have an evidential and moral perspective of divine moral effort unknown to people who choose to remain outside. They will know the morally powerful character and leading of God firsthand, while the people outside will not.

The divine leading is not human self-leading because the moral depth of the leading is not resident in typical humans. This becomes clear, and the plot thickens, once we acknowledge that the divine leading moves in a direction atypical for humans: love of enemies as willing, typically with compassion, what is good for them. Jesus was clear about this demanding direction God takes, in keeping with God's perfect moral character:

> You have heard that it was said, "You shall love your neighbor and hate your enemy." But I say to you, Love your enemies and pray for those who persecute you, so that you may be children of your Father in heaven; for he makes his sun rise on the evil and on the good, and sends rain on the righteous and on the unrighteous. For if you love those who love you, what reward do you have? Do not even the tax collectors do the same? And if you greet only your brothers and sisters, what more are you doing than others? Do not even the Gentiles do the same? Be perfect, therefore, as your heavenly Father is perfect. (Matt 5:43–48; cf. Luke 6:32–36)[20]

According to Jesus, we must allow God's leading to guide us to love our enemies if we are to be children of God. He anchored this demand in God's character of moral perfection and offered no exceptions to the scope of divine love's demand.

Jesus showed his top priority in his naming the supreme command from God: "Hear, O Israel: the Lord our God, the Lord is one; you shall love the Lord your God with all your heart and with all your soul and with all your mind and with all your strength" (Mark 12:29–30; cf. Matt 22:37–38). The love commanded is reflective of God's character and contributes to being a child of God. It goes deeper than mere behavior to the "heart," "soul," and "mind" of a person. It also is dependent love for humans, given its reliance on God's perfect character of unselfish love. Neglect of the love commanded and the resulting human defilement before God have a similar inward source, according to Jesus: "It is what comes out of a person that defiles. For it is from within, from the human heart, that evil intentions come: sexual immorality, theft, murder, adultery, avarice, wickedness, deceit, debauchery, envy, slander, pride, folly. All these evil things come from within, and they defile a person" (Mark 7:20–23). Jesus is thus concerned with matters deeper than mere behavior.

Jesus used the parable of the prodigal son to illustrate God's quest for divine-human reconciliation even with people opposed to God's perfectly loving ways (Luke 15:11–32).[21] He also manifested the love in question with his befriending and eating with social outcasts of questionable moral standing. In addition, he expected the same of his followers (Matt 25:34–45). So sharing in God's moral character, with due cooperation, may be personally integrating with divine goodness, but it is not easy or casual for typical humans. Given wayward human moral tendencies, we should not expect acquaintance or cooperation with a God of perfect goodness to be easy or casual. Instead, we should expect a moral struggle with dissonance for the sake of realizing divine goodness in our lives. We need to consider how divine hiding bears on such a struggle and on divine vindication.

Divine Hiding and Seeking

Talk of divine hiddenness is ambiguous between talk of *God's hiding* something about God, for whatever reason, and talk of *humans doing* something that, intentionally or unintentionally, hides or obscures evidence regarding God. The book of (second) Isaiah suggests the first option: "Truly, you are a God who hides himself, O God of Israel, the

Savior" (Isa 45:15). Likewise from Jesus: "At that time Jesus said, 'I thank you, Father, Lord of heaven and earth, because you have hidden these things from the wise and the intelligent and have revealed them to infants; yes, Father, for such was your gracious will'" (Matt 11:25–26; cf. Luke 10:21).[22] *God* is doing the hiding here, actively, and one result is divine hiddenness regarding evidence of God for some humans at some times. It does not follow, of course, that God hides from all humans at all times.

The second kind of divine hiddenness stems from human obstruction, intentional or unintentional, of God's intended self-manifestation. This alternative assumes that God is not coercive of human wills in divine self-manifestation but allows for human obstruction of it (and thereby of God) for themselves. Since God seeks agreeable and responsible cooperation from humans in their redemption as divine-human reconciliation, divine coercion of humans would defeat the purpose. So, God's gambit for redemption takes the risk of human neglect, opposition, and rejection toward God. The kind of righteous love God seeks fits with that gambit; it allows for human freedom to ignore or reject divine love. Jesus on the cross illustrates this lesson with tragic clarity.

God's occasional hiding would stem from perfect redemptive caring toward humans. It would aim to bring humans to reconciliation with God at an opportune time, perhaps when their resistance is vulnerable. Divine hiding can give relevant humans needed room to experience life without God's presence. It also can help people apprehend life's difficulty and even long-term futility without God present to them. In doing so, it would avoid a divine intervention that further alienates some humans from God.

Some humans would resent God's interfering in their affairs, despite good divine intentions at work. Timing thus matters in divine self-manifestation because humans are not always ready to cooperate with it or even to tolerate it. God, of course, would not want any person to choose final rejection of God and would offer divine self-revelation accordingly. This can include God's postponing self-revelation for a person until that person is more receptive.

Divine self-manifestation to wayward humans typically aims at their cooperative redemption in reconciliation with God. The issue of why God is not more transparent in self-manifestation, including transparent to more people, belongs in this context. If I am not agreeable toward the cooperative redemption on offer, I easily could ignore, reject, or distort the relevant evidence for it, owing to my lacking a perspective of divine righteousness. God then could take the initiative in self-hiding from me until a better, more opportune time for my reconciliation. Alternatively, I could prompt the hiddenness of relevant divine evidence by ignoring or rejecting any initial self-manifestation from God, and God could allow my negative response. Part of God's allowing it would be God's refraining from self-manifestation to me for the time being in order to avoid my deeper alienation.

We now can see how some people could find themselves without definite evidence of God's reality. God could honor, at least for a time, their preference not to have such evidence. God thus could postpone giving such evidence to them, owing to their not being willing to respond in a constructive way. Their lacking the evidence of a God they would neglect is, however, no basis for general agnosticism or atheism. Other people still could have definite undefeated evidence of God's reality and goodness, given their cooperation with the divine intervention in their moral experience.

People opposed to divine intervention could get an initial moral challenge from God, and thus initial tentative evidence, but their opposition, whether through indifference or rejection, could leave them with an absence of definite divine evidence. In this regard, God would allow for human resistance to divine self-manifestation and the definite evidence it can supply. This option fits with God's seeking the agreeable reconciliation rather than the alienation of humans toward God.

Many inquirers have neglected the redemptive aim of divine self-manifestation and its evidence as well as the divine vindication it supplies to humans. They have thought of the evidence of God's reality as being suited to observers indifferent to cooperation with God's will. They thus have tended to ignore human sharing in God's moral character as relevant to the salience of the relevant evidence. In doing so, they have contributed to divine hiddenness, either by obscuring divine evidence themselves or by prompting God to hide relevant evidence until a more opportune redemptive time. In either case, they have excluded themselves from being in a trustworthy position to assess relevant evidence of divine self-manifestation and self-vindication. Their uncritical neglect of their untrustworthy position has made their epistemic situation inadequate to discern God's reality and goodness. Much of the literature on divine hiddenness favoring atheism suffers on this front.

A person resistant to sharing in God's moral character, through unwillingness to cooperate, will tend to be an untrustworthy observer of available evidence of God's reality. Such unwillingness amounts to pushing away, or at least ignoring, the evidence, instead of receiving it for what it is intended to be: a reconciliatory source of human cooperation with God's morally powerful character and will. Pushing the evidence away, without cooperation, will leave people devoid of experiencing God's power as motivating and guiding them toward God's perfect goodness.

Jesus told a story with an important but widely neglected lesson: "If they do not listen to Moses and the prophets, neither will they be convinced even if someone rises from the dead" (Luke 16:31). His point was that observing striking phenomena pertinent to God from outside of cooperation with God's self-presented will blocks people from the cogency of divine intervention. It leaves them without the experienced divine power that moves a person, via intended cooperation with it, to be reasonably convinced of its reality. The result is a kind of divine hiddenness that does not support a general skepticism about divine evidence; it does not count against God's reality or goodness.

Inquirers often fail to find adequate evidence for commitment to a God worthy of worship. This failure often results from their looking in the wrong places. The relevant evidence is not in the nature of causation, the complexities of nature, a concept of God, or some elaborate argument. As long as inquirers neglect the divine challenge and invitation grounded in moral experience, they will miss the focal evidence and its effort to attract people to share in God's moral character and will.

We see the role of a redemptive challenge in the following invitation attributed to Jesus: "I am standing at the door, knocking; if you hear my voice and open the door, I will come in to you and eat with you, and you with me" (Rev 3:20). Note the role of being willing to hear and open the door. This is the equivalent of welcoming God's moral character and will, with willingness to cooperate with this perfect character and will manifested in human experience. Inquirers who neglect this live option for salient evidence of God do not give such evidence a fair hearing. They suffer from a neglect or bias that misses out on the distinctive interpersonal and redemptive nature and intention of the evidence in question.

Some inquirers prefer not to engage the kind of morally challenging evidence from a God worthy of worship. A god of deism seems more convenient, morally at least, and no god at all may be even more convenient, in the short run anyway. In any case, a God worthy of worship is socially unsettling, given human moral tendencies. Jesus thus said, "Do you think that I have come to bring peace to the earth? No, I tell you, but rather division!" (Luke 12:51; cf. Matt. 10:34–37). God's ultimate aim would be peace among people of good will, but without good human will, human clashes with God are inevitable, and they call for human cooperation with God.

God does not sacrifice genuine moral goodness for human convenience or agreement. Instead, God allows divine goodness to prompt divisions among people for the sake of their being attracted to cooperate with this goodness. In the divisions, people can, and perhaps even should, come to see the special value of divine goodness and the ultimate futility of alternatives to it. The evidence of God comes to people in the midst of such divisions and creates moral dissonance for them. Moral conflict and struggle mark the context of that evidence. God, however, intends the dissonance to be redemptive for the moral good of all people involved.

Conclusion

We now face some questions: Are we humans hiding from God and God's redemptive effort, at least at times? Is our manner of supposedly disengaged inquiry about God designed to protect our hiding from God? Do we choose, with our morally casual manner of inquiry, to remain unmoved by God's moral character while nonetheless appointing ourselves as evaluators of God's reality and vindication? Are we open to the prospect that God resides at a level of reality that is morally deeper than our typical level and that this directly bears on the results of our inquiry about God?

Human inquirers about God should face the previous self-reflective questions, for the sake of acquiring truth and avoiding error regarding God and themselves. In facing these questions, with due moral courage and candor, we may find that inquiry about God, if done right, goes deeper into reality than many inquirers assume. We need to pursue, in this connection, the matter of a God's-eye standpoint for human inquiry and divine self-vindication among humans.

CHAPTER TWO

Vindication from a God's-Eye Standpoint

Let the same mind be in you that was in Christ Jesus.

—Philippians 2:5

We have the mind of Christ.

—1 Corinthians 2:16

INQUIRERS DO NOT all share a single standpoint for evaluating God's reality or self-vindication. Some evaluate, for instance, from a standpoint of a supposed purely physical universe, and, as a result, God's reality and self-vindication do not receive approval. Some others evaluate from a standpoint of a supposed world where values are just human constructions or subjective feelings, and, similarly, God's reality and self-vindication do not fare well. In addition, there are many other standpoints for evaluating God's reality and self-vindication, and their results vary widely.

This chapter offers a fair-minded approach to assessing the reality of God and divine vindication. It gives special attention to the prospect of a "God's-eye standpoint" for assessment available to humans. The chapter supports the viability of a God's-eye standpoint for humans in what the apostle Paul calls "the mind of Christ." It contends that this standpoint draws from influential volitional and affective traits of God's personality, including "the fruit of the Spirit." This standpoint also contributes to a trustworthy assessment of divine self-vindication.

God's-Eye Standpoint

A God's-eye standpoint is not "a view from nowhere" because the notion of God differs from a notion of "nowhere." Instead, it is a view from *God's* perspective, even if it is often neglected by humans. If the divine perspective is real, then, it is not "nowhere," and its reality is not just a matter of opinion. Many people in monotheistic traditions, as noted previously, use the term *God* as an exalted title entailing in any titleholder worthiness of worship and thus perfect moral goodness as righteousness. If an actual God's-eye standpoint exists, then God exists. We will identify important but widely neglected evidence for such a standpoint and its bearing on divine vindication.

We will examine whether human discernment of God's reality and vindication in goodness benefits from human participation in a God's-eye standpoint. We would gain nothing by simply begging the question of God's existence or of the existence of a divine standpoint. That approach would be arbitrary from the standpoint of needed supporting evidence. It would ignore a pressing legitimate question: Why should we, if we aim for true belief rather than false belief, assume that God exists or that there actually is an available divine standpoint? Perhaps we should not assume this but instead withhold judgment on the matter.

The issue of relevant evidence for divine reality is controversial and merits careful attention. We can give it such attention by attending to the availability of evidence regarding an actual divine standpoint. We shall do so by considering what a divine standpoint would include, if real. Our assessment will consider the bearing of human volition and affect on receiving pertinent evidence of divine personality traits in moral experience. This topic merits serious consideration from various theistic traditions, in the light of evidence from biblical history and present religious experience.

Religious epistemology often suffers from lack of specificity in a relevant concept of God. It thus can leave us with an unanswered question, "Which god?" We shall correct for this problem by attending to the recurring biblical notion of God as perfectly righteous. The latter notion will illuminate the divine standpoint and its being shared by some humans. It will set important parameters for the kind of evidence we should expect for divine reality and goodness. Without such parameters, religious epistemology will suffer a serious kind of indeterminacy from conceptual vagueness. We shall use relevant biblical material to clarify a pertinent notion of God and an important idea of knowing God, without begging questions about the veracity of the biblical material.

Divine Standpoint in the Jewish Scriptures

A recurring biblical theme and command is that humans are to be "holy" (*qadōsh*) as God is holy: "I am the Lord your God; consecrate yourselves therefore, and be holy, for I am holy. . . . For I am the Lord who brought you up out of the land of Egypt, to be your God; you shall therefore be holy, for I am holy" (Lev 11:44–45). The commands of the Lord express the holiness of God and thus are to be observed (Lev 19:36–37; cf. Lev 20:26, 1 Pet 1:16), even if their formulations progress over time with more rigor and depth. Such holiness based in divine righteousness, we shall see, is at the center of the God's-eye standpoint for apprehending divine reality.[1]

Various biblical writers show concern for the perspectives from which humans view reality and make decisions. For instance, the author of Deuteronomy reports, "Moses summoned all Israel and said to them, "You have seen all that the Lord did before your eyes in the land of Egypt, to Pharaoh and to all his servants and to all his land, the great trials that your eyes saw, the signs, and those great wonders. But to this day the Lord has not given you a mind to understand or eyes to see or ears to hear" (Deut 29:2–4). The writer suggests that God needs to give humans "a mind to understand or eyes to see or ears to hear." This mind will enable them to "understand" the things God does in human experience and history, such as in the exodus of God's people from Egypt. This mind also will amount to God somehow giving people a standpoint for apprehending reality, at least regarding some of God's actions in the world. To benefit our religious epistemology, we need to explore how God can do this and how humans are to respond.

The book of Isaiah names the problem, noted above in Deuteronomy, of human seeing with a deficit in relation to God:

> He [the Lord] said, "Go, and say to this people:
> "Hear and hear, but do not understand;
> see and see, but do not perceive."
> Make the heart of this people fat,
> and their ears heavy,
> and shut their eyes;
> lest they see with their eyes,
> and hear with their ears,
> and understand with their hearts,
> and turn and be healed." (Isa 6:9–10)

Something important to God was missing from the seeing and hearing by the people in Isaiah's audience. So, to "understand with their hearts," in their current condition, would not be an adequate corrective.

Sometimes the moral attitude of human hearts does not enable them to "turn and be healed" in the righteous way desired by God. Something more than mere turning is needed, then, to meet God's expectation for the people to be adequately healed. It would miss God's standard for divine healing if people resisted cooperation with the morally robust, righteous standard for their divine healing. So, God is willing to obscure their perception of reality until they yield, as God desires, to a righteous divine standpoint.[2]

We need to clarify what God seeks among humans in their standpoint for apprehending divine reality and relating to God. Isaiah offers an answer with a divine promise for the future regarding divine righteousness:

> There shall come forth a shoot from the stump of Jesse,
> and a branch shall grow out of his roots.

> And the Spirit of the Lord shall rest upon him,
> the spirit of wisdom and understanding,
> the spirit of counsel and might,
> the spirit of knowledge and the fear of the Lord.
> And his delight shall be in the fear of the Lord.
> He shall not judge by what his eyes see,
> or decide by what his ears hear;
> but with righteousness he shall judge the poor,
> and decide with equity for the meek of the earth; . . .
> Righteousness shall be the girdle of his waist,
> and faithfulness the girdle of his loins. (Isa 11:1–5, RSV)

The divine remedy for human deficits in seeing, hearing, knowing, and understanding, as well as wisdom, counsel, and might, is a divine provision that offers a corrective standpoint for humans, namely, "the Spirit of the Lord." This Spirit, according to divine promise, will come to "rest upon" a person, and a result will be "righteousness" and "faithfulness" in that person. The promise for this person is that they "shall not judge by what his eyes see, or decide by what his ears hear, but with righteousness" from the unique standpoint of God's Spirit. (We shall see that this consideration is central to the apostle Paul's religious epistemology.)

The Spirit of the Lord aims to challenge a human problem of "the heart" that results in a deficit in human discernment of and commitment to the Lord, according to the book of Isaiah (Isa 29:13–14). The Lord sends the Spirit to challenge human wisdom and discernment at odds with divine wisdom and understanding. The divine aim is to take humans to a better standpoint for apprehending and understanding the reality and actions of God in human experience and history. An interpersonal moral conflict results.

According to the book of Isaiah, God promises correction to the people of Israel (Isa 29:22–24). God seeks to correct people who "err in spirit" by bringing them to receive understanding and instruction from God. This intended correction occurs through God's offering them a standpoint for apprehending divine reality and work among them, courtesy of the Spirit of the Lord working in human experience. Even so, the process is complicated by human indifference and resistance.

The book of Isaiah extends the needed work of God's Spirit beyond an appointed individual to the people of God more generally, for the sake of bringing divine righteousness to them:

> [Once] the Spirit is poured upon us from on high, . . .
> Then justice will dwell in the wilderness,
> and righteousness abide in the fruitful field.
> And the effect of righteousness will be peace,
> and the result of righteousness, quietness, and trust forever.
> (Isa 32:15–17, RSV)

The author has in mind righteousness from God and is thinking of human trust in God, both prompted by "the Spirit" of God. The author thus names a crucial role for God's Spirit in bringing people to their needed righteousness and trust in relation to God. Various Jewish prophets shared this perspective.

The book of Isaiah recognizes a role for God's Spirit in attracting a needed human commitment to God. It represents God to say to Israel:

> I will pour water on the thirsty land,
> and streams on the dry ground;
> I will pour my Spirit upon your descendants,
> and my blessing on your offspring.
> They shall spring up like grass amid waters,
> like willows by flowing streams.
> This one will say, "I am the Lord's,"
> another will call himself by the name of Jacob,
> and another will write on his hand, "The Lord's,"
> and surname himself by the name of Israel. (Isa 44:3–5, RSV)

This promise of the Spirit extends into the future, bearing on the "descendants" or "offspring" of Israel. Even if a singular appointed individual arises to represent God's Spirit of righteousness, the people of God are expected to share in the same Spirit, complete with full commitment to God. We thus see the importance of individuals affirming with commitment "I am the Lord's."

The book of Jeremiah indicates what God desires for the people of God regarding their inward status and knowledge: "I will give them a heart to know that I am the Lord; and they shall be my people and I will be their God, for they shall return to me with their whole heart" (Jer 24:7). God desires the people to have "a heart to know that I am the Lord," and this heart is offered to them by God. They are to apprehend the Lord from the standpoint of a heart received from God, thus enabling them to know that the Lord is unique and authoritative. We may think of the "heart" from God to include God's standpoint for apprehending divine reality. It is a unity of intellect, volition (will), and affect involving the whole person, as suggested by the Deuteronomic command to *love* God from the heart (Deut 6:5).[3]

The book of Ezekiel connects God's giving a new heart to humans with giving them a new spirit: "I will give them one heart and put a new spirit within them; I will remove the heart of stone from their flesh and give them a heart of flesh, so that they may follow my statutes and keep my ordinances and obey them. Then they shall be my people, and I will be their God" (Ezek 11:19–20; cf. Ezek 36:26–27). Ezekiel sees the human need, inwardly, for divine aid in obeying God aright and in being the faithful people of God.[4] He agrees with Jeremiah and Isaiah on this hard-won lesson in the history of Israel.

Ezekiel draws a key connection between the sending of God's Spirit to people to be "within you" and their "knowing" that God has acted: "I will put my spirit within you, and you shall live, and I will place you on your own soil; then you shall know that I, the Lord, have spoken and will act, says the Lord" (Ezek 37:14). Ezekiel's idea of God's Spirit thus suggests a divine standpoint shared within people for their knowing, courtesy of this Spirit, that God is acting in their experience as their Lord. This important idea recurs in the epistemology regarding God found in various New Testament writers, particularly Paul and John.

We turn to them for their elucidation of this idea and its role in divine self-vindication among humans.

Divine Standpoint in Paul and John

The apostle Paul gives a central role to the Spirit of God (with special focus on God as active among people) in human apprehension of the reality and goodness of God. He writes to the Corinthian Christians, "No one comprehends what is truly God's except the Spirit of God. Now we have received not the spirit of the world but the Spirit that is from God, so that we may understand the gifts bestowed on us by God. And we speak of these things in words not taught by human wisdom but taught by the Spirit, interpreting spiritual things to those who are spiritual. Those who are unspiritual do not receive the gifts of God's Spirit, for they are foolishness to them, and they are unable to understand them because they are spiritually discerned" (1 Cor 2:11–14).

Paul's claim about "spiritual discernment" finds a basis in God's Spirit for human understanding or knowing the things of God: "We have received not the spirit of the world but the Spirit that is from God, so that we may understand the gifts bestowed on us by God." If what God gives to humans are typically "gifts" from God (1 Cor. 4:7), the role of God's Spirit will be extensive in humans understanding or knowing the things given by God to them. (Chapter 7 returns to this topic.)

Paul suggests an important contrast in knowing things regarding God: "From now on, therefore, we regard no one from a human point of view [literally, *according to flesh*; κατὰ σάρκα]; even though we once knew Christ from a human point of view [κατὰ σάρκα], we no longer know him in that way. So if anyone is in Christ, there is a new creation [καινὴ κτίσις]: everything old has passed away; look, new things have come into being! All this is from God, who reconciled us to himself through Christ and has given us the ministry of reconciliation" (2 Cor 5:16–18). Paul contrasts two kinds of knowing: knowing according to "flesh" and knowing according to "new creation." The NRSV translation "from a human point of view" attempts to capture Paul's notion of knowing "according to flesh," where "flesh" in this context is the human factor susceptible to opposing God. Paul has in mind his previous "knowing" of Christ as a false messiah who failed to represent God. He reports that "we no longer know him in that way."

Paul's improved way of knowing Christ is based not on "flesh" but on "new creation" from God.[5] This new creation emerges from God's Spirit, as Paul suggests: "It is God who establishes us with you in Christ and has anointed us, who has put his seal on us and given us his Spirit in our hearts as a down payment" (2 Cor 1:21–22; cf. 2 Cor 5:5; Gal 4:6, 6:1). The coming of God's Spirit as a "seal on us" is a down payment for the later fullness of a new creation and gives us a divine standpoint now for knowing God.

The Spirit's epistemological work, including giving evidence of God, has a temporal feature of "now but not fully yet." For now the Spirit "in our hearts" serves as an installment from God on what God will bring about completely later, namely, the fullness of divine righteousness throughout the new creation. So, the new creation as God's kingdom is already present in initial form: "The kingdom of God is . . . righteousness and peace and joy in the Holy Spirit" (Rom 14:17; cf. 1 Cor 4:20). The latter remarks concern the present and not just the future.

Paul has in mind the new creation in fullness when he speaks of "the glory about to be revealed to us" (Rom 8:19). He adds,

> The creation waits with eager longing for the revealing of the children of God, for the creation was subjected to futility, not of its own will, but by the will of the one who subjected it, in hope that the creation itself will be set free from its enslavement to decay and will obtain the freedom of the glory of the children of God. We know that the whole creation has been groaning together as it suffers together the pains of labor, and not only the creation, but we ourselves, who have the first fruits of the Spirit, groan inwardly while we wait for adoption, the redemption of our bodies. (Rom 8:19–23)

The "first fruits of the Spirit" are the first fruits as a voucher of "the glory about to be revealed to us," that is, God's new creation in full "redemption," including "the freedom of the glory of the children of God."

God currently vouchsafes, by the Spirit of God experienced at work now in human life, the forthcoming fullness of righteousness in new creation. Paul takes this experience to be marked by a conflict between the Spirit and human flesh, with a pivotal decision left to humans. He comments, "Those who live according to the flesh set their minds on the things of the flesh, but those who live according to the Spirit set their minds on the things of the Spirit. To set the mind on the flesh is death, but to set the mind on the Spirit is life and peace" (Rom 8:5–6). This key decision about "setting one's mind" raises the question of what "things of the Spirit" Paul has in mind.

Paul's Letter to the Galatians clarifies the conflict facing people with "desires of the flesh" in relation to God's Spirit and new creation:

> Through the Spirit, by faith, we eagerly wait for the hope of righteousness. . . . Live by the Spirit, I say, and do not gratify the desires of the flesh. For what the flesh desires is opposed to the Spirit, and what the Spirit desires is opposed to the flesh, for these are opposed to each other, to prevent you from doing what you want. . . . Now the works of the flesh are obvious: sexual immorality, impurity, debauchery, idolatry, sorcery, enmities, strife, jealousy, anger, quarrels, dissensions, factions, envy, drunkenness, carousing, and things like these. . . . By contrast, the fruit of the Spirit is love, joy, peace, patience, kindness, generosity, faithfulness, gentleness, and self-control. There is no law against such things. If we live by the Spirit, let us also be guided by the Spirit. (Gal 5:5, 16–23, 25)

We should acknowledge the relation of the fruit of the Spirit to human living and being guided by the Spirit and thereby to divine self-vindication via humans. We also should recognize its close relation to the self-giving character of Jesus Christ (Gal 5:24).

Paul's talk of "the hope of righteousness" connotes the hope of full righteousness in the fulfilled new creation that will completely vindicate God. This hope, according to Paul, is grounded now in the following experience: "Because you are children, God has sent the Spirit of his Son into our hearts, crying, 'Abba!, Father!'" (Gal 4:6). The result now is an ongoing conflict during God's effort toward full righteousness in complete new creation: "What the flesh desires is opposed to the Spirit, and what the Spirit desires is opposed to the flesh, for these are opposed to each other." The experiential evidence for the Spirit thus arises now in a context of conflict over divine righteousness for humans, with God seeking to be a rectifier for human renewal in righteousness.

The Spirit of God offers a standpoint for human knowledge of God and for divine vindication in the aforementioned manifested fruit for humans: "The fruit of the Spirit is love, joy, peace, patience, kindness, generosity, faithfulness, gentleness, and self-control." This lesson of a divine standpoint, courtesy of God's Spirit in "the fruit of the Spirit," is widely neglected by theologians and philosophers of religion. It captures, however, the center of Paul's epistemology, as we have noted in connection with Romans 5:5. Hope in God, like faith in God, does not "put us to shame" because it has a basis of distinctive evidence in the primary fruit of the Spirit: "God's love" poured into our moral experience, particularly into our "hearts." The love in question includes divine forgiveness offered to humans and can be experienced directly by attentive, receptive humans.

H. R. Mackintosh has commented on the interpersonal directness of God's relating to cooperative humans in forgiveness, or pardon:

> The reality of pardon, imparted by God, can never be demonstrated to one who has not known it from within, nor can it be shown to follow necessarily from any rational notion of God that might figure in metaphysical argumentation. . . . It can nonetheless be experienced as something borne in upon the mind that submits itself, with candour. . . . It is the breaking of eternity into time, the intervention of a love beyond all

> measure, a supernatural event not deducible by any human calculus from the nature of the universe but rather the spontaneous and unanalysable deed of God. We do not reach it by hard thinking; we are confronted by it. It emerges from pure love as an inexplicable gift to the unworthy which conveys the solution of our sorest problems.[6]

Human conscience can have a central role in such direct experience because the forgiveness in question can be experienced in it.

Mackintosh rightly notes the importance of "the mind that submits itself, with candour" to the divine forgiveness on offer. This submitting is a voluntary, volitional feature among (some) humans, enabling the offer of forgiveness to come to fruition in their experienced reconciliation with God. The forgiveness offered is a release from divine condemnation, and this release demands a person's starting anew, free of being condemned, toward righteousness in relationship with God. (The next section returns to this topic.)

Paul relates "the heart" closely to human "conscience": "[Gentiles] show that what the law requires is written on their hearts, as their own conscience also bears witness, and their conflicting thoughts will accuse or perhaps excuse them" (Rom 2:14). He thus holds that one's conscience reflects one's heart on some matters regarding God. He also holds that God's Spirit confirms in conscience some things regarding God: "I am speaking the truth in Christ—I am not lying; my conscience confirms it by the Holy Spirit" (Rom 9:1). In this regard, God's Spirit sometimes provides a divine standpoint in human conscience for discerning divine truth, reality, and goodness. This lesson is central to Paul's understanding of human knowledge of God and divine actions.

Paul thinks of God's Spirit as functionally equivalent to the Spirit of Christ, with both being set on human renewal in divine righteousness. He writes to the Roman Christians, "You are not in the flesh; you are in the Spirit, since the Spirit of God dwells in you. Anyone who does not have the Spirit of Christ does not belong to him. But if Christ is in you, then the body is dead because of sin, but the Spirit is life because of righteousness" (Rom 8:9–10). Paul's notions of "the Spirit of God in you" and "Christ in you" figure in his key idea of "having the mind [νοῦν] of Christ" (1 Cor 2:16; cf. 1 Cor 15:45). His talk of "the mind of Christ" is to be understood in terms of "the Spirit" of Christ (in keeping with Paul's role for the Spirit in 1 Cor 1:12) while preserving personal identity for individual humans and for Christ. We may think of such talk of "the mind of Christ" as connoting the moral conscience and character of Christ shared by humans.[7]

The ethical volitional features of "having the mind of Christ" are explicit in Paul's following remark to the Philippian Christians:

> Let the same mind be [φρονεῖτε] in you that was in Christ Jesus,
> who, though he existed in the form of God,
> did not regard equality with God
> as something to be grasped,
> but emptied himself,
> taking the form of a slave,
> assuming human likeness.
> And being found in appearance as a human,
> he humbled himself
> and became obedient to the point of death—
> even death on a cross. (Phil 2:5–8)

The "mind of Christ," according to Paul, includes obedience to God and not just reflection or reasoning about God. It thus is shared by humans with a volitional and ethical component on their part, going beyond a merely intellectual or contemplative process to cooperation with divine righteousness. (The ethical significance of "the mind of Christ" is confirmed in 1 Cor 3:1–4.)

In 1 Corinthians 2:16, Paul mentions "the mind of Christ" in relation to his interpretation of Isaiah 40:13: "Who has directed the spirit of the Lord or as his counselor has instructed him?" The answer to this rhetorical question is: No mere human. The question is important to

Paul because he endorses God's supreme authority in giving evidence of divine reality and goodness to humans. He thus remarks to the Corinthians, "My speech and my proclamation were made not with persuasive words of wisdom but with a demonstration of the Spirit and of power, so that your faith might rest not on human wisdom but on the power of God" (1 Cor 2:4–5). The relevant power is the power of God's Spirit for new creation in divine righteousness over moral failure and death (2 Cor 5:16–21). Faith and hope in God, according to Paul, are to rest (i.e., be based) on such divine power, including divine love (Rom 5:5), rather than on "human wisdom" that disregards such power.[8] (Chapter 7 returns to this matter.)

The power in question stems from divine lordship, including intended divine guidance and vindication toward righteousness. It underlies Paul's focus on knowing God as one's Lord rather than on mere factual knowledge that God exists. We may call such knowing "lordship knowledge" because it includes attitudinal and behavioral conformity to God as Lord of human knowers, with the aim of divine-human reconciliation and vindication in righteousness (see 2 Cor 4:5, 5:16–21). God supplies in human experience the needed evidence, through the fruit of the Spirit, to authenticate divine reality and goodness, and a result is a divine challenge favoring human repentance before God (Rom 2:4).

The relevant evidence, as suggested, comes from divine self-manifestation to humans (Rom 10:20) via divine personality traits in what Paul calls "the fruit of the Spirit." Those traits show the unique moral power of God, and they serve as the evidential base of faith in God. They manifest divine "power through human weakness," thereby enabling God to emerge as the source of life-giving power for humans.[9] Such power is founded on divine righteous love and the other fruit of the Spirit, and Paul finds it exemplified perfectly in Jesus Christ as the image (εἰκών), power (δύναμιν), and righteousness (δικαιοσύνη) of God (2 Cor 4:4; 1 Cor 1:24, 30; cf. Gal 5:24). So, the mind of Christ, as understood by Paul, has the kind of divine power that can anchor well-grounded human commitment to God.

The divine power in question enables God to be *self-authenticating* (of divine reality and goodness) in human experience in a way that mere propositions or beliefs cannot be. God does so by self-presenting unique features of the divine moral character to humans in their moral experience, including conscience. In doing so, God challenges, with the power of intended divine moral influence, humans to be renewed in cooperative character formation toward the experienced moral character of God.

Mere propositions and beliefs do not have the intentional causal power to self-authenticate in the way used by God. Given the divine moral power that can be manifested by humans, Paul says to the Corinthian Christians, "You yourselves are our letter, written on our hearts, known and read by all, and you show that you are a letter of Christ, prepared by us, written not with ink but with the Spirit of the living God, not on tablets of stone but on tablets that are human hearts" (2 Cor 3:2–3). The Spirit of God thus can witness to the reality and goodness of divine power through cooperative humans.

The author of John's Gospel, in agreement with Paul, finds a divine standpoint for humans in the intervening Spirit of God. He represents Jesus as saying, "I will ask the Father, and he will give you another Advocate [παράκλητον], to be with you forever. This is the Spirit of truth, whom the world cannot receive because it neither sees him nor knows him. You know him because he abides with you, and he will be in you. . . . The Advocate, the Holy Spirit, whom the Father will send in my name, will teach you everything and remind you of all that I have said to you" (John 14:16–17, 26). God's Spirit, according to John's Jesus, is the standpoint for being taught the things of God by God. This Spirit comes to humans to represent the departed Jesus as God's prior advocate. The Spirit thus aims to bring the reality and the truth about God and Jesus to humans.

John's Jesus continues on the role of God's Spirit for apprehending divine reality: "I still have many things to say to you, but you cannot bear them now. When the Spirit of truth comes, he will guide you into all the truth, for he will not speak on his own but will speak whatever he hears, and he will declare to you the things that are to come. He will glorify me because he will take what is mine and declare it to you" (John 16:12–14). Jesus signals a special time of God's Spirit at work after he (Jesus) has departed. The Spirit, he promises, "will guide you into all truth" by revealing things about God and Jesus. This Spirit also will reveal some things regarding what God plans to accomplish in the future.

John's Gospel gives the Spirit an important role in supplying convicting knowledge to humans regarding God: "I tell you the truth: it is to your advantage that I go away, for if I do not go away, the Counselor [παράκλητος] will not come to you; but if I go, I will send him to you. And when he comes, he will convict the world concerning sin and righteousness and judgment: concerning sin, because they do not believe in me; concerning righteousness, because I go to the Father, and you will see me no more; concerning judgment, because the ruler of this world is judged" (John 16:7–11, RSV). The Spirit's "convicting concerning righteousness," according to John, is positive, promoting not only the avoidance of unrighteousness (or sin) but also the human move to cooperate with conformity to divine righteousness.[10] It thus is not limited to confirming human guilt for sin.

The Johannine tradition gives a special role to the anointing (including teaching) by God's Spirit that saves its members from dependence on outsiders for knowledge of God and divine action: "As for you, the anointing that you received from [the Holy One] abides in you, so you do not need anyone to teach you. But as his anointing teaches you about all things and is true and is not a lie, and just as it has taught you, abide in him" (1 John 2:27). Abiding in God includes conforming to the divine standpoint of teaching provided by God's Spirit, without wandering to opposing teaching from outsiders. The challenge from the latter teaching was evidently a real threat in the Johannine community to giving God a due role of authority and preeminence, including in epistemology regarding God.[11] Such a challenge persists widely today for religious commitment to God. We thus need to further clarify the significance of adopting God's

Spirit as a divine standpoint for apprehending God in divine action and vindication.

Responding to the Spirit's Standpoint

It is one thing for there to be a divine standpoint of God's Spirit available to humans. It is another thing for people to adopt such a standpoint in response to evidence for it in their moral experience. A Platonic approach would make the adoption a matter centrally of intellectual insight, or "contemplation by the understanding," shared by God and humans.[12] This is inadequate, however, from the perspective of Paul and the writer of John's Gospel (as well as the author of Deuteronomy; cf. Deut 11:26–28, 30:15). In their perspective, human volition in cooperative decision toward righteousness has a central role in the ideal response to indicators of God's reality and goodness.[13] In addition, humans voluntarily can avoid taking the divine standpoint of God's Spirit; that is, they can "quench the Spirit" (1 Thess 5:19; cf. Eph 4:30).

Paul writes, "I appeal to you therefore, brothers and sisters, on the basis of God's mercy, to present your bodies as a living sacrifice, holy and acceptable to God, which is your reasonable act of worship. Do not be conformed to this age, but be transformed by the renewing of the mind, so that you may discern what is the will of God—what is good and acceptable and perfect" (Rom 12:1–2). Paul seeks being "transformed by the renewing of the mind, so that you may discern what is the will of God." The desired "renewing of the mind" toward God and divine righteousness is not purely or even centrally intellectual or contemplative in Paul's perspective. Instead, it stems from "presenting your bodies as a living sacrifice, holy and acceptable to God" in response to divine "mercy" or goodness in human experience (cf. Rom 2:4).[14] This amounts to presenting *yourself* to God as a voluntary and cooperative response toward divine righteousness expressed in your life.

Paul makes an appeal to the Roman Christians: "Do not let sin reign in your mortal bodies, so that you obey their desires. No longer present your members to sin as instruments of unrighteousness, but present yourselves to God as those who have been brought from death to life, and present your members to God as instruments of righteousness. . . . Do you not know that, if you present yourselves to anyone as obedient slaves, you are slaves of the one whom you obey, either of sin, which leads to death, or of obedience, which leads to righteousness?" (Rom 6:12–13, 16). Human self-presenting to God is volitional toward cooperating with divine righteousness and not purely intellectual or reflective. Paul takes it to be a matter of "obedience [to God] which leads to righteousness," in response to God's self-manifested goodness. So, this is not a matter of mere intellectual contemplation or awareness analogous to Plato's intellectual apprehension of the forms. It calls for human "turning to the Lord" (2 Cor 3:16) in responsive and cooperative obedience, the heart of repentance and faith before God, or what Paul calls "the obedience of faith" (Rom 1:5, 16:26).[15]

We have clarified Paul's central role for the divine Spirit and corresponding fruit. We now may understand Paul's talk of presenting ourselves to God to include presenting ourselves to God's Spirit in cooperative response to corresponding intervening fruit of the Spirit. This response includes a cooperative direct relation to God's self-manifested personality traits of love, joy, peace, patience, kindness, generosity, faithfulness, gentleness, and self-control. We thus present ourselves to God when we intend to conform to or cooperate with those personality traits presented in our own lives, thereby enabling them to come to fruition in our moral experience and character formation.[16] An important result, given a divine redemptive purpose, is our imaging or reflecting the righteous moral character of God, if imperfectly. An equally important result is our coming to know God through direct acquaintance and responsive cooperation with the self-manifested fruit of God's Spirit as the personality traits of God.

We humans suitably apprehend God's reality and goodness through God's self-manifested love in our experience, when we present ourselves to be conformed to it, ideally wholeheartedly in thought, will, and affect. As a result, when we resist forgiving others in the manner of forgiveness required by divine love, we resist not only divine forgiveness but also God. We then block divine love from coming to fruition in our experience and thereby obscure evidence for God and for divine moral power otherwise available to us. The problem in that case is our failure to adopt the standpoint of God's Spirit for apprehending and knowing God. This failure can result from various purposes of ours at odds with God's moral character, thus "quenching" the Spirit of God in the divine effort to renew us as part of the new creation in righteousness. Such a failure thereby hinders divine vindication through human cooperation with God.

The author of John's Gospel emphasizes a human volitional component that is cooperative in responding to and adopting the standpoint of God. He represents Jesus as saying, "I can do nothing on my own. As I hear, I judge, and my judgment is just because I seek to do not my own will but the will of him who sent me" (John 5:30). This "seeking to do the will of him who sent me" recalls Gethsemane, where Jesus showed his priority for his volitional resolve to obey God's expressed will, even when suffering and death result (Mark 14:36). John has Jesus link his co-valuing with God to co-judging with God: "My judgment is true, for it is not I alone who judge but I and he who sent me" (John 8:16, RSV). Since divine judging has intellectual, volitional, and affective components, we may think of Jesus as sharing in those divine components and thus cooperatively responding to and adopting a divine standpoint for judging reality.

John portrays Jesus to endorse a cooperative volitional component in knowing God's reality and action: "Anyone who resolves [θέλῃ] to do the will [θέλημα] of God will know whether the teaching [of mine] is from God or whether I am speaking on my own" (John 7:17). "Resolving to do the will of God" is explicitly volitional in cooperation, in the way Jesus was volitional in cooperation with God in Gethsemane. It thus takes us beyond merely intellectual reflection or contemplation to cooperation with divine righteousness. It calls for the will-based commitment of a person to God and God's will in response to this will expressed in human moral experience.

The author of 1 John represents the Johannine tradition of volitional obedience to God in relation to the Spirit of God: "All who keep his commandments abide in him, and he in them. And by this we know that he abides in us, by the Spirit which he has given us" (1 John 3:24, RSV). The divine Spirit, in John as in Paul, is the source of human knowledge of God's reality and activity in human experience and life. "Abiding" in God, according to the Johannine tradition, includes adopting God's standpoint for discerning divine reality and actions. The fruit from God manifested in a cooperative life is a sign of following God, and it is promoted by the Spirit of God, who points to Jesus after his departure (John 8:5, 8, 26). This pointing includes recommending conformity to the mind (or spirit) of Christ.

The fruit of God's Spirit expresses God's moral will, at least in a *de re* manner. A volitional resolve to conform to this fruit in human experience, including conscience, is a way to resolve to do God's will. Our response to the experienced fruit of the Spirit thus becomes our own Gethsemane experience, in the wake of Jesus's pivotal decision to do God's self-giving will based in unselfish love. In addition, we can make such decisions about God's will without knowing it *as God's will* (with knowing *de re*, without theological *de dicto* content).[17] Lack of awareness of the manifested fruit of the Spirit as *God's* intervention with divine personality traits leaves many people assuming that they have no evidence of God's reality or goodness. They are mistaken, however, if they have had awareness of the manifested fruit of the Spirit in their moral experience, including conscience.

John's Gospel links God's revealing of Jesus to humans with the kind of response they will offer to God and Jesus: "Judas (not Iscariot) said to him, 'Lord, how is it that you will reveal yourself to us and not to the world?' Jesus answered him, 'Those who love me will keep my word, and my Father will love them, and we will come to them and make our home with them. Whoever does not love me does not keep my words, and the word that you hear is not mine but is from the Father who sent me'" (John 14:22–24).

The revelation of Jesus to humans, by God and Jesus, looks for human obedience and love toward God and Jesus in response.

If there is no prospect for obedience and love toward God among some humans, God may have no good purpose in revealing Jesus to them. In this regard, there are divine moral expectations for human knowing of God and God's work among humans. These expectations do not demand human earning of God's approval. Instead, they demand that relevant human moral attitudes fit with God's revealed moral character in a way that allows for cooperation with God toward righteousness in relationship.

We now see a key difference between mere factual knowledge that God exists and what we have called "lordship knowledge" of God. The latter knowledge has an irreducible moral component owing to its requirement of cooperation with divine righteousness. Mere factual knowledge that God exists, as typically understood, has no such requirement. The mind of Christ, given its robust moral character, fits well with lordship knowledge of God. It thus reflects the moral attitude of Jesus toward God in Gethsemane, with his personal commitment to God's righteousness.

Adopting the divine standpoint of God's Spirit demands two components in human response: candid attentiveness and resolute cooperation. Paul recommends the following attentiveness to what is good: "Whatever is true, whatever is honorable, whatever is just, whatever is pure, whatever is lovely, whatever is gracious, if there is any excellence, if there is anything worthy of praise, think about these things" (Phil 4:8, RSV). Thinking *about* these things *de re* requires attending to them in experience; it thus is not abstract speculation regarding them. Paul's injunction fits with the teaching of Jesus to attend to God's goodness manifested in human experience (Matt 6:26–32). In Paul's thinking, such attending ideally prompts people to turn to God in sincere cooperation with divine goodness (Rom 2:4).

Adopting the divine standpoint of God's Spirit calls for applying value priorities fitting God's expressed will, including the manifested fruit of the Spirit. Paul thus remarks:

> Whatever gain I had, I counted as loss for the sake of Christ. Indeed I count everything as loss because of the surpassing worth of knowing Christ Jesus my Lord. For his sake I have suffered the loss of all things, and count them as refuse, in order that I may gain Christ and be found in him, not having a righteousness of my own, based on law, but that which is through faith in Christ, the righteousness from God that depends on faith; that I may know him and the power of his resurrection, and may share his sufferings, becoming like him in his death, that if possible I may attain the resurrection from the dead. (Phil 3:7–11, RSV)

Paul's challenge is to "count everything [else] as loss" in comparison with knowing God and Christ, with the kind of lordship knowing identified above. He thus speaks of his goal to "know [Christ] and the power of his resurrection" in order to "attain the resurrection from the dead." (Chapter 8 returns to the crucial role of divine resurrection in God's self-vindication.)

Paul's suggested value priority enables wholehearted commitment to and cooperation with God and the fruit of the Spirit. A perfect God would not settle for half-hearted commitment given its vacillating ways between good and bad. Divine vindication through humans seeks their full commitment to God and divine righteousness. This aim sets a high expectation of humans, but we should expect as much from a God of perfect righteousness.

Humans have a power deficit from their moral weakness relative to divine righteousness. Paul is clear on this deficit and on human need of the Spirit's aid in adopting a divine standpoint: "The Spirit helps us in our weakness; for we do not know how to pray as we ought, but the Spirit himself intercedes for us with sighs too deep for words. And he who searches the hearts of [humans] knows what is the mind of the Spirit, because the Spirit intercedes for the saints according to the will of God" (Rom 8:26–27, RSV). Suitably responding to the Spirit, then, depends on the Spirit interceding in human prayer to God for divine aid.

"The Spirit intercedes . . . according to the will of God," and this divine action includes interceding according to the fruit of the Spirit. The gift of this fruit is unearned by humans, but it still is hard-won by humans in a struggle for its reception, given human moral weakness. Here, again, we see a key difference between the basis of lordship knowledge of God and mere factual knowledge that God exists. Divine vindication through humans does not come easily for them.

Humans, as previously noted, must overcome conflicts of their "flesh" with the righteous divine power offered in the fruit of the Spirit. The Spirit seeks to lead them to this goal (Rom 8:14; Gal 5:18), courtesy of the manifested fruit of the Spirit in their moral experience. This divine intentional activity indicates the intentional agency and thus personhood of God in human experience, including in conscience. Humans are, however, inconsistent in allowing God to lead in this way and thus to be their Lord. Even though God offers them the needed power to preserve responsible human agency, they are divided in their response to the fruit of the Spirit, as they often are in conscience.

The divine requirement is not perfection now in adopting the divine standpoint, given that humans are at best works in progress. Paul remarks, "Not that I have already obtained this or am already perfect; but I press on to make it my own, because Christ Jesus has made me his own. Brethren, I do not consider that I have made it my own; but one thing I do, forgetting what lies behind and straining forward to what lies ahead, I press on toward the goal for the prize of the upward call of God in Christ Jesus" (Phil 3:12–14). Adopting the divine standpoint in God's Spirit is thus a work in progress at best. We now fall short of perfection in this area, even if our intentions are commendable. As a result, human attentiveness and cooperation remain as partly unfulfilled divine expectations. They can be part of the Spirit's down payment with the corresponding fruit, but they will come to perfect fruition only in the fullness of time.

Our being works of renewal in progress toward full righteousness does not challenge the reality of God's own standpoint of full righteousness. God's perfect righteousness can show up in human experience while we cloud it and hinder it in part with our unrighteous ways. This idea underlies Paul's remark that "we have this treasure in clay jars, so that it may be made clear that this extraordinary power belongs to God and does not come from us" (2 Cor 4:7). The relevant power of divine righteousness, including the divine standpoint in the mind of Christ, can coexist in humans with their moral deficits, as long as they intend to cooperate. Incompleteness in having the mind of Christ, then, does not entail lacking the mind of Christ. As a result, typical humans can benefit, morally and epistemologically, from having the mind of Christ. They can also represent, if imperfectly, divine vindication in righteousness, although full righteousness for humans awaits the fullness of time.

The perspective of this chapter enables us to understand an evidential basis in moral experience for direct, or noninferential, knowledge of God. Such knowledge can serve as a cognitive basis for inferential knowledge of God, such as testimonial evidence. We cannot digress now to the familiar (but troubled) arguments of natural theology for God's existence, but we can acknowledge evidence in moral experience prompting a person to adopt a divine standpoint in the mind of Christ. Various ideas of (and inferences regarding) a first cause, designer, fine-tuner, and source of consciousness need not conflict with the approach developed here, and that is an epistemological benefit of this approach. Even so, we do well to put the most resilient evidence first.

The relevant evidence of God's reality and goodness in the experienced fruit of the Spirit brings us directly to the divine moral character that makes God worthy of worship: to what makes God *God*. This fruit manifests the perfect righteousness of God (Phil 1:11) and thus represents the existence and goodness of God to human experience, even when humans fail to recognize this. So, we do not face a chasm, as in much natural theology, between the relevant evidence and who God truly is, particularly as perfectly morally good.[18] This chasm blocks any straightforward inference from nature or natural evolution to the reality or goodness of God.

We have noted the relevance of an inference to a best available explanation, or abduction, in our presenting evidence regarding God from the moral experience of some people. Presenting such evidence is not the same as simply having such evidence. Suppose that the best available explanation of the experienced fruit of the Spirit for a person includes a causally influential role for divine guidance toward righteousness, in the absence of undermining considerations. In that case, this person will have a responsible epistemic means of presenting the relevant evidence. The sciences often present their evidence with such explanatory support, and nothing in principle bars a similar approach for experience of God and the mind of Christ in the present context.

Best available explanations can, and do, vary relative to varying evidence among people, and this holds for the sciences as well as religious experience. Even so, some people find that their experience of the relevant fruit of the Spirit is evidently intentional in a manner suited to their divine moral guidance toward righteousness. As a result, they are in a position to offer an abductive inference to present their evidence in question on behalf of divine reality and goodness. We have no way to rule out this prospect, and it merits careful attention for the sake of elucidating human moral experience. Giving it such attention can contribute to serious attention to the kind of epistemological perspective we have identified in the apostle Paul and John's Gospel.[19] It also can shed light on the nature of divine self-vindication through humans in righteousness.

Conclusion

At best, we humans now know in part and adopt in part the divine standpoint in God's Spirit, including in the mind of Christ. Even so, the standpoint is arguably available despite human moral shortcomings. As people conform to the divinely offered fruit of the Spirit, they take on the mind of Christ (at least *de re*) and come to know God directly in lordship knowledge (at least *de re*). If humans ignore or oppose the fruit's reality, as a result of their imperfection of some kind, the result will be to their detriment, morally and epistemologically. They thus will fail to let God be God and Lord in their lives.

In restoring the prospect of humans having the divine standpoint and the mind of Christ, we will make room for a distinctive approach to apprehending divine reality. In doing so, we will bring hope not only for knowing God now as Lord, courtesy of the manifested fruit of the Spirit, but also for our knowing God later "as we are known," in the fullness of time. That will be the time of the new creation in the fullness of the Spirit's standpoint and the corresponding fruit. The divine standpoint for apprehending reality aright then will be at hand fully for humans, supplementing and fulfilling their having the mind of Christ in part now. Divine self-vindication in righteousness through humans will then be fully realized as they fully image God's moral character. We need to clarify what God seeks to show and accomplish in this arduous effort.

CHAPTER THREE

Vindication Through Interpersonal Showing

> *I will prove the holiness of my great name which has been profaned among the nations, which you have profaned in their midst. Then the nations will know that I am the Lord, declares the Lord God, when I prove myself holy through you in their sight.*
>
> —Ezekiel 36:23

THE PREVIOUS CHAPTERS have introduced divine self-vindication through the topics of divine self-revealing (and hiding) and a God's-eye standpoint available to humans in their appropriating the fruit of God's Spirit. The latter appropriating occurs in a context of God's seeking to show (or "prove") something to humans, even if they typically overlook this. People often ask what they can prove about God, but they rarely ask what God aims to prove or show to or about them. This striking omission calls for correction for the sake of responsible inquiry about God and divine self-vindication in righteousness.

We shall see that the answer to the question of what God aims to show to humans guides the answer to the question of what humans are able to prove or, less strictly, confirm about God. The needed answer will arise in the light of a recurring but underappreciated biblical theme about what God vindicates in the presence of human distrust, avoidance, and alienation toward God. God aims to show that God alone is perfectly righteous but nonetheless can justify initially resistant people who cooperate in a re-creative process toward righteousness in relationship to God. This consideration lies at the heart of divine self-vindication.

The process in question includes the divine effort to make people worthy of God and God's good news of unmerited divine approval for them. This perspective has been widely neglected by theologians, biblical interpreters, and philosophers of religion. In clarifying it, we can make some sense of God's ways of self-vindication in the world. This chapter uses the term *proof* in a familiar sense of *confirmation*, in a way that does not require the kind of deductive inference found in mathematical or logical proof.

Divine Showing Through Humans

The book of Job leaves many readers puzzled about God. It is, however, clear on one thing: God prompted the challenges, frustrations, and suffering faced by Job. Beginning with Job 1:8–12, the book of Job develops the perspective that God did so because God had something to show among humans, even inviting the accuser (*Satan*) to contribute. Thus,

> The Lord said to the accuser, "Have you considered my servant Job? There is no one like him on the earth, a blameless and upright man who fears God and turns away from evil." Then the accuser answered the Lord, "Does Job fear God for nothing? Have you not put a fence around him and his house and all that he has, on every side? You have blessed the work of his hands, and his possessions have increased in the land. But stretch out your hand now, and touch all that he has, and he will curse you to your face." The Lord said to the accuser, "Very well, all that he has is in your power; only do not stretch out your hand against him!" . . . Job did not sin or charge God with wrongdoing. (Job 1:8–12, 22)

What does God seek to prove or show here? The answer is initially unclear to Job but becomes clear over time. Part of the answer is found in Job's following remark about God: "Though he kill me, yet I will trust in him" (Job 13:15, NRSV margin). God seeks to show that Job trusts God but not for Job's benefits resulting in this earthly life. More generally, God aims to show that Job is worthy of a trustworthy God, including worthy of God's trust in Job to be loyal to God.

We began with a passage from Ezekiel that captures God's strategy for divine "proof" as interpersonal showing in vindication, now in paraphrase: I [God] will prove myself righteous through the people of God in the sight of the nations. Walther Eichrodt comments on Ezekiel's statement of God's character proof, "If Israel can still possess any sort of hope, it must have as its sole basis the certainty that God's fidelity to his own intrinsic nature (and that is precisely what is ultimately meant by the hallowing of his name) must necessarily lead to the sanctifying and renewing [God's] people. . . . His holiness must receive recognition and honour and the worship that is its due. . . . What is at stake is not an impressive position for Israel but the justification of God's claim to reveal himself to the world as its God."[1] Ezekiel affirms that God proves or shows God holy through the people of God, thus involving them in the promised divine proof as vindication in righteousness.

God aims to show that the people of God are worthy representatives of the vindication of divine righteousness, as they show God's worthiness of being loved, trusted, and obeyed, despite the pains and losses in their lives. We may think of God's holiness as perfect righteousness. The divine effort for the vindication in such righteousness has mixed results among people. Ezekiel, however, portrays God to be motivated by love for God's people, despite their unfaithfulness (Ezek 16:8–15). The divine righteousness to be shown by God, then, is righteous love.

The divine vindication of the worthiness of God's people is complicated by its intended inward component. Ezekiel, we have noted, puts the divine promise in terms of a "new heart" and a "new spirit": "A new heart I will give you, and a new spirit I will put within you, and I will remove from your body the heart of stone and give you a heart of flesh. I will put my spirit within you and make you follow my statutes and be careful to observe my ordinances" (Ezek 36:26–27; see Ezek 11:19). This is a divine plan for the inward renewal of God's people, going beyond their mere behavior. It is a matter of "a new heart" and "a new spirit" for the people of God, courtesy of God's re-creative power. Such renewal includes a new will and new attitudes, at least toward God, but this consideration does not reach the core motivator announced by Ezekiel.

Ezekiel goes beyond a new human will and attitude by having God promise, "I will put my spirit [*ruach*] within you." This is a matter of God renewing people without coercing them. Eichrodt comments, "The spirit of God permeates each individual member of the people of God so as to carry out an inward transformation through which the regenerate power of God's purity and holiness lays hold of the most intimate part of man's nature and assimilates it to the nature of God. Here we see the new importance of the individual member of the people to the coming people of God, and how he is aroused to a feeling of responsibility for realizing God's plan of salvation."[2] This "feeling of responsibility [by the people of God] for realizing God's plan of salvation" includes a willingness to become worthy of God and God's plan of righteous salvation for humans. It also includes a new willingness to show, with one's life and its deepest motivations, God's worthiness of being Lord. The latter willingness is a central feature of the redemptive work of the Spirit of God in people willing to cooperate with God.

Ezekiel is clear and even emphatic about the reality of individual human responsibility before God and a corresponding voluntary role for humans in turning to God in repentance. He portrays God as follows:

> A child shall not suffer for the iniquity of a parent nor a parent suffer for the iniquity of a child; the righteousness of the righteous shall be their own, and the wickedness of the wicked shall be their own. But if the wicked turn away from all their sins that they have committed and keep all my statutes and do what is lawful and right, they shall surely live; they shall not die. None of the transgressions that they have committed shall be remembered against them, for the righteousness that they have done they shall live. Have I any pleasure in the death of the wicked, says the Lord God, and not rather that they should

> turn from their ways and live?. . . . Yet you say, "The way of the Lord is unfair." Hear now, O house of Israel: Is my way unfair? Is it not your ways that are unfair?. . . . Repent and turn from all your transgressions; otherwise iniquity will be your ruin. Cast away from you all the transgressions that you have committed against me, and get yourselves a new heart and a new spirit! Why will you die, O house of Israel? For I have no pleasure in the death of anyone, says the Lord God. Turn, then, and live. (Ezek 18:20–23, 25–32)

This passage distinguishes God's way ("my way") from human ways ("your ways"). God disowns causal and moral responsibility for human ways, including for their decisions and actions. (This contrast is at the center of chapter 7.)

God urges wayward humans to "repent and turn from" their unrighteous ways. Such repentance as a cooperative turning to God is a way to "get yourselves a new heart and a new spirit," and this result, we have seen, is courtesy of God. So, according to Ezekiel, humans have a responsible voluntary role in receiving what is needed to become worthy of God and thereby to show God's righteous character among humans.

Hindering Divine Showing: Distrust and Alienation

The opening chapters of the book of Genesis, along with many other biblical writings, identify human alienation from God stemming from misplaced distrust (and fear) toward God. According to Genesis, God commanded that Adam and Eve not eat of the fruit of the tree in the middle of the garden. Nonetheless, "when the woman saw that the tree was good for food and that it was a delight to the eyes and that the tree was to be desired to make one wise, she took of its fruit and ate, and she also gave some to her husband, who was with her, and he ate" (Gen 3:6). The serpent had said to her, "God knows that when you eat of it your eyes will be opened, and you will be like God, knowing good and evil" (Gen 3:5).

A suggestion of Eve's thinking is that God's command intended to withhold something good from Adam and Eve, namely, something that would "make one wise" in a way that involves "knowing good and evil." Adam and Eve, by that thinking, did not trust God to supply what was good for their being wise. Their faith in God's goodness thus lapsed, and their distrust resulted in their alienation from God. That is, they moved out of a cooperative relationship with God.

God responded to human distrust with damage control to protect righteous life: "The Lord God said, 'See, the humans have become like one of us, knowing good and evil, and now they might reach out their hands and take also from the tree of life and eat and live forever'—therefore the Lord God sent them forth from the garden of Eden, to till the ground from which they were taken. He drove out the humans, and at the east of the garden of Eden he placed the cherubim and a sword flaming and turning to guard the way to the tree of life" (Gen 3:22–24). God's decision "to guard the way to the tree of life" represents a divine concern for *how* humans approach God.

Humans are to approach God as their guiding Lord, without their self-designed shortcuts that demote God as Lord. In short, they are not to "play God" in the area of what a good life is for them. Divine righteousness and approval are to be the guide for humans, and they need to learn this lesson, if often via the hard way. So, God puts humans, for their own good, under instructive duress that limits their harmful exercise of self-control over life.

According to Ezekiel, God confronts in the people of God the kind of human rebellion found in Genesis:

> Thus says the Lord God: This is Jerusalem; I have set her in the center of the nations, with countries all around her. But she has rebelled against my ordinances and my statutes, becoming more wicked than the nations and the countries all around her, rejecting my ordinances and not following my statutes.

> Therefore thus says the Lord God: Because you are more turbulent than the nations that are all around you and have not followed my statutes or kept my ordinances and have not even acted according to the ordinances of the nations that are all around you, therefore thus says the Lord God: I, I myself, am coming against you; I will execute judgments among you in the sight of the nations. (Ezek 5:5–8)

God thus warns Ezekiel, "The house of Israel will not be willing to listen to you, for they are not willing to listen to me, because all the house of Israel have a hard forehead and a stubborn heart" (Ezek 3:7). In this regard, God's people have a "heart" problem, and the divine solution must work at the inward place of the human heart.

Ezekiel represents God to face the human resistance directly, as a problem of idolatry in demoting God as Lord: "Thus says the Lord God: Repent and turn away from your idols, and turn away your faces from all your abominations. For any of those of the house of Israel or of the aliens who reside in Israel who separate themselves from me, taking their idols into their hearts and placing their iniquity as a stumbling block before them and yet come to a prophet to inquire of me by him, I the Lord will answer them myself" (Ezek 14:6–7). The core of the resistance is the human tendency to put something other than the Lord in the place of the Lord's guiding authority.

God's directness in response to human idolatry as demoting God's lordship has a clear aim: "So that the house of Israel may no longer go astray from me nor defile themselves any more with all their transgressions. Then they shall be my people, and I will be their God, says the Lord God" (Ezek 14:11). When people inquire of God in a context of idolatry, according to Ezekiel, God will take responsibility for a direct reply, and it may include corrective judgment for the good of the inquirers. The corrective feature is the divine effort to save people from their going "astray" from God. It is not destructive condemnation of humans.

The pressing issue for God's people and others is: Why should we suppose that God is trustworthy, given the surrounding frustrations, temptations, and evils in human life? God promises to answer directly, according to Ezekiel, with showing divine trustworthiness in righteousness. God aims to counter distrustful human alienation from God (allowed by God) and build trust with showing divine worthiness, including divine trustworthiness in righteousness. We need to clarify how this aim proceeds. A key factor, often neglected, is that God's showing divine worthiness in righteousness includes an intended corresponding showing of human worthiness, courtesy of God. The two go together, for the good of all involved.

Advancing Divine Showing: Becoming Worthy of God

The apostle Paul illuminates our understanding of what God seeks to show to humans in divine self-vindication: "We dealt with each one of you like a father with his children, urging and encouraging you and pleading that you lead a life *worthy* [ἀξίως] *of God*, who calls you into his own kingdom and glory" (1 Thess 2:11–12, italics added; see Col 1:10). We will unpack the crucial but widely neglected idea of living worthy of the God who shows divine and human (for some humans) worthiness of respect for righteousness.

The Epistle to the Ephesians, whether authored or just heavily influenced by Paul, identifies some divine expectations for the worthiness of God's people: "I beg you to walk in a manner worthy [ἀξίως] of the calling to which you have been called, with all humility and gentleness, with patience, bearing with one another in love, making every effort to maintain the unity of the Spirit in the bond of peace: there is one body and one Spirit, just as you were called to the one hope of your calling, one Lord, one faith, one baptism, one God and Father of all, who is above all and through all and in all. But each of us was given grace according to the measure of Christ's gift" (Eph 4:1–7). The "worthiness" in question thus depends on the unmerited gift of the fruit of God's Spirit (love, peace, patience, gentleness, etc.; see Gal 5:22–23) and the divine grace that supplies it. On this basis, we will clarify what God aims to show to and for humans for the sake of vindicating God and the people of God.

Drawing from Jesus and Paul, along with the previous lessons from Job and Ezekiel, we may consider that God has the following to show to and for humans in vindication:

1. God alone is perfectly good or righteous (Mark 10:18; Rom 3:25–26).
2. God nonetheless justifies, with divine approval and without condoning evil, imperfect humans ("the ungodly") who, despite their initial distrust, cooperate with God through faith in God (Rom 4:4).
3. The divine approval through faith, including trust, in God, relies on a divine process of transformative grace in divine-human reconciliation: that of empowering humans to become, in relationship with God, worthy of God and the gospel of their unearned divine approval (Phil 1:27; see Matt 10:37, Luke 15;11–32).
4. The latter approval graciously motivates their character formation by cooperation with the fruit of God's Spirit in the "obedience of faith" that includes both fellowship as Gethsemane-like moral rapport with God (Gal 5:22–23; Rom 1:5, 5:3–5; 2 Cor 13:14; Mark 14:34–36) and a human witness regarding God to a world in need of God (Phil 1:18, 27).

One result of the intended divine vindication, in Paul's language, is humans receiving, living out, and manifesting "the mind [= spirit] of Christ," if as an incomplete process in progress (1 Cor 2:16; Phil 2:5–8, 3:12–13).

God aims to show not only that God is trustworthy for righteous relationships but also that humans can willingly receive the righteous mind (spirit) of Christ. God does so to redeem the fallen world through building human trust in God and through humans showing, as living epistles of Christ, God's trustworthy righteousness to the world

(2 Cor 3:3; see Matt 5:16). We may use the following nonmathematical notion of proof (or showing) from the *Oxford English Dictionary:* "the action, process, or fact of establishing the truth of a statement; the action of evidence in convincing the mind." When we are concerned with a reality (say, a hope) that is not a statement, we may think of a proof (or showing) as confirming that reality with evidence.

God, as suggested, shows the righteousness of God's character in order to reconcile to God initially distrustful (and fearful) humans and enable them likewise to show, with their new lives, the unique reality, character, and worthiness of God to the world. In other words, we are able to show God to others with our lives when we enable God to show us worthy of God, by our faithful conformity to the fruit of the Spirit in faithful relationship to God. Paul thinks of this as our being "known by God" (Gal 4:9; 1 Cor 8:3), and it is what we have called "lordship knowledge" that puts God first in our decisions and lives (and not just factual knowledge that God exists). This perspective, particularly its aim regarding becoming worthy of God by the unmerited fruit of God's Spirit, has been widely neglected among theologians, biblical interpreters, philosophers of religion, and religious people more generally.

Restoring attention to what God aims to show among humans will aid in clarifying God's distinctive ways in the world, thereby adding credibility to those ways and to faith in God. God's having something to show is part of God's unique duty to be God, that is, a God who is worthy of worship and thus morally perfect and who will vindicate God's righteous character for the benefit of receptive inquirers. God's duty prompts, in turn, a human duty to honor God's duty and thus to cooperate with the divine effort to have people willingly conform to the fruit of God's Spirit, in faithful relationship to God. Humans thus can become co-showers of God's goodness with God, through their lives sharing in and manifesting the fruit of God's Spirit, for the good of all concerned. They thus can show God to be worthy of being their righteous God. This cycle of moral vindication aims to include all people, but it can meet human resistance and rejection.

Inquiry about God should raise the question of whether we humans are *willing* to be shown worthy of a perfectly righteous God. If we are willing, we can assess *how* willing we actually are. Are we willing come what may? Do we thus let Jesus in Gethsemane set the standard of worthiness for us? If so, his prayer to God in Gethsemane, "Not my will, but Your will be done," becomes the key practical motivator for us in relating to God. Gethsemane, we shall see, is a focal place for God showing God to be worthy of both human trust and love and human co-showing of God.

Showing as a Gift of Grace Through Faith

Only a gift of divine grace can deflate human distrust toward God and build needed trust in God. It alone can defuse human fear and distrust by countering those tendencies with unmerited good from God. Such a gift has a role in attracting, without coercion, distrustful people to attend to and value the uniqueness of God and divine goodness, including trustworthiness for righteousness. At the center of divine grace is a gift of an unearned opportunity for humans to share and participate in God's righteous love, including the power to receive and manifest such love. So, this gift is not static but active. It invites people actively to join, in interpersonal relationship, God's effort to reconcile people to God and others. It thereby can renew people in a Christlike manner, individually and as a society.

In Gethsemane, God offers Jesus a "cup to drink," and the offer is pivotal for the relation of Jesus to God and to the divine plan to reconcile people to God. God asks Jesus to give his earthly life for God and God's plan by willingly being crucified in Jerusalem. Paul would add, "God proves [συνίστησιν] his love for us in that while we still were sinners Christ died for us" (Rom 5:8). Gethsemane shows how Jesus chose to be part of God's vindication, for the sake of demonstrating God's righteous self-giving love for wayward people. Jesus resolved to do God's will by putting it above his initial request ("remove this cup from me," Mark 14:36), thus letting God be his God and Father over his life and death. This faithful obedience proves Jesus's commitment to be God's trustworthy Son, who bears and manifests divine righteous love for all concerned.

Paul names the obedience of Jesus as a central feature in divine approval of him, as he showed God's righteous trustworthiness with his death (Phil 2:8). He also instructs God's people to follow suit with the same kind of loyal obedience found through their sharing "the mind" of Christ (Phil 2:5). In doing so, according to Paul, you "work out your own salvation with fear and trembling; for God is at work in you, both to will and to work for his good pleasure" (Phil 2:12–13, RSV). Such "working out," in Paul's thought, is a matter of receiving divine grace and not earning approval by God. In addition, God's working is not a matter of coercing human wills to conform to God. Paul acknowledges that humans can "quench" the working of God's Spirit in their lives (1 Thess 5:19). (Chapter 6 returns to the latter topic.)

Paul puts divine righteousness at the center of God's vindication for humans. He begins by acknowledging God's aim for a vindication: "Let God be [shown] true, as it is written, 'so that you may be justified [δικαιωθῇς; vindicated] in your words and you will prevail when you go to trial [κρίνεσθαί]'" (Rom 3:4). "Shown" is elliptical here (likewise NASB), and Paul clearly has it in mind with his reference, alluding to Psalm 51:4, to being vindicated when going to judgment or "trial."

Paul sums up the gift of grace in God's showing of divine righteousness to humans: "Since all have sinned and fall short of the glory of God, they are now justified by his grace as a gift, through the redemption that is in Christ Jesus, whom God put forward as a sacrifice of atonement by his blood, effective through faith. He did this to demonstrate [ἔνδειξιν; prove] his righteousness, because in his divine forbearance he had passed over the sins previously committed; it was to demonstrate at the present time his own righteousness, so that he is righteous and he justifies the one who has the faith of Jesus" (Rom 3:23–26). The divine grace of Gethsemane, working through the resolute cooperation of Jesus, thus led to the divine grace of Calvary, with Jesus again representing the face of the self-giving righteous God toward wayward humans. The divine gift, in each case, is in what God freely offers to attract humans to receive righteous life with God over final death without God.

Faith, according to Paul, is the cooperative reception of the gift of divine grace, and it includes trust in God, after the model of Abraham (Rom 4:3). So, it is not simply the acceptance of theological information, however important the information. Paul adds with regard to human "works" as human earnings, "To one who works, wages are not reckoned as a gift but as something due [ὀφείλημα]. But to one who does not work but trusts him who justifies the ungodly, such faith is reckoned as righteousness" (Rom 4:4–5). So, God in grace credits Abraham-like faith as righteousness approved by God.

The credit from divine grace through faith is not fictional credit because the faith in question receives God's righteousness in character formation, if only imperfectly and in part. Such faith at least begins the divine process of showing a human to be righteous before God, courtesy of divine grace. In the absence of such grace through faith in God, humans would have no viable option for their divine approval or vindication.

A gift of divine grace through faith is God's way to include, without condoning evil, humans in divine righteousness. This gift thus includes humans initially distrustful and alienated from God in the divine effort to re-create a fallen world. In such grace, God uses faith, including trust, as a basis for humans receiving divine power for re-creating them to recognize and value God's trustworthiness for righteousness. God's vindication thus offers humans, as a gift, the power to discern this effort as coming from God for their benefit. (The following section clarifies how divine power can come to fruition in human lives through trust in God.)

The gift of divine grace in Jesus coheres with God's aim to have people become worthy of God and God's vindication of divine righteousness. Their becoming worthy of God is through their receiving, in cooperative relationship with God, a gift of credited approval from God and not through their earning divine approval. In receiving this gift, they receive God and God's unique power to manifest character formation reflective of divine righteousness. We turn to this feature of God's vindication.

Showing in the Fruit of the Spirit

Ezekiel, as noted, offered a divine promise of God responding directly to people who inquire of God and divine righteousness (Ezek 14:7). We shall see how God uses God's own manifested personality traits, in the fruit of the Spirit, to respond directly to humans, offering them an opportunity to become "worthy of God" and of their divine calling. A cooperative reply to that fruit is a worthy response to God that leads to character transformation toward God's unique moral character, including the mind of Christ. It also enables divine self-vindication of righteousness in the lives of cooperative people.

Ephesians 4:1–3, we noted, indicates that becoming worthy of God's calling to a righteous relationship expects human conformity to "the unity of Spirit." This unity relies on cooperation with the following "fruit of the Spirit" (using language from Galatians 5:22–23): love, gentleness, peace, and patience. These are divine moral-character traits, in Paul's thinking, and are manifested directly at times in human experience, including in moral conscience, courtesy of God's Spirit. Love tops the list of Paul's portrayal of the fruit in Galatians, and it recurs in Paul's understanding of how God directly relates to people, including in their suffering. Humans can respond to such love with cooperation, rejection, or indifference.

Paul, we have seen, recognizes divine love to come to people through God's Spirit to counter their suffering and shame (Rom 5:3–5; see 2 Cor 5:14). He thinks of such love to emerge from God's intervening directly in human experience and thus to ground hope and faith in God. Such an intervention of God's Spirit, according to Paul, is a down payment on what God will deliver in fullness later (2 Cor 1:22, 5:5; see Rom 8:23; Eph 1:13–14). For now, Paul holds, God's experienced goodness aims to lead people to repentance before God (Rom 2:4), whereby they cooperate with God and the manifested fruit of God's Spirit. This is the divinely empowered path to become worthy of God and God's effort toward human renewal in redemption.

We have seen that God's self-giving love and mercy, according to Paul, call for human reciprocating in self-sacrifice to God through full obedience (Rom 12:1–2). The transformation in renewal of the mind comes not just from contemplation but also from presenting oneself sacrificially (with self-giving) to God in response to God's manifested goodness, including mercy. This is a matter of the human will, as noted, beyond mere contemplation (see Rom 6:13). Active loyal obedience to God is central to the divine goal of vindication, after the model of Jesus's faithful response to God in Gethsemane.

Paul notes a cognitive benefit of self-giving to God that leads to divine renewal of a human mind: human discernment of "what is the will of God—what is good and acceptable and perfect." The manifested fruit of the Spirit reflects God's moral will, and in cooperating with that fruit, a person enables it to come to maturity or fruition in reflecting God's moral will. In this regard, people see God's vindication by participating in it, that is, by participating cooperatively in the fruit of the Spirit as it comes to fruition in their lives. We thus may say that those cooperative in heart will see God.

Some critics will object that the intended divine vindication is too hard, given human moral weakness. Humans lack the power to sustain and to manifest the morally demanding fruit of God's Spirit, particularly love toward enemies. We can grant this objection as long as we are talking simply about human power. The availability of divine power for humans, however, offers a different opportunity, where they can be empowered by God to live by, including to manifest, the fruit of God's Spirit. Offering such moral power in relationship, God can strengthen cooperative people morally, without condoning human waywardness in complacency or opposition toward righteousness.

As the fruit becomes empowering in human lives, humans can recognize God to be trustworthy in actively promoting righteousness. The fruit can intentionally lead them to cooperate with God, despite the challenges from human life.[3] So, God can build human trust, uncoercively, by the attractive qualities of God's own personality traits, manifested in the fruit of the Spirit. Humans thereby can become co-showers or co-vindicators with God of divine righteousness. God's vindication enables their participating in the vindication as witnesses to God's unique moral character of perfect righteousness, including unselfish love.

Conclusion

God would be negligent if humans were left without a witness to God's reality and goodness. They would be left with a dubious option of an ungrounded leap in the dark, without needed guidance in how and where to leap. That would not be biblical faith in God. Biblical faith is a response, directly or indirectly, to divine intervention with distinctive qualitative features characteristic of God. Ezekiel, as noted, announced the role of divine proof or showing in the people of God, including with God's direct response to human inquiry about God.

God's showing and direct response, as seen, rely on the qualitative features Paul calls "the fruit of the Spirit." When humans allow this fruit to form their moral character, they become co-vindicators and co-showers with God of divine righteousness. They thereby join with God in vindicating God's moral character as righteous and trustworthy for righteous relationships. Interpreters of divine action should accommodate this lesson to unify the biblical storyline and clarify how God vindicates God and God's people. Their efforts will bear fruit for interpreters of divine action in human history and experience.

CHAPTER FOUR

Vindication with Moral Direction

Obeying the commandments of God is everything.

—1 Corinthians 7:19

THE PREVIOUS CHAPTERS have explained how divine self-vindication works through the cooperation of humans in their moral-character transformation toward divine righteousness. We now turn to how God guides such transformation by means of moral commands that promote righteousness among humans. Many people in Jewish, Christian, and Islamic monotheistic traditions testify to their experience of being commanded by God to do something or to be a certain way that promotes righteousness. We need to ask if such testimony is credible in some cases and, if so, on what ground.

A central thesis of this chapter is that human testimony to divine commanding is credible in some cases. It finds a suitable ground for this testimony in the morally purifying experience of human conscience. The chapter looks to the Jewish Bible, the New Testament, and the *Qur'an* for relevant testimony to righteous divine commanding experienced by humans. The commands in question are not abstract or merely theoretical but are grounded in human moral experience and are potentially motivating for righteous action. The chapter doubts that God would be God if there were no divine commands given directly to receptive people in their moral experience. It contends that God would not be a morally righteous guide worthy of worship by humans in the absence of God's directly commanding people in their experience.

Jewish, Christian, and Islamic versions of monotheism have long maintained that God is fully holy as perfectly righteous, or morally good. Divine righteousness is not limited to God's internal moral character. Instead, it moves outward to interaction with humans for the sake of their redemption or salvation as reconciliation to God in a righteous relationship. In doing so, it aims to guide people to cooperative repentance, faith, and obedience toward God. An intended result is volitional submission to God, thus giving God's moral will normative supremacy over human wills. We shall explore how God presents the divine moral will to humans via divine commanding in human moral experience, including conscience. We shall see how this divine effort figures in the self-vindication of God in cooperative human lives.

Divine Commanding in the Jewish Bible

Gerhard von Rad has commented, "There is absolutely no concept in the Old Testament with so central a significance for all the relationships of human life as that of *tzedaqah* [righteousness]."[1] Alan Richardson adds, "Righteousness is for the Hebrews the fundamental character of God."[2] We need to clarify what this righteous character involves. P. T. Forsyth has suggested that God's character of perfect righteousness grounds both divine holiness and divine love: "Holiness is the foundation of divine love and the bloom on divine righteousness."[3] I concur with this suggestion and will present relevant evidence from Jewish monotheism, which implies that there is just one true God.

An important testimony in the Jewish Bible to direct experience of God occurs in the book of Isaiah:

> In the year that King Uzziah died, I saw the Lord sitting on a throne, high and lofty, and the hem of his robe filled the temple. Seraphs were in attendance above him; each had six wings: with two they covered their faces, and with two they covered their feet, and with two they flew. And one called to another and said, "Holy, holy, holy is the Lord of hosts; the whole earth is full of his glory."

> The pivots on the thresholds shook at the voices of those who called, and the house filled with smoke. And I said, "Woe is me! I am lost, for I am a man of unclean lips, and I live among a people of unclean lips, yet my eyes have seen the King, the Lord of hosts!" (Isa 6:1–5)

The reference to "a man of unclean lips" and "a people of unclean lips" is instructive. Its use here contrasts the intervening "Lord of hosts" with the inferior moral state of Isaiah and his fellow Jews. It points to a superior moral state of the Lord and honors this status.

A previous chapter of the book of Isaiah portrays the moral state of the Lord of hosts:

> The Lord of hosts is exalted by justice,
> and the Holy God shows himself holy by righteousness [*tzedaqah*]. . . .
> Woe to those who drag iniquity along with cords of falsehood,
> who drag sin along as with cart ropes,
> who say, "Let him make haste;
> let him speed his work
> that we may see it;
> let the plan of the Holy One of Israel hasten to fulfillment,
> that we may know it!"
> Woe to those who call evil good
> and good evil,
> who put darkness for light
> and light for darkness,
> who put bitter for sweet
> and sweet for bitter!
> Woe to those who are wise in their own eyes
> and shrewd in their own sight!
> Woe to those who are heroes in drinking wine
> and valiant at mixing drink,
> who acquit the guilty for a bribe
> and deprive the innocent of their rights! (Isa 5:16, 18–23)

Isaiah thus calls for attention and honoring toward the righteousness of the Lord of hosts as God's distinctive moral character.

Isaiah identifies divine righteousness with "good" rather than "evil," with "light" rather than "darkness." He also calls for patience toward seeing the fulfillment of "the plan of the Holy One." In addition, he challenges people who are "wise in their own eyes and shrewd in their own sight," without their depending on the righteous wisdom of the Lord.

The book of Isaiah promises a future fulfillment in righteousness for the people of God:

> A spirit from on high [will be] poured out on us,
> and the wilderness [will] become a fruitful field,
> and the fruitful field [will be] deemed a forest.
> Then justice will dwell in the wilderness
> and righteousness abide in the fruitful field.
> The effect of righteousness will be peace,
> and the result of righteousness, quietness and trust forever.
> My people will abide in a peaceful habitation,
> in secure dwellings, and in quiet resting places. (Isa 32:15–18)

Divine righteousness aims for such peace and faithfulness among the people of God. Its goal is a righteous society of the people of God under God's perfect righteousness in relationship with God. It aims to motivate human hope in the ultimate victory of God in divine righteousness shared by cooperative humans.

The book of Isaiah presents God as challenging human anti-God ways, calling for a responsible, candid human reply and even a trial with them:

> I alone am the one
> who blots out your transgressions for my own sake,
> and I will not remember your sins.
> Accuse me; let us go to trial;

set forth your case, so that you may be proved right.
Your first ancestor sinned,
and your mediators rebelled against me. (Isa 43:25–27)

This passage identifies God's motive in extending divine righteousness, including forgiveness, to humans "for my own sake." God thus seeks to uphold God's own perfect moral character, and this aim is foundational for the God of Isaiah. From this motive, coupled with divine love, God brings divine righteousness and forgiveness to wayward humans for their salvation as reconciliation with God. Interpreters thus do well not to ignore the integrity of God's own goodness in the divine redemption of humans.

Isaiah assigns responsibility to humans for receiving and cooperating with divine righteousness: "If you are willing and obedient, you shall eat the good of the land, but if you refuse and rebel, you shall be devoured by the sword, for the mouth of the Lord has spoken" (Isa 1:19–20). God takes responsibility for trying to purify the people of God morally while maintaining their responsibility to cooperate with God in receiving and manifesting divine righteousness.

Here is the challenge:

Therefore says the Sovereign, the Lord of hosts, the Mighty One of Israel:
Surely I will pour out my wrath on my enemies
and avenge myself on my foes!
I will turn my hand against you;
I will smelt away your dross as with lye
and remove all your alloy.
And I will restore your judges as at the first
and your counselors as at the beginning.
Afterward you shall be called the city of righteousness,
the faithful city.
Zion shall be redeemed by justice,
and those in her who repent, by righteousness.

> But rebels and sinners shall be destroyed together,
> and those who forsake the Lord shall be consumed.
> (Isa 1:24–28)

The divine motive toward the people of God is their purification in righteousness as they relate to God: "I will smelt away your dross as with lye and remove all your alloy."

The divine goal is that the people of God be "redeemed . . . by righteousness," for those "who repent." So, the desired purification brings divine righteousness to inhabit and form the people of God in a repentant relationship with God. This is a kind of interpersonal moral catharsis for God's people, and it amounts to a moral theophany incarnate in these people.

The message of God as righteous and as spreading righteousness echoes throughout the Jewish Bible, beyond the book of Isaiah. The prophet Malachi, for instance, continues a theme from Isaiah by connecting God's coming to humans with the divine moral refining of them as a means to righteousness: "[The Lord] is like a refiner's fire and like fullers' soap; he will sit as a refiner and purifier of silver, and he will purify the descendants of Levi and refine them like gold and silver, until they present offerings to the Lord in righteousness" (Mal 3:2–3; cf. Zech 13:8–9; Ps 66:10–12). Divine moral agitation of humans through refining, or purifying, them aims at human righteousness in relationship with God. We will not adequately understand divine action toward humans apart from such divine agitation for righteousness. If we neglect this kind of agitation, we will neglect the moral commands at the center of God's righteous character.

Divine righteousness has priority even over worship ceremonies in the Jewish Bible. The prophet Amos represents God speaking to God's people:

> I hate, I despise your festivals,
> and I take no delight in your solemn assemblies.
> Even though you offer me your burnt offerings and grain offerings,

> I will not accept them,
> and the offerings of well-being of your fatted animals
> I will not look upon.
> Take away from me the noise of your songs;
> I will not listen to the melody of your harps.
> But let justice roll down like water
> and righteousness like an ever-flowing stream. (Amos 5:21–24)

God refuses to receive, and even hates, human worship coupled with human unrighteousness. Human worship of God is to be motivated by human cooperation with divine righteousness, thus reflecting God's unique moral character of righteousness. Otherwise, it is counterfeit and displeasing to God.

Divine righteousness extends beyond ethics to bear on human knowledge of God, as the book of Jeremiah reports:

> Did not your father eat and drink
> and do justice and righteousness?
> Then it was well with him.
> He judged the cause of the poor and needy;
> then it was well.
> Is not this to know me?
> says the Lord. (Jer 22:15–16)

Doing righteousness, according to Jeremiah, is integral to knowing the Lord. Such knowing, then, is practical and not merely speculative or theoretical. It is morally robust in its dependence on divine righteousness and the human doing of such righteousness.

The emphasis on divine righteousness stems from a divine preference for human life over death. The book of Ezekiel represents God's preference coupled with severe consequences for human disobedience: "Have I any pleasure in the death of the wicked, says the Lord God, and not rather that they should turn from their ways and live? But when the righteous turn away from their righteousness and commit iniquity and do the same abominable things that the wicked do, shall they live? None of the righteous deeds that they have done shall be remembered, for the treachery of which they are guilty and the sin they have committed, they shall die" (Ezek 18:23–24). Human life, then, depends on cooperation with divine righteousness for its avoiding death, by God's standard of righteous life. This is the result of God's righteous character as the standard for worthwhile human life.

The divine way of promoting righteousness includes the divine "leading" of willing humans in a moral direction. Psalm 23 characterizes God as a divine shepherd: "He leads me in paths of righteousness for his name's sake" (23:3, RSV). This leading includes commanding by God and other moral means. The psalmist indicates divine guidance in his experience as he moves to prayer to God in the second person: "Thou art with me; Thy rod and Thy staff, they comfort me" (23:4, RSV). The rod and staff are the shepherd's means of guiding, safeguarding, and rescuing the sheep. The psalmist treats them as symbolic for divine moral guidance, including by God's good commanding. The psalmist thus identifies a vital result from God: "Surely goodness and mercy shall follow me all the days of my life" (23:6).

The Jewish Bible offers a summary of the role of divine commanding with a life-or-death challenge: "See, I have set before you this day life and good, and death and evil. If you obey the commandments of the Lord your God which I command you this day, by loving the Lord your God, by walking in his ways, and by keeping his commandments and his statutes and his ordinances, then you shall live and multiply" (Deut 30:15–16). The good life in question is a righteous life in cooperation with God. The recurring idea of divine guiding into righteousness continues in the Christian New Testament.

Divine Commanding in New Testament Experience

The place of divine commanding for the sake of righteousness among humans is prominent in the New Testament, particularly in the writings of the apostle Paul. Paul asks, "Do you presume upon the riches of

[God's] kindness and forbearance and patience? Do you not know that God's kindness is meant to lead you to repentance?" (Rom 2:4). This repentance demands human turning to a righteous relationship with God. Paul adds that "[the Gentiles] show that what the law [of God] requires is written on their hearts, while their conscience also bears witness and their conflicting thoughts accuse or perhaps excuse them" (Rom 2:15). God, according to Paul, is at work in human conscience to draw people to God on the basis of their needing a life guided by divine righteousness. This work includes divine moral commands in human conscience.

Paul takes divine righteousness to be received by a human response that goes beyond merely obeying the requirements of the divine law. He explains,

> The righteousness of God has been manifested apart from law, although the law and the prophets bear witness to it, the righteousness of God through faith in Jesus Christ for all who believe. For there is no distinction; since all have sinned and fall short of the glory of God, they are justified by his grace as a gift, through the redemption which is in Christ Jesus, whom God put forward as an expiation by his blood, to be received by faith. This was to show God's righteousness, because in his divine forbearance he had passed over former sins; it was to prove at the present time that he himself is righteous and that he justifies him who has faith in Jesus. (Rom 3:21–26, RSV)

Paul's message includes the claim that "[humans] are justified by [God's] grace as a gift" and not by anything they have earned. Being thus justified is God's approval of humans without condoning their evil. Paul holds that human moral failure in relation to God blocks any avenue to God through human earning of approval. Human righteousness, given its moral failure, does not meet the divine standard of righteousness, in Paul's perspective.

Paul acknowledges an alternative to human earning of divine approval in human faith, or trust, in God and finds a basis in the experience of Abraham in the book of Genesis. He explains, "What then shall we say about Abraham, our forefather according to the flesh? For if Abraham was justified by works, he has something to boast about, but not before God. For what does the scripture say? 'Abraham believed God, and it was reckoned to him as righteousness' [Gen 15:6]. Now to one who works, his wages are not reckoned as a gift but as his due. And to one who does not work but trusts him who justifies the ungodly, his faith is reckoned as righteousness" (Rom 4:1–5, RSV). Paul holds that, given human failure to satisfy the divine standard of perfect righteousness, God finds a merciful and morally responsible way for humans to be justified or approved before God. Without condoning evil, God credits righteousness to them on the basis not of their (failed) earning but of their faith, or trust, in God, who seeks to lead them into a righteous relationship. As a result, Paul claims that "all who are led by the Spirit of God are children of God" (Rom 8:14; see also Gal 5:18, 25).

We need to clarify what Paul calls "the gift of grace" from God in the divine crediting of righteousness to humans. This gift is interpersonal and experiential, not abstract or speculative. The salvific or redemptive gift, at its center, is *God* graciously coming to humans to lead them, with their faithful cooperation, into an ever-deepening filial relationship of experienced reconciliation with God.

Paul portrays the salvific gift to bring filial adoption to humans from God: "You did not receive a spirit of slavery to fall back into fear, but you received a spirit of adoption. When we cry, 'Abba! Father!,' it is that very Spirit bearing witness with our spirit that we are children of God, and if children, then heirs: heirs of God and joint heirs with Christ, if we in fact suffer with him so that we may also be glorified with him" (Rom 8:15–17; see Gal 4:6–7). God "bears witness" to the people of God, according to Paul. This witness affirms and confirms the status of cooperative people as children of God in God's family. The hallmark of this family is its undergoing salvation toward righteous relationships with God and other humans. This family is thus a work in progress.

Paul summarizes his message of the good news of divine grace in relation to divine reconciliation and righteousness: "In Christ God was reconciling the world to himself, not counting their trespasses against them, and entrusting the message of reconciliation to us. So we are ambassadors for Christ, since God is making his appeal through us; we entreat you on behalf of Christ: be reconciled to God. For our sake God made the one who knew no sin to be sin, so that in him we might become the righteousness of God" (2 Cor 5:19–21). "Be reconciled to God" sums up Paul's understanding of the goal of God's gift of grace. This imperative is a divine command, in Paul's understanding, even for the people of God. If people have been justified or approved by God, through credited righteousness in faith, they still may lack full reconciliation with God. They therefore may need deeper reconciliation.

Paul thinks of God's salvific gift in terms of "life" with God: "Those who live according to the Spirit set their minds on the things of the Spirit. To set the mind on the flesh is death, but to set the mind on the Spirit is life and peace. . . . The Spirit is life because of righteousness" (Rom 8:6, 10). Paul has in mind "life and peace" with God (Rom 5:1), and he finds the needed source in "the Spirit" of God, with God seeking human cooperation with this source.

Paul finds divine motivating power for righteousness among humans in the fruit of the Spirit listed previously (Gal 5:22–23). Such fruit of the Spirit, manifested in human experience, is not a set of principles, concepts, or ideas. We have noted that it is, in Paul's approach, a divine presentation of the moral character, or personality, traits of God, shown by God in human moral experience. It is thus an experienced feature of God in action, bringing God's moral character into human experience. As a result, it serves as direct experiential evidence of God's presence and goodness.

Paul, we noted, is clear about the role of divine love from the fruit of the Spirit in the basis of faith and hope in God (Rom 5:5). Paul's talk of "not putting us to shame," as suggested, concerns evidential, or epistemic, shame. He rejects such shame on the basis of available evidence of

God from divine love shown in human moral experience ("poured into our hearts" through God's Spirit). Paul finds the same Spirit at work in human moral conscience, challenging and guiding people, including himself. He writes, as noted, to the Roman Christians, "I am speaking the truth in Christ—I am not lying; my conscience confirms it by the Holy Spirit" (Rom 9:1). God's Spirit works in conscience, according to Paul, to confirm what is true and good and thus real.

Paul gives a decisive role to God's Spirit in revealing knowledge of God to humans: "God has revealed to us through the Spirit, for the Spirit searches everything, even the depths of God. For what human knows what is truly human except the human spirit that is within? So also no one comprehends what is truly God's except the Spirit of God. Now we have received not the spirit of the world but the Spirit that is from God, so that we may understand the gifts bestowed on us by God" (1 Cor 2:10–12). The Spirit of God brings not only God's gifts to humans, including cognitive gifts, but also some understanding of those divine gifts.

Divine gift-giving involves the moral searching of humans by God's Spirit, in a manner recognized by Psalm 139:

> O Lord, you have searched me and known me.
> You know when I sit down and when I rise up;
> you discern my thoughts from far away.
> You search out my path and my lying down
> and are acquainted with all my ways.
> Even before a word is on my tongue,
> O Lord, you know it completely.
> You hem me in, behind and before,
> and lay your hand upon me.
> Such knowledge is too wonderful for me;
> it is so high that I cannot attain it. (Ps 139:1–6)

Humans cannot attain such knowledge on their own. It must come as a gracious gift from God, who mercifully intervenes in human experience to bring moral goodness and guidance to receptive people in need.[4] Even so, human reception of this gift requires a life-or-death moral struggle to conform to what God offers.

The divine challenge to human unrighteousness leads to the following command from Paul to the Corinthian Christians: "Let us cleanse ourselves from every defilement of flesh and of spirit, making holiness perfect in the fear of God. . . . Godly grief produces a repentance that leads to salvation and brings no regret, but worldly grief produces death" (2 Cor 7:1,10). The desired moral cleansing or catharsis is not a self-help program, given its dependence on the power of God's Spirit: "If you live according to the flesh, you will die, but if by the Spirit you put to death the deeds of the body, you will live" (Rom 8:13). Such a struggle against unrighteous "deeds of the body" is part of repentance before God. This struggle, according to Paul, includes keeping God's commands. Therefore, "circumcision is nothing, and uncircumcision is nothing, but obeying the commandments of God is everything" (1 Cor 7:19). Paul thus recognizes no inherent conflict between obedience and credited righteousness through faith.

According to the book of Acts, Paul's preaching at Athens included a divine command to repent: "While God has overlooked the times of human ignorance, now he commands all people everywhere to repent" (Acts 17:30). The author of Acts may be a bit creative in representing some of the earliest Christian preaching, but he captures an actual theme from Paul here (see Rom 2:4). The divine command to repent extends to human conscience as long as humans, according to Paul, do not "by their injustice [or, unrighteousness] suppress the truth" in this area (Rom 1:18). Humans, then, have a voluntary role in responding to a divine command to repent. They are not pawns of God, in Paul's thought.

According to Paul, problems of suppressing divine truth emerge from a human will resistant to, but in need of, the cooperative receiving of divine transformation in moral catharsis. He encourages, as we noted, a correction by presenting oneself to God for renewal (Rom 12:1–2).[5] This appeal goes beyond hard thinking to difficult acting before God, in cooperation with God's Spirit.

Paul couples the needed renewing of the human mind to presenting oneself to God. He gives such presenting a central role in the commanded repentance and moral catharsis in righteousness (Rom 6:12–14). His talk of "grace," in this connection, signifies divine intentional power to lead people to righteousness in relationship with God and thus to life with God rather than moral death. The command to "present yourselves to God" indicates that the key relation is interpersonal (divine-human) and not just a matter of human behavior. It bears on who we are in relation to God and not just on what we think or do.

Actions matter, of course, but God is after persons in their righteous relationships with God (and others). These relationships include grounded trust in God, as in the case of Abraham (Rom 4:1–5), even if this trust occurs in the context of a very limited understanding of God and divine purposes. God commands such trust for the good of humans in relation to God. In doing so, God works in human moral experience, including conscience, to attract a voluntary commitment from humans toward divine righteousness. Such a commitment will contribute to the divine effort of self-vindication through cooperative humans. It will enable them to manifest who God really is, in the goodness of righteousness.

Divine Commanding in the *Qur'an*

The religion of Islam follows Jewish and Christian monotheism in giving a priority to divine commands in relation to humans. We shall document this lesson in order to highlight the centrality of divine commands in the main variations on Abrahamic monotheism. As the religion of absolute submission to Allah, or God, Islam finds its basis in the following prayer in the *Qur'an*: "Our Lord, . . . make us submissive to You, and from our descendants a community submissive to You" (2:128).[6] A related rhetorical question, combining obedience and faith, is: "Who is better in religion than he who submits himself wholly to God, and is a doer of good, and follows the faith of Abraham the Monotheist?" (*Qur'an* 4:125; see also 31:22, 72:14).

The *Qur'an* contrasts God with the one who commands evil and associates the people of God with doing "good on earth": "O people! Eat of what is lawful and good on earth, and do not follow the footsteps of Satan. He is to you an open enemy. He commands you to do evil and vice, and to say about God what you do not know" (2:168, 169). An important lesson is that God does not command people "to do evil and vice" but commands "what is lawful and good on earth."

The *Qur'an* associates righteousness with belief in God: "Righteousness does not consist of turning your faces toward the East and the West. But righteous is he who believes in God, and the Last Day, and the angels, and the Scripture, and the prophets. Who gives money, though dear, to near relatives, and orphans, and the needy, and the homeless, and the beggars, and for the freeing of slaves; those who perform the prayers, and pay the obligatory charity, and fulfill their promise when they promise, and patiently persevere in the face of persecution, hardship, and in the time of conflict. These are the sincere; these are the pious" (*Qur'an* 2:177). The *Qur'an* does not limit divine righteousness to Muslims but makes it available to Jews and Christians: "Those who believe, and those who are Jewish, and the Christians, and the Sabeans—any who believe in God and the Last Day, and act righteously—will have their reward with their Lord; they have nothing to fear, nor will they grieve" (2:62).

Islam, according to the *Qur'an*, is the original monotheism of which Abraham was a proponent: "Abraham was neither a Jew nor a Christian, but he was a Monotheist, a Muslim. And he was not of the Polytheists" (3:67). It also aims to include Moses and Jesus under the religion of Allah: "He [Allah] prescribed for you the same religion He enjoined upon Noah, and what We inspired to you, and what We enjoined upon Abraham, and Moses, and Jesus: 'You shall uphold the religion, and be not divided therein'" (42:13).

The *Qur'an* portrays a formative religious experience for Muhammad as follows:

> It is but a revelation revealed.
> Taught to him by the Extremely Powerful.

> The one of vigor. He settled.
> While he was at the highest horizon.
> Then he came near and hovered around.
> He was within two bows' length, or closer.
> Then He revealed to His servant what He revealed.
> The heart did not lie about what it saw.
> Will you dispute with him concerning what he saw? (53:4–12)

Such an experience prompted Muhammad to convey the contents of the *Qur'an* as the word of God, as a communication from God through him. This experience anchored his conviction that he was called to be God's final prophet to humans.

The *Qur'an* characterizes the divine revelation to Muhammad as follows:

> Read [or: Proclaim]: In the Name of your Lord who created.
> Created man from a clot.
> Read [or: Proclaim]: And your Lord is the Most Generous.
> He who taught by the pen.
> Taught man what he never knew. (96:1–5)

The report here is that God, the "most generous" Creator, is using Muhammad, as a prophetic messenger, and his pen to reveal divine things previously unknown to humans. This report accompanies the religious experience of Muhammad, and it led to the formation of Islam as a religious way of life, as submission to God and divine commands.

Allah's revelation to Muhammad, according to the *Qur'an,* came with "clear signs" of divine involvement in the process, but some people rejected these signs (2:97–99). We need to clarify what kind of "sign" of God was central to Muhammad's religious experience.

The experience of *being commanded (by Allah)* anchors Muhammad's formative religious experience. The following summary statement focuses his experience: "The guidance of Allah is the guidance, and we are commanded to surrender [or submit] to the Lord of the universe" (*Qur'an* 6:71). The *Qur'an* puts Allah's status as the one who commands on an equal footing with Allah's status as the Creator: "Your Lord is Allah; He who created the heavens and the earth in six days, then established Himself on the Throne. The night overtakes the day, as it pursues it persistently; and the sun, and the moon, and the stars are subservient by His command. His is the creation, and His is the command. Blessed is Allah, Lord of all beings" (7:54). This is a strong sense of "command" because it involves a kind of divine control over the objects of the command (sun, moon, and stars, for instance). A command need not have such control, but Allah's command does, at least in some cases, according to the *Qur'an*.

The signs of Allah to humans are "within yourselves," and they should be clear to those who pay attention:

> And on earth are signs for the convinced.
> And within yourselves. Do you not see?
> And in the heaven is your livelihood, and what you are promised.
> By the Lord of the heaven and the earth, it is as true as the fact that you speak. (51:20–23)

An important question is: How are the signs of Allah "within yourselves"? An answer will guide us toward where to look for the intervention of Allah in human experience.

According to the *Qur'an*, having signs "within yourselves" involves Allah's "calling" people to himself through his Messenger, the Prophet Muhammad, who represents "clear revelations" from Allah as "most compassionate":

> Believe in Allah and His Messenger, and spend from what He made you inherit. Those among you who believe and give will have a great reward.

> What is the matter with you that you do not believe in Allah, when the Messenger calls you to believe in your Lord, and He has received a pledge from you, if you are believers?
> It is He who sends down upon His servant clear revelations, to bring you out of darkness into the light. Allah is Gentle toward you, Most Compassionate. (57:7–9)

Allah's commanding people to submit in obedience and worship is an experience that many people report to have or feel, and it motivates their commitment to Allah in a faithful Islamic way of life. Such commanding was at the experiential center of Muhammad's life, and it accounted for his proclaiming the message of the *Qur'an*.

The *Qur'an* goes beyond the view that God hides from some people, including in their experience, to the stronger view that God "leads astray" or "misguides" some people: "We have appointed only angels to be wardens of the Fire, and caused their number to be a stumbling block for those who disbelieve; so that those given the Scripture may attain certainty; and those who believe may increase in faith; and those given the Scripture and the believers may not doubt; and those in whose hearts is sickness and the unbelievers may say, 'What did Allah intend by this parable?' Thus Allah leads astray whom He wills, and guides whom He wills" (74:31).

In a similar vein, "Whomever Allah desires to guide, He spreads open his heart to Islam; and whomever He desires to misguide, He makes his heart narrow, constricted, as though he were climbing up the sky. Allah thus lays defilement upon those who do not believe" (6:125). This is a kind of divine judgment, and it raises the question of who wills human unbelief first, Allah or humans. The matter is controversial, but some interpreters assume that the Islamic missionary movement depends on individual people needing to make a responsible, voluntary decision about the message offered.

The central role of divine command in the *Qur'an* relies on a notion of the law of God: "We revealed to you the Book, with truth, confirming the Scripture that preceded it, and superseding it. So, judge between them according to what Allah revealed, and do not follow their desires if they differ from the truth that has come to you. For each of you we have assigned a law and a method" (5:48). The divine law in question is the updated, clarified version (relative to past versions, such as the Mosaic law) based on the commands of the *Qur'an*.

Submitting to Allah is law-based, according to the *Qur'an,* and the relevant law emerges in Allah's unique revelation to Muhammad. The *Qur'an* endorses "reward," "earning," and "wages" from God on the basis of divine law and human submission to God, for instance, "Whoever submits himself to God, and is a doer of good, will have his reward with his Lord—they have nothing to fear, nor shall they grieve" (2:112). This kind of submission includes active striving for obedience on the part of humans: "The human being attains only what he strives for. And . . . his efforts will be witnessed. Then he will be rewarded for it the fullest reward. And that to your Lord is the finality" (53:39–42). These remarks suggest that humans are not mere pawns of the will of God. They evidently have an active voluntary role in responding to God's will in their lives.

The *Qur'an* portrays God as crediting humans on the basis of what they "earn" from God: "God does not burden any soul beyond its capacity. To its credit is what it earns, and against it is what it commits" (2:286). In a similar vein, "How about when We gather them for a Day in which there is no doubt, and each soul will be paid in full for what it has earned, and they will not be wronged?" (3:25). This talk of "earning" assumes payment from God for human merit.

The theme of God's paying wages and increasing grace to humans on the basis of their good works arises as follows: "As for those who believe and do good works, He will pay them their wages in full, and will increase His grace for them. But as for those who disdain and are too proud, He will punish them with an agonizing punishment. And they will find for themselves, apart from God, no lord and no savior" (*Qur'an* 4:173). Similarly, "He [Allah] will pay them their dues in full, and will increase them from His bounty" (35:30). Such talk of "dues" relies on a notion of humans earning or meriting something from God, including increased divine grace for them.

The wages-earning approach of the *Qur'an* to submission to God differs from some Jewish perspectives and Paul's approach to divine-human atonement (even though the latter portray God to give rewards to humans). A law-based theism could reject human earning of God's approval on the ground that human obedience to divine laws is simply a fitting response to God's goodness and a way to accommodate this goodness. In Muhammad's approach, however, good human life will require human earning from God on the basis of human submission to God in obedience. Such varying theistic interpretations of obeying divine commands generate controversy, but they share acknowledgment of the reality of divine commanding in human experience. They also share commitment to the general importance of integrating a human life under submission to God's commanding will.

The *Qur'an* connects the proper divine-human relationship to divine grace and love that seek human love in response: "O you who believe! Whoever of you goes back on his religion—God will bring a people whom He loves and who love Him, kind toward the believers, stern with the disbelievers. They strive in the way of God, and do not fear the blame of the critic. That is the grace of God; He bestows it upon whomever He wills. God is Embracing and Knowing. Your allies are God, and His Messenger, and those who believe—those who pray regularly, and give charity, while bowing down" (5:54–55). The people of God are thus "a people whom He loves and who love him." The role of such love, divine and human, goes beyond any merely external behavior to what motivates a divine-human relationship. It extends to inward psychological and volitional factors in human action toward relating to God.

Suitable human motivation toward God bears on two prominent religious practices commanded by God in Islam: pilgrimage (*hajj;* to Mecca) and prayer (*salat;* five times each day). God announces to Muhammad, "We showed Abraham the location of the House: Do not associate anything with Me; and purify My House for those who circle around, and those who stand to pray, and those who kneel and prostrate. And announce the pilgrimage to humanity. They will come to you on foot, and on every transport. They will come from every distant point. That they may witness the benefits for themselves, and celebrate the name of God during the appointed days" (*Qur'an* 22:26–28). The command to "purify My House" calls for moral catharsis among humans. The practices of pilgrimage and prayer depend on purity and celebration in human motivation toward God. Such commanded practices are, then, to be properly motivated inwardly and are not to be merely external practices.

God expects sacrificial offerings to God to conform to the purified motives of pilgrimage and prayer, in keeping with "righteousness" and the "good news" of divine guidance for humans:

> Those whose hearts tremble when God is mentioned, and those who endure what has befallen them, and those who perform the prayer and spend from what We have provided for them. We have made the animal offerings emblems of God for you. In them is goodness for you. So, pronounce God's name upon them as they line up. Then, when they have fallen on their sides, eat of them and feed the contented and the beggar. Thus We have subjected them to you, that you may be thankful. Neither their flesh, nor their blood, ever reaches God. What reaches Him is the righteousness from you. Thus He subdued them to you, that you may glorify God for guiding you. And give good news to the charitable. (*Qur'an* 22:35–37)

God thus expects a divine command for sacrificial offerings to God to prompt human gratitude to God for the goodness in the offerings. Such offerings are to express righteousness and gratitude toward God on the basis of the divine guidance given to humans. They thus underwrite the good news of God's guiding righteousness.

The *Qur'an*, we have noted, portrays righteousness at the human level in terms of belief in God coupled with sincere actions pleasing to

God (2:177). Righteousness for humans is faith in God joined with sincere conduct commanded by God. This is the center of the holy life commanded by God through Muhammad, and it is the way to absolute submission to God. According to the *Qur'an*, then, divine commands figure in human experience of God, and they serve to manifest among humans the kind of righteousness characteristic of God. They thus can contribute to the vindication of God as righteous among obedient humans who manifest God's righteous character.

Answering Divine Commands

We have identified a central role for divine commands in Jewish, Christian, and Islamic monotheism, with a divine expectation of an obedient human response. An important divine goal is to have God's moral character represented and vindicated in obedient human lives. A pressing question, however, is whether humans have the moral strength to handle divine commands adequately, given God's morally perfect character and commands.

Humans tend to be morally weak at times, and their weakness can yield a conflict between them and God's morally perfect character and commands. A result is their falling short, at least at times, of perfect obedience to God and divine commands. God can be merciful, but divine mercy does not always result in perfect human obedience to God. We need some explanation of how this problem is to be resolved, for the sake of human representation of God's moral character.

Some inquirers might respond by representing humans as mere coerced pawns of God's "sovereign, all-controlling" will, as if human cooperation had no role. That position, however, would preclude genuine *human* submission to God. It would entail God's will and power submitting to God's fully dominating and controlling will. In that case, genuine human responsibility would be suffocated, and genuine, voluntary human agency would be extinguished. Interpersonal human response to God then would be an illusion at best. God would have a monopoly on decision-making. This prospect does not fit well with the felt voluntary character of typical moral decision-making among humans. It also does not fit well with the role of divine injunctions to humans in the Jewish, Christian, and Muslim scriptures.

We should consider that, by a divine standard, acceptable human submission to God's command can be imperfect in some cases. Needed divine mercy toward humans would allow for such an option, given moral weakness in humans. Even if perfect obedience is an ideal, to be realized in the future (Matt 5:48), divine compassion and mercy do not include the condemnation of humans simply for their imperfect repentance, faith, or obedience toward God. A merciful divine response would be more tolerant than such condemnation, without condoning human evil.

In his parable of the prodigal son, Jesus portrays God to be "filled with compassion" and eager to receive the returning prodigal son with forgiveness and even joy (Luke 15:20). He remarks, "I tell you, there will be more joy in heaven over one sinner who repents than over ninety-nine righteous persons who need no repentance" (Luke 15:7). A similar theme emerges in the Jewish Bible: "To the Lord our God belong mercy and forgiveness, but we have rebelled against him and have not obeyed the voice of the Lord our God by following his laws, which he set before us by his servants the prophets" (Dan 9:9–10; see also Ps 130:4). The *Qur'an* characterizes God likewise, "God, the Gracious, the Merciful," adding, "Forgiver of sins, Accepter of repentance, . . . Bountiful in bounty" (40:3).

Jesus shows awareness of moral imperfection among God's people in his parable of the two debtors (Luke 7:40–50). He acknowledges God's forgiveness of "a woman in the city who was a sinner," despite her obvious status of moral imperfection (Luke 7:37). He does not portray God's forgiveness as demanding human perfection in repentance, faith, or obedience. At the same time, he discourages humans from boasting in their repentance, faith, or obedience, advising, "When you have done all that you were ordered to do, say, 'We are worthless slaves; we have done only what we ought to have done!'" (Luke 17:10). So, the God of Jesus is forgiving without condoning evil, and this God allows for human imperfection in responding cooperatively.

H. R. Mackintosh has commented on the divine compassion at work in the forgiveness of humans, as represented by Jesus in relation to the "woman in the city who was a sinner": "To [Jesus] the wish for reconciliation was enough. Repentance settled all accounts. He will not keep her waiting, or put her on probation, nor will he spoil his gift by cruel reminders of the past."[7] This comment takes us in the right direction, but I propose that we replace "the wish for reconciliation" with "the sincere cooperative commitment to reconciliation." A "wish," as commonly understood, is too weak to support the kind of often challenged faith or trust in God needed for interpersonal human reconciliation with God.

The divine commands in search of human repentance, faith, and obedience are not abstract or merely theoretical. They include uncoercive nudging, attracting, or drawing in human conscience, aiming to motivate humans in voluntary cooperation with God's manifested will in their moral experience. Paul thus advises, as noted, "Work out your own salvation with fear and trembling, for it is God who is at work in you, enabling you both to will and to work for his good pleasure" (Phil 2:12–13, RSV). This talk of "working out" signifies human moral struggling to cooperate with God's manifested will, such as in the aforementioned fruit of the Spirit. It does not presume human earning or meriting of God's approval.

Paul holds that God works uncoercively in human conscience to guide people toward righteousness in relationships with God and other humans. This leaves room for a voluntary, responsible human response. As people cooperate with God, the fruit of God's Spirit comes to maturity or fruition with salience and motivational power in their moral experience and lives. The evidence of God's presence and goodness thus gains clarity for cooperative people. Such evidence can contribute to the vindication of divine righteousness through humans.

Mackintosh, we have noted, identifies the interpersonal directness of divine relating to cooperative humans, particularly in forgiveness or pardon sought through a divine command to repentance.[8] The role of human conscience is crucial here because it can bring a person into an I-Thou acquaintance with God and the fruit of the Spirit. It thus can give a person an opportunity to yield, in repentance, trust, and obedience, to God's direct offer of forgiveness that seeks a righteous relationship with God.

A divine command to repent has a goal. It aims to attract human reception of divine forgiveness toward reconciliation with God. This reception will involve a related divine expectation: for humans to forgive others as God forgives them. The Lord's Prayer thus requests of God, "Forgive us our debts, as we also have forgiven our debtors" (Matt 6:12). This request is supplemented with: "If you forgive others their trespasses, your heavenly Father will also forgive you, but if you do not forgive others, neither will your Father forgive your trespasses" (Matt 6:14–15). The latter prospect of God's not forgiving is an indicator of the wide-reaching nature of divine forgiveness, which is intended to be extended. It is not a grudging strategic threat to humans.

Divine forgiveness aims to be universal in scope and shared similarly by its human recipients. It is thus a divine-human relation that requires the human offering of forgiveness without limits from its recipients. (Whether people will *receive* the universal offering of forgiveness is an open issue.) If we accept or practice a limited, exclusive version of forgiveness, we are accepting or practicing a counterfeit rather than the real article from God. Genuine divine forgiveness excludes no willing recipients who are sincere about participating in its intended universality of scope. As a result, people can exclude divine forgiveness for themselves when they withhold it from other people. This consideration enables us to see that the Lord's Prayer does not offer a grudging attitude toward offering forgiveness. Instead, it assumes universality of scope for divine forgiveness offered and for being shared by humans who receive it.

Some people choose to reject or ignore divine forgiveness, but this does not preclude a divine offer of genuine forgiveness to them. Divine seeking of universal forgiveness does not entail that all people will receive this forgiveness. Some people oppose or ignore the divine-human reconciliation sought through divine forgiveness. They thus do not value the forgiveness on offer. Sometimes they do not see the real need of it, given a failure to recognize their alienation from God or its harmfulness. As a result, God's offer of forgiveness is not attractive to them.

Divine forgiveness is central to advancing the kind of reconciliation that can lead to a universal society grounded in righteousness. It thus can contribute to divine self-vindication in the lives of that society's members. Lack of valuing such a society can figure in a person's not valuing the divine forgiveness on offer. In that case, God's effort toward divine-human reconciliation will not be attractive to that person.

Divine commands aim to overcome human alienation from God, for the sake of divine-human reconciliation. They thus join with divine expectations for a cooperative moral response from humans. God can command, to this end, even love of God and others among humans, and humans can respond voluntarily in a cooperative manner. God intends the manifested fruit of the Spirit to lead and empower people in the needed direction toward reconciliation with God.

People can, and often do, resist God, but the divine challenge including a divine command is real nonetheless. Its reality and goodness offer a gift and a moral challenge for anyone willing to be reconciled to, and guided by, God. They also offer salient evidence of God's compassionate and righteous reality. In doing so, the divine challenge in divine commands can contribute to the vindication of God in the lives of cooperative humans. It can draw them into cooperation with God in a way that manifests and empowers divine righteousness in their lives.

Conclusion

We have seen that divine commanding recurs throughout the scriptural traditions of Judaism, Christianity, and Islam. This chapter has contended that such commanding provides an important, if widely neglected, basis for evidence of God's reality and goodness. The evidence provided, however, is sensitive to human receptivity to it in terms of a cooperative response in repentance, faith, and obedience. Human conscience, in particular, supplies an area for direct I-Thou human acquaintance with the commanding God behind the relevant evidence in the moral experience of conscience.

The evidence in question includes the fruit of God's intervening Spirit in human experience, such as love, joy, and peace. It comes to fruition in salience and motivating power as people cooperate with its moral leading or guiding toward moral catharsis for a righteous relationship with God. This chapter supports the lesson that, from the standpoint of divine righteousness, theology without moral catharsis is empty, and moral catharsis without theology is blind. It also supports the lesson that divine self-vindication can benefit from human cooperation with the divine commands experienced. So, the commanding God presented is the vindicating God set on universal divine-human reconciliation for the good of all concerned.

CHAPTER FIVE

Vindication for Righteous Splendor

Be perfect as your heavenly Father is perfect.

—Matthew 5:48

IN DIVINE SELF-VINDICATION for righteousness, God shares divine "glory" (*kabōd*) with humans. We need to clarify this claim and reconcile it with the biblical claim that God does not share divine glory with humans. This chapter offers a resolution of the apparent conflict on the basis of a biblical conception of divine glory as inexhaustible perfect goodness. It proposes that divine glory could, in principle, be shared in either of two contrasting ways: with humans controlling ownership over it and without such ownership.

The chapter finds widely neglected importance of divine glory in relation to voluntary human cooperation with God in sharing in it without controlling ownership. As a result, divine perfect (defect-free) goodness inhabits a context of imperfection in human moral defects. The chapter explains that this context does not preclude divine glory but can advance its value and salience. It also finds the apostle Paul and the author of John's Gospel to agree on a voluntary human role in sharing in divine glory and on a central role of this sharing in God's salvific "gospel of the glory of Christ" (2 Cor 4:4).

Divine Glory in the Jewish Bible

Talk of divine glory emerges early in the Pentateuch, and it recurs in the historical writings, the prophetic writings, and the Psalms. The book of Exodus is seminal here. Its talk of divine glory points to something that can be observed by God's people. Moses and Aaron promise the

Israelites, "In the morning you shall see the glory of the Lord, because he has heard your complaining against the Lord" (Exod 16:7). The elaboration is: "As Aaron spoke to the whole congregation of the Israelites, they looked toward the wilderness, and the glory of the Lord appeared in the cloud" (Exod 16:9). We should ask how, or in virtue of what, it appeared in the cloud.[1] What, in other words, does the glory of the Lord "look" like?

The book of Exodus clarifies what indicates the glory of God: "The glory of the Lord settled on Mount Sinai, and the cloud covered it for six days; on the seventh day he called to Moses out of the cloud. Now the appearance of the glory of the Lord was like a devouring fire on the top of the mountain in the sight of the Israelites" (Exod 24:16–17). If this was an initial indicator of the glory of the Lord, we should ask how it differed from other mountaintop fires. We may assume that "the glory of the Lord" has unique features for a unique God that distinguish it from most fires.

A key indicator of the unique divine features, as noted in chapter 1, arises from a request of Moses to see God's glory:

> Moses said [to the Lord], "Please show me your glory [*kabōd*]." And he said, "I will make all my goodness [*tub*] pass before you and will proclaim before you the name, 'The Lord', and I will be gracious to whom I will be gracious and will show mercy on whom I will show mercy." "But," he said, "you cannot see my face, for no one shall see me and live." And the Lord continued, "See, there is a place by me where you shall stand on the rock, and while my glory passes by I will put you in a cleft of the rock, and I will cover you with my hand until I have passed by; then I will take away my hand, and you shall see my back, but my face shall not be seen." (Exod 33:18–23)

The writer of Exodus, as suggested, conveys an important insight: God identifies "all my goodness passes before you" with "my glory passes by [you]." God thus leaves Moses with an understanding of glory in terms of divine perfect goodness, as the splendor, grandeur, excellence, and majesty of God's perfect goodness.

The approach of Exodus conflicts with an understanding of divine glory as just the spectacular activity of a storm god or a powerful amoral god.[2] Divine glory harbors moral robustness without defect, according to the God of Moses. Terence E. Fretheim thus remarks, "[God's talk of goodness here] carries the matter beyond any simple tangible manifestation to a statement about *what kind of God this is*. What will serve as *a more genuine sign* to Moses is not some direct view of God but a specific indication of the 'good' character of this one who has given the divine name 'Yahweh' to Israel."[3] Moses experiences the glory of God's perfectly good character, but he does not see God's face. The latter omission indicates that God is not fully comprehended by Moses. Even so, he does experience divine glory as the unique goodness self-presented by God.

Planning to leave Mount Sinai, Moses set up the tabernacle of the Lord, and the cloud of divine glory occupied it: "The cloud covered the tent of meeting, and the glory of the Lord filled the tabernacle. Moses was not able to enter the tent of meeting because the cloud settled upon it, and the glory of the Lord filled the tabernacle" (Exod 40:34–35). A lesson here is that divine glory is not limited to Mount Sinai or any geographic location. Instead, it is with God and the people of God, wherever their journey takes them. The divine glory is nomadic: "For the cloud of the Lord was on the tabernacle by day, and fire was in the cloud by night, before the eyes of all the house of Israel at each stage of their journey" (Exod 40:38). A change of location, then, is compatible with the presence of divine glory.

The previous chapter cited chapter 6 of the book of Isaiah to illustrate direct experience of God, but its relevance now concerns the relation between divine glory and the goodness of and from God. It contrasts divine glory and "people of unclean lips," that is, the "holy" righteousness of God and the unrighteousness of the people of God (Isa 6:1–5). This is not a contrast merely of divine power with human weakness. It rests, as previously noted, on a striking moral difference between God and humans, between moral superiority and moral inferiority.

The book of Isaiah directly relates divine glory to a concern for righteousness, beginning with some rhetorical questions from God:

> Is not this the fast that I choose:
> to loose the bonds of wickedness,
> to undo the thongs of the yoke,
> to let the oppressed go free,
> and to break every yoke?
> Is it not to share your bread with the hungry,
> and bring the homeless poor into your house;
> when you see the naked, to cover him,
> and not to hide yourself from your own flesh?
> Then shall your light break forth like the dawn,
> and your healing shall spring up speedily;
> your righteousness shall go before you,
> the glory of the Lord shall be your rear guard. (Isa 58:6–8, RSV)[4]

The glory of the Lord, according to the book of Isaiah, seeks to build divine righteousness among humans, despite their habitual resistance. Divine glory and its righteousness are thus seen in joint conflict with wayward humans.

The divine righteousness inherent to divine glory contravenes static morality. It includes the *active* divine effort to save wayward people, to bring them into a righteous relationship with God. According to the book of Isaiah, God stirs up trouble for humans in order to promote righteousness and salvation toward divine-human reconciliation among them:

> I am the Lord, and there is no other.
> I form light and create darkness,
> I make weal and create woe,
> I am the Lord, who do all these things.
> Shower, O heavens, from above,
> and let the skies rain down righteousness;

> let the earth open, that salvation may sprout forth,
> and let it cause righteousness to spring up also;
> I the Lord have created it. (Isa 45:6–8, RSV)

Creating woe here is not doing evil; it is agitating among humans for their benefit toward righteousness and salvation in divine-human reconciliation. This is part of the glory of the Lord, according to the book of Isaiah.

The divine effort toward righteousness in salvation is not limited to Israel, according to the book of Isaiah. It aims to attract all people:

> The foreigners who join themselves to the Lord,
> to minister to him, to love the name of the Lord,
> and to be his servants,
> every one who keeps the sabbath, and does not profane it,
> and holds fast my covenant—
> these I will bring to my holy mountain,
> and make them joyful in my house of prayer;
> their burnt offerings and their sacrifices
> will be accepted on my altar;
> for my house shall be called a house of prayer
> for all peoples.
> Thus says the Lord God,
> who gathers the outcasts of Israel,
> I will gather yet others to him
> besides those already gathered. (Isa 56:6–8, RSV)

The promise to "all peoples" is striking, recalling the divine promise to Abram (Abraham) to have all families of the earth blessed through him (Gen 12:3). So, divine righteousness and its salvation are explicitly transnational (see Isa 66:18–19).

The book of Ezekiel concurs with the idea of intended divine glory for all peoples: "I will set my glory among the nations; and all the nations shall see my judgment which I have executed, and my hand which I have laid on them. The house of Israel shall know that I am the Lord their God, from that day forward" (Ezek 39:21–22). This scope is fitting for a God worthy of worship and thus morally perfect.

Psalm 85 relates divine glory to righteousness and salvation in divine love and faithfulness, thus integrating some key features:

> Surely his salvation is at hand for those who fear him,
> that glory may dwell in our land.
> Steadfast love and faithfulness will meet;
> righteousness and peace will kiss each other.
> Faithfulness will spring up from the ground,
> and righteousness will look down from the sky.
> Yea, the Lord will give what is good,
> and our land will yield its increase.
> Righteousness will go before him,
> and make his footsteps a way. (Ps 85:9–13, RSV)

This is a remarkable summary of the rich goodness involved in divine glory. It resists any attempt to reduce such glory to mere power, light, or living presence. The power of divine glory encompasses the power of righteousness and its reliance on the divine goodness of salvation, love, and faithfulness. It thus fits with what we have seen in the books of Exodus and Isaiah.

Given the previous biblical passages, I dissent from Abraham Heschel's purely functional approach to divine glory: "The glory is the presence, not the essence of God; an act rather than a quality; a process not a substance. Mainly the glory manifests itself as a power overwhelming the world."[5] We shall see that the divine glory is not an overwhelming or coercive power in the way Heschel suggests. Instead, it can be opposed and frustrated by humans. In addition, it is integral to the moral character of God and thus is no mere act or function of God. It includes the inherent moral perfection of God and therefore figures in God's worthiness of worship, that is, in God's being truly God.

Talk of the glory of God, going beyond talk merely of divine morality or goodness, serves an important purpose for various characters and writers of the Jewish scriptures. It captures the reality of their experience of God's moral character as inexhaustibly profound, illuminating, challenging, and renewing in relation to cooperative humans. It thus accommodates an important difference between God's actively righteous moral character and the static rules and norms of familiar morality.

God's moral character of glory, being profoundly intentional and active, is not static or fully comprehensible by humans. It thus can challenge human moral complacency or presumed moral completeness. Human recognition of divine glory enables us to see that God can always go deeper in moral profundity for humans, even leaving older moral teachings surpassed by deeper divine glory. We shall see how Paul recruits this consideration in relation to the transition from the old to the new covenant.

A key issue concerns how divine glory relates to cooperative humans, with regard to their participation in it. Is it selfish rather than shared from a divine point of view? The book of Isaiah offers some relevant comments:

> I am the Lord; that is my name;
> my glory I give to no other,
> nor my praise to idols. (Isa 42:8)
>
> For my own sake, for my own sake, I do it,
> for why should my name be profaned?
> My glory I will not give to another. (Isa 48:11)

Such comments suggest that God is selfish with divine glory, being unwilling to share it with, or give it to, other persons. They raise the question of whether divine glory is compatible with unselfish love in its presentation and circulation among humans. Is it something to be announced by God but limited to God?

Some biblical writers, including Paul and the author of John's Gospel, reject any suggestion that divine glory goes unshared by God. They hold that humans can, and sometimes do, share in divine glory and that human cooperation with God bears significantly on this sharing. Perhaps, then, they would interpret the aforementioned passages from Isaiah to bear on the giving of divine glory to humans without giving them *controlling* ownership of it. We shall explore relevant evidence that makes the latter interpretation plausible, at least from the perspectives of Paul and the author of John's Gospel.

Divine Glory in Paul and John

Paul tells the Corinthian Christians that his "ministry of righteousness excels in glory," even in more glory than that found in the Mosaic covenant (2 Cor 3:9). He adds, "Whenever someone turns to the Lord, the veil ['over their hearts'] is taken away. Now the Lord is the Spirit, and where the Spirit of the Lord is, there is freedom. But we all, with unveiled faces, looking as in a mirror at the glory of the Lord, are being transformed into the same image from glory to glory, just as from the Lord, the Spirit" (2 Cor 3:16–18, NASB). Paul's language of "from glory to glory" indicates divine glory, or splendor, shared with humans.

Victor Paul Furnish correctly observes, "Paul's association here of *the Lord* with *the Spirit* shows that he is still thinking of God himself (see especially 'the Spirit of the living God,' v. 3) as the ultimate source of that *splendor* [= glory] with which not only the Pauline apostolate but also the life of every believer is being infused."[6] In such "infusion," according to Paul, divine glory is being shared with cooperative humans, that is, those humans who "turn to the Lord." So, the transformation of responsive humans by God's glory is interpersonal and voluntary, not mechanical and coercive. Divine glory, according to Paul, invites and encourages human turning to God without extinguishing voluntary human agency.

The veil needing removal blocks people from apprehending the glory aright, in the absence of their turning to the Lord in heartfelt, sincere repentance. This consideration recalls the deficit in human attitude toward God from chapter 6 of Isaiah. God commands Isaiah, "Make the mind of this people dull, and stop their ears, and shut their eyes, so that they may not look with their eyes and listen with their ears and comprehend with their minds and turn and be healed" (Isa 6:10). (John 12:39–41 cites this passage and relates it to divine glory.) Without the suitable moral attitude from the human heart (or volitional and affective center) toward God, the turning to God would be relatively superficial. It would fail to align a human heart with God's moral will. In particular, suitable love toward God would be lacking. So, God aims to block humans turning to God before people are ready to obey God sincerely from their hearts. The veil needing removal, then, is not merely intellectual, a matter of thinking. It has volitional and affective features that bear on turning to God aright.

Paul represents the risen Jesus Christ as a focal place for divine glory and for human response to such glory. He is, according to Paul, "the Lord of glory" (1 Cor 2:8; see Eph 1:18 on "the God of our Lord Jesus Christ, the Father of glory"). In addition, "It is the God who said, 'Light will shine out of darkness,' who has shone in our hearts to give the light of the knowledge of the glory of God in the face of Christ" (2 Cor 4:6). Paul does not mean the physical face of the historical Jesus; instead, he has in mind the Jesus of history who "became a life-giving Spirit" (1 Cor 15:45). This is the Christ of whom the Epistle to the Colossians says, "God chose to make known how great among the gentiles are the riches of the glory of this mystery, which is Christ in you, the hope of glory" (Col 1:27; cf. Gal 4:19).

Paul's talk of "the face of Christ" concerns the direct presence of the Spirit of the risen Christ, whom Paul closely associates with the Spirit of God (Rom 8:9–10). He thinks of the relevant Spirit as characterized by "righteousness" (Rom 8:10). He also thinks of the Spirit of God, as noted, to be the divine source of bringing divine glory to cooperative humans (2 Cor 3:17–18).

Evil, according to Paul, can block people from seeing the glory of God in Christ: "If our gospel is veiled, it is veiled to those who are perishing. In their case the god of this world has blinded the minds of the unbelievers, to keep them from seeing clearly the light of the gospel of the glory of Christ, who is the image of God" (2 Cor 4:3–4). Paul also recognizes the prospect, and the reality, of humans frustrating the glory of God among them. He recognizes a moral component in divine glory that enables him to say, "All have sinned and fall short of the glory of God" (Rom 3:23). Frustrating divine glory, furthermore, is included in what he opposes with this injunction: "Do not quench the Spirit" (1 Thess 5:19; cf. Eph 4:30). (Chapter 6 returns to this topic.)

We have noted that Paul regards the transformation from "glory to glory" to originate from "the Spirit, the Lord" (2 Cor 3:18). So, quenching the Spirit will result in frustrating the glory of God among humans. Paul also holds that humans can "nullify the grace of God" owing to their attitudes toward divine righteousness (Gal 2:21). When they do so, they frustrate the divine glory inherent in righteousness by divine grace (the latter grace being compatible with an expectation of human cooperation). In addition, when they fail to "turn to the Lord" (2 Cor 3:16), they frustrate the divine glory on offer in the transformation, from glory to glory, that arises through such turning (cf. Rom 2:4).

Paul follows the book of Isaiah in representing God as saying, "I will destroy the wisdom of the wise, and the discernment of the discerning I will thwart" (1 Cor 1:19; cf. Isa 29:14). He adds, "Has not God made foolish the wisdom of the world? For since, in the wisdom of God, the world did not know God through [its] wisdom" (1 Cor 1:20–21; cf. Isa 55:8–9). This perspective echoes part of the book of Isaiah:

> You felt secure in your wickedness;
> you said, "No one sees me."
> Your wisdom and your knowledge
> led you astray,
> and you said in your heart,
> "I am, and there is no one besides me." (Isa 47:10)

Divine glory has and exhibits an incomprehensible splendor that cannot be explained by the wisdom of the world. It thus disturbs worldly wisdom, seeking to destroy it, for the good of "the wise" and "the discerning," who are "led astray." By transcending human understanding, while bringing unique goodness, divine glory challenges, by way of sharp contrast, the wisdom of the world. Whether it attracts "the wise" to God, however, depends on their priorities and their willingness to be led by God. (Chapter 7 returns to this topic.)

Paul acknowledges the goal-directed leading by God with divine glory: "Our slight, momentary affliction is producing for us an eternal weight of glory beyond all measure, because we look not at what can be seen but at what cannot be seen, for what can be seen is temporary, but what cannot be seen is eternal" (2 Cor 4:17–18). Divine glory aims to yield "glory beyond all measure" for receptive humans in the fullness of time, and it does so through ongoing pain and suffering now. Such intentional leading brings a measure of divine glory to cooperative humans now but not in its fullness for them. So, there is a "now but not yet (fully)" feature to the sharing of divine glory, just as there is with the arrival of the divine kingdom in Jesus.

The goal-directedness of divine glory, as suggested previously, seeks the glory of the freedom of God's people, according to Paul (Rom 8:20–21). Here again the ultimate divine goal for glory is eschatological, to be realized in the fullness of time but also realized in part now. Full human freedom from sin and death, according to Paul, awaits God's appointed time in the future, but a measure of its glory is available to humans now. In its goal-directedness, or intentionality, toward moral perfection for recipients, divine glory exceeds any static or impersonal moral standard. In settling for static or impersonal morality, we would neglect divine glory and its active, intentional righteousness.

Paul thinks of divine glory as both transcendent and immanent relative to humans. Its transcendence is that of God as creator and sustainer of the created world. Its immanence is found in God's personality traits self-manifested in human experience and life, at least where humans are cooperative toward God. These traits, we have noted, are "the fruit of the Spirit" of God and represent Christ's moral character (Gal 5:22–24). Such fruit is not static or impersonal; instead, it includes features of the active moral character of God in human life (cf. Rom 5:5; 2 Cor 5:14). It actively manifests, as suggested, what Paul characterizes as "God who is at work in you" (Phil 2:13). This work to manifest the divine fruit in humans is interpersonal, morally challenging, and thus uncoercive toward human wills. As a result, Paul uses injunctions to promote it, thereby assuming a voluntary human response.

The salvific or redemptive work of God, according to Paul, aims to have the glory of God realized perfectly with cooperative welcome in human lives, individually and socially. This is an ultimate goal, realized only in part now, given the imperfections of human life in relation to God. So, Paul writes, "Since we have these promises [from God], beloved, let us cleanse ourselves from every defilement of flesh and of spirit, making holiness perfect in the fear of God" (2 Cor 7:1; cf. 2 Cor 12:9). He thus asks the Corinthian Christians, "Do you not know that you are God's temple and that God's Spirit dwells in you?," adding that this temple is holy. Paul has in mind the kind of righteous holiness, in contrast with human unrighteousness, that we observed in chapter 6 of Isaiah in connection with God's manifested glory. Such holiness stems from the divine glory that extends outward to wayward humans, for the sake of their salvation as reconciliation with God. We find a related idea in Matthew's Jesus: "Be perfect as your heavenly Father is perfect" (Matt 5:48).

Paul connects his "gospel of the glory of Christ" (2 Cor 4:4) to a divine triumph, in accordance with his theology of the cross. This connection fits with his understanding of divine self-vindication in righteousness. Paul remarks to the Corinthian Christians, "Thanks be to God, who in Christ always leads us in triumphal procession [θριαμβεύοντι] and through us spreads in every place the fragrance that comes from knowing him" (2 Cor 2:14). This remark follows on the heels of Paul's comment on his preaching the good news of Christ's death and resurrection: "When I came to Troas to proclaim the good news of Christ, a door was opened for me in the Lord" (2 Cor 2:12; for his overview of the good news, see 1 Cor 15:1–6). Paul thus suggests that his proclaiming the good news of Christ includes God's leading him in "triumphal procession," in a victory parade.[7]

Some commentators have questioned the translation of "triumphal procession," but the relevant idea of triumph or victory is explicit elsewhere in Paul's undisputed letters. Paul writes to the Roman Christians, "Who will separate us from the love of Christ? Will affliction or distress or persecution or famine or nakedness or peril or sword? As it is written, 'For your sake we are being killed all day long; we are accounted as sheep to be slaughtered.' No, in all these things we are more than victorious [ὑπερνικῶμεν] through him who loved us" (Rom 8:35–37). We can replace *victorious* with *triumphant* here without loss of meaning. This consideration fits well with Paul's suggestion of triumph in 2 Corinthians 2.

We have noted that, under suspicion of his apostleship by some of the Corinthians, Paul connects his ministry of the gospel of Christ with glory from God on the basis of Exodus 34 (2 Cor 3:9, 16, 18). He claims, "If there was glory in the ministry of condemnation, much more does the ministry of justification [better: *righteousness*; δικαιοσύνης] abound in glory!" (2 Cor 3:9). Paul has in mind divine glory received by humans through his gospel and ministry of divine righteousness. This glory, he suggests, is superior to the self-exaltation offered by his critics at Corinth because this glory comes "from the Lord," that is, from God.[8]

Two considerations are noteworthy. First, Paul has in mind a divine transformation of humans into divine glory now and not merely in the eschatological future. Victor Paul Furnish rightly observes, "For [Paul], transformation means conformity to the image of Christ (Rom 8:29). . . . Expressed otherwise, it means Christ being formed in the believer (Gal 4:19), a transformative event which faith receives and affirms already in the present (Gal 2:20) as 'a new creation' (2 Cor 5:17). . . . Hellenistic and apocalyptic Jewish notions have coalesced here, only to emerge as the distinctive Pauline view that the believer's transformation into a new being has both a present and a future aspect."[9] This observation is important because it entails that the divine glory in human life acknowledged by Paul is experienced now and not just in the future. Inasmuch as this current glory includes human sharing in the resurrection life of Christ (as it does, in Paul's thinking; see Rom 6:11, 13), this resurrection life is shared now among the people of God. (Chapter 8 returns to this topic.) Such glory and life, however, are irreducible to the cross of Christ, even if the cross is the divinely approved way to them.

Second, the transformation in question is not mechanical or coercive but depends, as noted previously, on voluntary human "turning to the Lord." Furnish thus remarks, "To turn to the Lord would mean, in the context of Paul's preaching, to acknowledge and receive one's reconciliation with God through Christ."[10] The turning and receiving here are not merely intellectual or contemplative; they go beyond mere intellectual acknowledgment of the Lord and are akin to repentance in the presence of the Lord. We find a hint toward this in Paul's aforementioned comment to the Roman Christians: "Do you not realize that God's kindness is meant to lead you to repentance?" (Rom 2:4).[11] This consideration coheres with the fact that faith in God includes volitional and affective, and not just intellectual, features, in Paul's thought.

Paul's confirmation of a voluntary human role in receiving divine grace and its glory comes from the live options of humans frustrating the grace of God and quenching the Spirit of God. He writes to the Galatian Christians, "I do not nullify [ἀθετῶ] the grace of God, for if righteousness comes through the law, then Christ died for nothing" (Gal 2:21). His claim assumes that a person can voluntarily set aside or frustrate an offer of divine grace and glory in "the gospel of the glory of Christ."

A voluntary option for humans is expressed in Paul's injunction to the Thessalonian Christians: "Do not quench [σβέννυτε] the Spirit . . ., but test everything; hold fast to what is good; abstain from every form of evil" (1 Thess 5:19, 21–22). Like testing moral scenarios, holding fast to what is good and abstaining from evil are voluntary human options;

so also not quenching God's Spirit is a voluntary human option. If these were not voluntary human options, Paul's injunction would be pointless, simply beside the point.

Inasmuch as God's Spirit is the source of divine glory for humans, as noted in 2 Corinthians 3, a voluntary human response to the Spirit bears on whether people face and receive the Spirit's glory on offer. Humans, in Paul's language, must "turn to," rather than away from, the Spirit of divine glory. In this regard, we do not have a complete analogy with the original creation story in Genesis, despite Paul's allusion to it in 2 Corinthians 4:6 and 5:17. As a result, we must qualify Ernst Käsemann's following remark: "The cross [of Christ] shows that the true God alone is the creator who works from nothing, who continually draws creation out of chaos and who has hence constantly manifested himself since the beginning of the world as the raiser of the dead."[12] Even if God "works from nothing" in the ultimate power of resurrection in new life, the *reception* of that power by responsible human agents will depend on *their* voluntary response, positive or negative, to the divine power on offer. As a result, Paul takes humans to be accountable before God.[13]

A number of commentators have shied away from Paul's acknowledgment of a voluntary human role in receiving the glory of God offered in the death and resurrection of Christ. A familiar worry is that such a role would threaten divine grace by introducing a need for a human "work" in voluntarily "turning to the Lord."[14] Paul, in contrast, does not shy away from talk of "turning to the Lord" or corresponding injunctions calling for a voluntary human response to receive the divine glory on offer. He evidently recognizes that in Exodus 34, Moses's going before the Lord was voluntary, a genuine choice by Moses (Exod 34:34, LXX). As a result, interpreters of Paul are well advised to follow Rudolf Bultmann's sound advice that we should not confuse "deeds of obedience" in Paul's thought with "works" as earning approval from God.[15] An obedient active response to God need not be a "work" aimed at earning divine approval. (Chapter 6 returns to the topic of a voluntary human role in responding to divine action in human experience.)

Even if divine glory is to be received voluntarily now, we still have the question of what unifies divine glory in the cross and divine glory in the resurrection. Paul's answer, following the book of Isaiah (e.g., 6:1–5, 58:6–8), puts perfect divine righteousness at the center of the unifying divine glory. A hint arises in his following remark to the Roman Christians: "Now, apart from the law, the righteousness of God has been disclosed and is attested by the Law and the Prophets, the righteousness of God through the faith of Jesus Christ for all who believe. For there is no distinction, since all have sinned and fall short of the glory of God" (Rom 3:21–23). Paul is thus thinking of an important connection between the righteousness of God and the glory of God.

Divine righteousness being "disclosed and attested," according to Paul, is a corrective to "falling short of the glory of God." He thus suggests that such righteousness is integral to divine glory available to humans, to be received by "the faith of [or in] Jesus Christ for all who believe."[16] Paul recognizes two aspects of the righteousness offered: righteousness in dying to sin and death on the cross and righteousness in being raised to life in resurrection, beginning with Jesus and being shared with his followers now.

Paul's suggestion connecting righteousness and glory fits with his reflection on the book of Exodus (particularly 34:29–35) in 2 Corinthians 3. We have noted an important theme of Exodus 33 portraying divine glory in terms of divine goodness (including divine righteousness), after Moses requests of God, "Show me your glory" (Exod 33:18–19). Paul's suggestion relating righteousness and glory is also confirmed by his comment to the Corinthian Christians that, with his gospel of cross and resurrection, "the ministry of righteousness abounds in glory" (2 Cor 3:9). He adds that with his "ministry of righteousness" and its gospel, "the permanent has come in glory" (2 Cor 3:11). This glory marks the cross and the resurrection, including for the present time in the lives of believers.

The contemporary glory in question does not stop at the cross, contrary to a suggestion of Ernst Käsemann. This glory seeks sharing in righteous *life*, the latter being more motivating with hope for life than any sharing merely in the cross and its death. Paul thus speaks of Jesus, who "was raised [to life] for our justification [δικαίωσιν]" (Rom 4:25; cf. Rom 6:4). This fits with Paul's comment that, regarding the provider of divine glory now for humans, "the Spirit is life because of righteousness [δικαιοσύνην]" (Rom 8:10). Similarly, Paul recognizes a divine goal that now "in [Christ] we might become the righteousness [δικαιοσύνη] of God" (2 Cor 5:21) and thereby reflect divine glory. It does not follow, however, that such glory is fully reducible to, or exhausted by, perfect righteousness, even though such righteousness is integral to the glory being realized now and later, in the fullness of time, for the people of God.

Divine glory, as the book of Isaiah (40:17, 45:24–25, 46:9–13) suggests, includes something weighty and rich in value that need not be fully comprehensible to humans. In addition, its powerful value as excellence can exceed mere divine righteousness in riches. Paul concurs with the book of Isaiah, as he mentions divine glory:

> O the depth of the riches and wisdom and knowledge of God!
> How unsearchable are his judgments and how inscrutable his ways!
> "For who has known the mind of the Lord?
> Or who has been his counselor?
> Or who has given a gift to him,
> to receive a gift in return?"
> For from him and through him and to him are all things. To him be the glory [δόξα] forever. Amen. (Rom 11:33–36; cf. Isa 40:13; 1 Cor 2:16)

2 Corinthians 3, as suggested, indicates a need for a human veil to be removed for perceiving the glory of God in the ministry of righteousness. The veil hides the glory from humans in need of "turning" to God. This raises the issue of what draws a receptive person to turn to the Lord and divine glory. Is there a distinctive manifestation of God that motivates and grounds the turning noted by Paul?

Käsemann remarks, "The theology of the cross and the theology of the Word belong together and are won or thrown away together.... According to Paul, whether one wants to hear or to see is what divides faith from superstition.... Apparently, in spite of the Reformation, we still have not learnt that faith derived from the Word and faith deriving from manifestations are two different things."[17] We need caution about the contrasting talk of "the Word" and "manifestations" here, given various biblical reports of manifestations of divine glory, courtesy of God's Spirit.

Käsemann gives prominence to "the Word of proclamation" as follows:

> Assurance of salvation only comes through preaching.... The cross helps no one who does not hear the word of the cross and ground his faith on that. The same is true of the resurrection, exaltation, and incarnation of Christ; it is true even of the historical Jesus. Faith in them is only possible via the Word of proclamation, not on the grounds of their historical reality, which is as ambiguous as our own lives.... It is the one who is risen who acts through the Word of proclamation, even when the theme of that proclamation is the "historical" Jesus.[18]

Even if God and the risen Jesus "act through the Word of proclamation," we need to consider how to avoid disappointment that we are receiving *mere* proclamation, devoid of divine power manifested to receptive humans. Talk, after all, is cheap.

Paul does not settle for *mere* proclamation, despite the importance he assigns to preaching (1 Cor 1:17–21; Rom 10:6–9). He identifies divine power that accompanies preaching of the gospel while not being reducible to mere preaching. For instance, he endorses, as noted, divine love as the basis of hope in God (Rom 5:5). Similarly, "The love of [better: from] Christ urges us on" (2 Cor 5:14). Divine love is the primary "fruit of the Spirit," in Paul's thinking (Gal 5:22), and it is thus a feature of divine self-manifestation to humans.[19]

The divine love in question, according to Paul, comes directly from God's Spirit and thus "does not put us to shame," from the standpoint of needed self-manifestation or self-evidence from God. It manifests God's unique moral character to human "hearts," courtesy of the Spirit, in a way that empowers "the Word of proclamation," thus taking it beyond mere proclamation or preaching. Paul therefore characterizes the gospel as "the power of God" (Rom 1:16–17), in relation to the power of divine righteousness.

Paul, we have seen, acknowledges a role for humans in responding to the power of God in the gospel in a cooperative manner. They are to let it, and help it, come to fruition rather than suppress its transforming power. In other words, humans are to cooperate with this power, thus "being led" by its Spirit toward conforming to it in righteousness (Rom 8:14–16; Gal 5:16–18). In that case, its unique intentional power of God will gain salience and stability in human life, indicating that it is God at work in humans (Phil 2:13). This consideration figures in Paul's various injunctions to yield in conformity to the leading of divine righteousness.

Käsemann comments that "the raising of Jesus from the dead counted from the outset as an enthronement and the Easter appearances were conceived of as being manifestations of the one who was already exalted. This earliest view involved the danger that the cross could appear as a mere transit point on the way to the exaltation."[20] Perhaps there is no precluding this "danger" (as a prospect), but the mere danger does not challenge the importance of divine self-manifestation in human experience. Paul, as chapter 1 noted, quotes the book of Isaiah, with God announcing self-manifestation to people: "I have shown myself [ἐμφανὴς ἐγενόμην] to those who did not ask for me" (Rom 10:20; cf. Isa 65:1). This fits well with Paul's view of self-manifested divine love toward receptive people (Rom 5:5; 2 Cor 5:21). As a result, we need not follow an exclusive contrast between divine self-manifestation and the "Word of proclamation." The two work together, at least at times, in Paul's thought.

The self-manifested divine love recognized by Paul is self-giving righteous love (Gal 2:20; 1 Cor 13:4–7) and not the stuff of dubious partners in crime. It thus figures in the glory of God on offer to humans. We therefore may think of the latter offered glory as grounded in a central feature of divine glory: the moral character of perfect love. As a result, Paul's aforementioned talk of "from glory to glory" has a basis in human experience receptive to the divine transformation of humans toward divine glory.

Paul acknowledges a hidden feature of divine glory and his gospel message, understandably given the conflicts he faced over them. Käsemann proposes that "[Christianity's] glory is hidden in being crucified with Jesus."[21] That is part of the story, but the matter is more complicated for Paul. He writes to the Corinthian Christians, "Even if our gospel is veiled, it is veiled to those who are perishing. In their case, the god of this world has blinded the minds of the unbelievers, to keep them from seeing clearly the light of the gospel of the glory of Christ, who is the image of God" (2 Cor 4:3–4). Evil in the world goes against the good news of divine glory in a way that obscures its reality and power for many people.

Paul's antidote to the veiling of divine glory includes humans turning away from evil to the Lord of glory. Paul sees a basis for the needed knowledge of glory in "the face of Christ": "It is the God who said, 'Light will shine out of darkness,' who has shone in our hearts to give the light of the knowledge of the glory of God in the face of Christ" (2 Cor 4:6). God, according to Paul, has "shone in our hearts" to anchor the needed knowledge in a presentation of the risen Christ. We have noted that such a presentation in our hearts includes divine love, including forgiveness, courtesy of God's Spirit.

The love in question indicates the divine self-giving, costly love in Christ, complete with motivating power that, according to Paul, "urges us on." It thus does not leave us "disappointed" for needed assurance and evidence regarding divine reality and goodness. Appropriating this motivating work depends, however, on one's "turning to the Lord" and "beholding the glory of the Lord," if as reflected in a mirror (2 Cor 3:18). So, the shared glory is interpersonal between God and responsible humans.

Paul's theology and gospel are irreducible to a "theology of the cross." Instead, a theology of triumph in divine "glory" captures his thinking and preaching while including as a feature a nonexclusive theology of the cross. Neglect of this lesson leaves Paul without grounded hope, in the present, for the full glory of the eschatological future. In contrast, sharing in the resurrection glory of Christ now, if only in part and not yet fully, grounds the hope in question. It also underwrites Paul's message of believers being "victorious" now in a "triumphal" procession of divine glory. We let Paul be Paul when we recognize his gospel of resurrection glory realized in part now but to be completed in the fullness of time.

If God does not triumph over evil with divine glory, God is morally deficient and therefore is not God. A key issue is: How does God triumph over evil? The difficult but true answer includes: God triumphs over evil by relying on the cooperation of humans in the process. An easy answer would be: Just go ahead and do it, God, and spare us humans. Instead, God chooses that we live through evil and join divine renunciation of it in its destructive presence. We thus come to know firsthand what we hate and renounce and what we love and confirm. We thereby have the rare opportunity to share in divine glory.

The author of John's Gospel shares Paul's understanding of divine glory as being morally perfect and thus uncoercive of humans in its being shared with them. The key role for voluntary human agency in receiving divine glory in Christ as "God's only son" emerges at the start of John's Gospel: "[Jesus] came to his own home, and his own people received him not. But to all who received him, who believed in his name, he gave power to become children of God, who were born, not of blood or of the will of the flesh or of the will of man, but of God. And the Word became flesh and lived among us, and we have seen his glory, the glory as of a father's only son, full of grace and truth" (John 1:11–14). God's glory, according to John's Gospel, is "seen" in Jesus as God's "only son, full of grace and truth." The talk of "grace and truth" points to God's moral character of glory. This glory on offer in Jesus is to be "received" by humans; they do not apprehend it aright without cooperative reception of it.

In a prayer to his "righteous Father," John's Jesus proclaims, "The glory which thou hast given me I have given to them, that they may be one even as we are one, I in them and thou in me, that they may become perfectly [τετελειωμένοι] one, so that the world may know that thou hast sent me and hast loved them even as thou hast loved me" (John 17:22–23, RSV). The divine glory "given" by God to Jesus aims at humans becoming "perfectly one" in a way that reflects God's glory and love. The perfection of divine glory and love among humans, according to John's Gospel, thus sets a goal for human development and salvation in reconciliation with God and humans. This reconciliation is individual and social for receptive humans.

John's Gospel identifies an important distinction between divine glory and human glory given by God. God's glory is inherent to God but not to humans. So, God's glory must be "given" to humans, as an unmerited gift, if they are to share in it. In addition, God "gives" divine glory to God's unique son, Jesus, who, in turn, gives this glory to humans who receive him as their Lord. A remarkable claim of John's Jesus is that God loves people in general ("the world") as God loves Jesus, his unique son.

John's Gospel, unlike the synoptic Gospels, has no isolated transfiguration story regarding Jesus. Jesus consistently shows divine glory in transfiguration, including through his "signs" of God's presence (beginning in John 2:11).[22] Even so, God's glory in Christ is no spectacle for mere human observation, according to John's Gospel. On the contrary, it presents a challenge that seeks voluntary human obedience (in cooperative faith) to divine righteousness.

John's Jesus links faithful obedience to divine glory: "Jesus answered, 'My teaching is not mine but his who sent me. Anyone who resolves to do the will of God will know whether the teaching is from God or whether I am speaking on my own. Those who speak on their own seek their own glory, but the one who seeks the glory of him who sent him is true, and there is nothing unjust in him'" (John 7:16–18).

Resolving to do God's will concerns God's moral will, the will Jesus experienced and faithfully obeyed in Gethsemane, despite his life being at stake. Jesus "seeks the glory of him who sent him" and expects his followers to do the same.[23] In doing so, they share in God's glory as an unmerited gift given to them.

According to John's Gospel, the self-giving death of Jesus is the focal point of divine glory in him: "Jesus answered them, 'The hour has come for the Son of Man to be glorified. Very truly, I tell you, unless a grain of wheat falls into the earth and dies, it remains just a single grain, but if it dies it bears much fruit. Those who love their life lose it, and those who hate their life in this world will keep it for eternal life. Whoever serves me must follow me, and where I am, there will my servant be also. Whoever serves me, the Father will honor'" (John 12:23–26). Jesus thus shares in God's glory when he obeys his Father in giving his life for God and God's people. His followers are expected to do the same and thus be honored by sharing in God's glory. So, Jesus's promise of his followers sharing in God's glory is realized in their serving God, with obedient love, as Jesus did.

Jesus asks Martha, the sister of Lazarus, "Did I not tell you that if you believed you would see the glory of God?" (John 11:40). The author of John's Gospel would generalize on this question to suggest that humanly apprehended glory of God is shared with those who faithfully obey God. John's Jesus thus prays to God in a promise to share divine glory with his followers: "I have made your name known to those whom you gave me from the world. They were yours, and you gave them to me, and they have kept your word" (John 17:6). Faith in God, for John as for Paul, is the kind of trusting and loving obedience that keeps God's word, after the model of Jesus, the obedient Son.

We cannot digress to a detailed comparison of Paul, John, and Isaiah on divine glory. We should note, however, their common Jewish background regarding divine glory in the theological life of ancient Israel. Even so, we can note some differences.

The book of Isaiah did not have the benefit of the realized Christology enjoyed by Paul and John in the wake of the ministry of

Jesus. In addition, as Richard Bauckham has noted, John's Gospel offers an "intensification" of Paul's understanding of glory and the cross of Christ: "In Philippians [2:6–11] the paradox which transforms the meaning of exaltation [to glory] is that the one who humiliated himself to the utmost is *therefore* exalted to the utmost. But in John the paradox intensifies: Jesus's self-humiliation actually is his exaltation [to glory] by God. . . . What it means to be God in God's sovereignty and glory appears in the self-humiliation of the one who serves."[24] Such intensification in John12:23 and 13:31–32 seems to be an actual Johannine emphasis.

Nonetheless, Paul and John share Christology regarding Jesus in a way that yields some common themes about glory. For example, Jesus shared in the richness of his Father's glory before his earthly life (2 Cor 8:9; John 17:4–5, 24), and Jesus's disciples, through faithful obedience, share in his glory now by grace, prior to their own bodily resurrection (2 Cor 3:16, 18; John 17:8, 22). We now can recruit the views of John and Paul to elucidate how divine glory is apprehended and shared by humans in divine self-vindication.

Glory Apprehended and Shared

Humans often neglect divine glory with its active moral perfection as defect-free goodness in salvific righteousness. In doing so, they omit something crucial for divine worthiness of worship and for human relating to God as worthy of worship. Divine glory, with its active moral perfection, merits unqualified commitment from humans in their obedience, trust, and love. Such glory, given its independence of any created agent or object, differs in authoritative status from the glory of created agents derived from and dependent on divine glory.

The unmerited gift of divine glory to cooperative humans relies for its being apprehended and shared in by them on their faithful and loving obedience to God. Such obedience is voluntary in its cooperatively conforming, to some extent, to the divine glory of God's moral character and will (even if they fail to acknowledge God, as God, at work; cf.

Matt 25:31–45). If humans seek to apprehend and share in divine glory, they are to obey God as God's will presents itself to them, such as in the offered fruit of God's Spirit, including in moral conscience. Such fruit is an experienced indicator of intentional divine perfection, even if experienced with only glimmers at times.

A relevant intentional feature is in the divine nudging of humans toward the goal of deeper righteousness on the basis of the offered fruit. How a person responds to this divine indicator will figure importantly in whether it comes to fruition in salience in that person's experience, that is, whether the person experiences its distinctive moral power in cooperation. For the sake of accountable human personhood, God yields to human persons the power to frustrate or to advance the expansion of divine glory in their experience (2 Cor 4:15).

Faithful obedience to God, according to Paul and John, has its highest reward in human sharing in divine glory. Humans then reflect that glory to some measure in their moral character and are thereby sustained in righteous life with God. To the extent that humans undervalue divine glory, they undervalue the motivating divine power behind faithful obedience to God (at least as a response to that power), with corresponding detrimental results for their lives. One such result bears on the human need to "turn to the Lord" in faithful obedience. This is no merely abstract or theoretical turning because, as suggested, it is a cooperative response to the manifested fruit of the Spirit as God's personality traits. Divine love heads the list, according to Paul, and its manifestation, as noted, is experienced evidence of God's reality and goodness that can ground hope and faith in God (Rom 5:5; cf. 2 Cor 5:14).

As humans cooperate with the manifested fruit of God's Spirit, they share in the divine perfect intention to bring divine glory to realization among humans. They thus experience firsthand the movement of this intention, and its reality, toward divine perfect goodness, and thus glory, among humans. God's power of glory on offer then moves toward fruition among them as they experience it firsthand and conform to it, at least to some extent. The voluntary role of this conforming leaves humans as responsible moral agents before God who lack controlling ownership over divine character traits of glory.

A recurring human impediment to recognizing divine glory is the human tendency to lose awareness and other apprehension of its moral perfection in the midst of life's abundant imperfections. Humans often allow the moral imperfections in their lives to obscure the presence of more or less subtle indicators of divine perfection. This amounts to losing recognition of God and divine glory in what is not God. It is common but harmful in relating to God. It can block a righteous human relationship with God, thus leaving people without a needed compass for a good, righteous life.

In the language of John's Gospel, people sometimes allow the world's darkness to "overtake" the light of divine glory. The author of John's Gospel thus remarks, "The light shines in the darkness, and the darkness did not overtake it," adding that this light is the glory of God in the life of Christ (John 1:5). Paul likewise would direct human focus to the impeccable divine goodness on offer: "Whatever is true, whatever is honorable, whatever is just, whatever is pure, whatever is pleasing, whatever is commendable, if there is any excellence and if there is anything worthy of praise, think about these things" (Phil 4:8; cf. Rom 2:4). This is an injunction to reflect carefully on the good things given to humans by God, in effect, to behold the glory of God (2 Cor 3:18). This is not, however, a recommendation for abstract speculation, which can distract inquirers from the self-manifested goodness and glory of God.

Paul is concerned not with arguments of natural theology but instead with being moved to turn to the Lord on the basis of divine "excellence" confronted firsthand in human experience. In this turning, a human voluntarily conforms to the divine glory on offer and shares in it. In that case, one becomes a co-valuer with God in and toward divine moral perfection. One thereby can become a living manifestation of divine goodness and glory.

Conclusion

Divine glory looms large in many biblical narratives, given God's worthiness of worship and inherent moral perfection. The excellence of God's character calls for language that goes beyond static morality to an active salvific morality personified and empowered by God. The latter is a morality driven by a divine intention to share divine glory with humans, without their controlling ownership, via their being reconciled to God, volitionally, affectively, and intellectually. This glory can coexist with human moral imperfection, as we "have this treasure in cracked earthen vessels." We honor God's exalted role in salvific morality by recognizing the central role of shared divine glory, the gift of grace that goes "from glory to glory" in the lives of cooperative humans. In doing so, we can see how divine self-vindication benefits from shared divine glory among humans. They have the privilege of manifesting divine goodness and thereby vindicating God as righteous, despite the surrounding evil and suffering.

CHAPTER SIX

Frustrating Divine Vindication

Let God be true.

—Romans 3:4

HUMANS RELATING TO God face many challenges, but a common thread emerges: Humans can, and sometimes do, resist letting God be God in their lives. God, of course, will be God in any case, but humans can obstruct or disallow God from being *their* God, that is, from being God in *their* lives. The result is distorted human life, underdeveloped toward the righteous character of God.

Humans have a certain amount of control over the extent of their evidence of God's reality and goodness. This chapter explains the main point of this control granted to humans. The ideal human control is to let God be God, particularly to let the Spirit of God be God's Spirit in one's moral and spiritual life. This consideration enables us to explain much of the variability in evidence for God's reality and goodness among humans.

Jesus and Paul show us, with their lives, the importance of the relevant challenge. A big question for humans, then, is to allow or disallow God to be God in human life as God's Spirit intervenes. We shall draw some neglected lessons from this question, showing that human accountability is more prominent than often assumed. We also shall note an important connection between divine self-vindication and freely receiving a gift of divine grace.

What Kind of God?

Jesus and Paul follow the Jewish prophets Isaiah and Jeremiah, among other prophets, in assuming that God is perfectly good, or holy, in keeping with being worthy of worship. Being thus good goes beyond simply wanting what is good for people; it includes intentional actions of goodwill, typically with compassion, toward people. We may call this *benevolent goodness*. It is what various biblical writers call *righteousness*, and it gives moral robustness to what many call *holiness*. We shall continue to use the word *God* as an honorific title requiring worthiness of worship and thus perfect righteousness. Such use enables us to illuminate some important aspects of human experience and life, including social life.

The book of Isaiah, we have seen, offers a morally robust understanding of divine holiness (Isa 6:1–3, 5). The holiness of the Lord, according to Isaiah, contrasts with the morally unclean lips of humans. It thus creates a sharp moral contrast between humans and the Lord. Divine holiness includes righteousness and promotes righteousness, thereby morally and spiritually challenging humans.

Throughout Isaiah 51, divine righteousness emerges as the basis of the deliverance and salvation of humans from what brings destruction to them. Such righteousness thus has an active role toward what is morally good and life-giving for humans, individually and socially. This active role of manifesting moral strength, according to various parts of the book of Isaiah, is unique to the Lord:

> Only in the Lord, it shall be said of me,
> are righteousness and strength;
> all who were incensed against him
> shall come to him and be ashamed. (Isa 45:24)

Being at odds with divine righteousness can lead to human shame. It is an uncooperative response to active moral strength from God, but it does not destroy this strength. Divine righteousness prevails over human resistance, at least in due course, even when humans endure in their resistance.

We need to talk of "in due course," because the divine promise of full righteousness is for the future. The book of Jeremiah, for instance, promises, "The days are surely coming, says the Lord, when I will raise up for David a righteous Branch, and he shall reign as king and deal wisely and shall execute justice and righteousness in the land. In his days Judah will be saved, and Israel will live in safety. And this is the name by which he will be called: 'The Lord is our righteousness'" (Jer 23:5–6). The book of Isaiah offers a similar divine promise for the future, focusing on divine righteousness reflected in the people of God: "For Zion's sake I [God] will not keep silent, and for Jerusalem's sake I will not keep quiet, until her righteousness goes forth like brightness, and her salvation like a torch that is burning. The nations will see your righteousness" (Isa 62:1–2). This promise offers divine self-vindication in the lives of the people of God as they reflect God's righteousness.

The righteousness sought by God, as previously suggested, has an inward feature emphasized by Jeremiah. The divine promise includes a new covenant with a new inward role for the law of God: "This is the covenant that I will make with the house of Israel after those days, says the Lord: I will put my law within them, and I will write it on their hearts, and I will be their God, and they shall be my people. No longer shall they teach one another or say to each other, 'Know the Lord,' for they shall all know me, from the least of them to the greatest, says the Lord, for I will forgive their iniquity and remember their sin no more" (Jer 31:33–34).

Inward righteousness comes with divine forgiveness, and this forgiveness can be directly experienced by humans. We now can grasp how the active divine goodness of righteousness works among humans and contributes to divine self-vindication, but more clarification is needed.

Active Divine Goodness

We should consider the question of how God is actively good among humans. This question is pivotal for assessing the reality and goodness of God, particularly with regard to divine self-vindication. Clearly, God does not aim to satisfy all human desires or even all "normal" human desires, such as those for health, wealth, and comfort. It should go without saying that human life is widely marked by illness, poverty, and discomfort, among many other kinds of suffering, and these are all allowed by God. God is responsible for allowing them to occur. Allowing, of course, is not to be confused with causing or even with ideally wanting.

In Matthew's Gospel, Jesus presents this command: "Seek first the kingdom of God and his righteousness, and all these things [some other good things] will be given to you as well" (Matt 6:33). This command suggests a needed ranking for the priority of good things to be sought. The command is for humans to prioritize good things as God prioritizes good things. The result is a serious moral challenge for humans, and they often need forgiveness for failing to meet it.

The divine moral challenge to humans takes a concrete form in Jesus's response to human suffering and death. In Luke's Gospel, Jesus raises questions about severe human suffering and loss, and he points to God's priority for humans:

> At that very time there were some present who told Jesus about the Galileans whose blood Pilate had mingled with their sacrifices. He asked them, "Do you think that because these Galileans suffered in this way they were worse sinners than all other Galileans? No, I tell you, but unless you repent you will all perish as they did. Or those eighteen who were killed when the tower of Siloam fell on them—do you think that they were worse offenders than all the other people living in Jerusalem? No, I tell you, but unless you repent you will all perish just as they did." (Luke 13:1–5)

Jesus clearly states that the suffering in question is not a special divine judgment for sin. He directs the inquiry to a different matter. At first, it seems that he is avoiding the issue of human suffering, but he actually has a special focus on God's top priority. This priority is: *lasting* human goodness with God through a repentant human relationship with God.

Goodness from God falls into four broad categories that contrast pairwise: temporary and lasting goodness, and interpersonal and non-interpersonal goodness. Non-interpersonal goodness from God arises when God gives good nonpersonal things to humans, such as sunshine and rain (Matt 5:45), even when they deny and otherwise disregard God's reality and goodness. Such goodness, being non-interpersonal, is not an integral part of an interpersonal relationship between God and the humans in question.

Jesus puts his primary focus, at least in Luke 13:1–5, on lasting interpersonal goodness from God. It stems from human repentance that can receive interpersonal reconciliation with God. Such repentance, as a response to a divine moral challenge, includes humans turning to God in a manner cooperative with God's expressed will. It is turning away from attitudes or actions at odds with God's manifested moral will or character. Humans thus at odds with God obstruct cooperative human reconciliation with God.

The interpersonal focus of the message of Jesus is difficult when we have a severe conflict between lasting goodness and temporary goodness for humans. For instance, the suffering and death of humans, such as in natural disasters, rightly attract our concern, especially when the humans are undeserving of the suffering. Consider a massive earthquake that results in human suffering and death but prompts some people to turn to God in repentance, leading to their lasting reconciliation with God. For this kind of case, Jesus appears to prioritize the lasting good of human repentance and reconciliation with God over the temporary human goods of health and comfort. Lasting human flourishing with God can come at the expense of temporary goods for humans, but it receives a top ranking by Jesus on the scale of good things from God.

Many people wonder whether God has a moral right to allow severe human suffering in order to bring some people to repentance and reconciliation with God. This issue applies to the suffering both of people who do not themselves repent and of people prompted to repent by the suffering (perhaps by the suffering of others). Some people find it unfair to have some suffer for the sake of the repentance of others, although it does seem that the repentance of some people is prompted by the suffering of others. Theists tend to hold that God has a moral right to use suffering in the latter manner. I shall not contest this view as long as the suffering is not cruel; our present focus, in any case, lies elsewhere.

Paul follows Jesus in focusing not on a full explanation of human suffering but instead on the goodness God seeks to bring out of suffering. He claims that God has an active role in frustrating some human wills by subjecting them to "futility," or failure (Rom 8:20–21). Such frustrating would bring about some human pain and suffering, and God would be the cause. In that case, God would be causally responsible for some human pain and suffering. It does not follow, however, that God causes *evil*. It would be a mistake to assume that all pain or suffering is evil.

As indicated, Paul claims that, according to God's aim with futility, "the creation itself will be set free from its enslavement to decay and will obtain the freedom of the glory of the children of God" (Rom 8:21). His talk of "the freedom of the glory of the children of God" is, we noted, eschatological, concerning God's future culmination of things regarding God's people. God's subjecting creation to futility aims at that future freedom for the children of God. It thus seeks to bring people to receive their becoming the children of God now, whereby full freedom from death and sin can be received from God in due course.

Paul, we noted, holds that God's future fulfillment for the people of God is partly realized in the form of a down payment now. God's Spirit makes the down payment in current human experience when people turn to God in repentance. Paul thus speaks of God, "who has put his seal on us and given us his Spirit in our hearts as a down payment" (2 Cor 1:22; cf. 5:5). This Spirit, according to Paul, brings people interpersonal confirmation and assurance of their being in a filial relation to God: "When we cry, 'Abba! Father!', it is that very Spirit bearing witness with our spirit that we are children of God" (Rom 8:15–16).

The filial relation in question depends on God's self-manifesting divine traits in human experience. Paul, we have seen, credits the Spirit of God in human hope in God having a grounding in divine love poured into our hearts (Rom 5:5). God's love for a person emerges in that person's experience and serves as reliable evidence that supports human hope and faith in God, owing to its indicating the reality and goodness of God. Paul thus speaks, as noted, of being urged on by love from Christ (2 Cor 5:14) and emphasizes this experienced love for his life: "The life I now live in the flesh I live by the faith of the Son of God, who loved me and gave himself for me" (Gal 2:20).

Paul does not limit divine manifestation to humans of the love from Christ to the historical self-sacrifice of Jesus on the cross. He finds, we have confirmed, the same love in currently experienced love from the intervening "fruit of the Spirit" of God and Christ. Interpreters have widely neglected the evidential value of this fruit regarding the reality and goodness of God and Christ. Many have treated the fruit as abstract values, but it is, in Paul's thought, a matter of God's active personality traits and thus *God* self-manifested in human experience. It is the self-manifestation of God in God's active moral character in human moral experience. It is, then, God self-authenticating God's reality and goodness for humans in their experience.

The fruit of the Spirit is central to the divine intentional leading of humans to divine righteousness (Rom 8:9–10, 14). Interpreters, however, have not given this intentional leading adequate attention. Such leading indicates a purpose, and this purpose includes a personal agent manifesting the fruit of the Spirit and leading people to cooperate in manifesting God's moral character. This leading indicates God's Spirit as active in value challenges from the fruit of Spirit toward reconciliation with divine righteousness and thus God.

The Gospel of John, we have noted, confirms the active role of God's Spirit in human moral experience, with a promise from Jesus regarding conviction concerning righteousness (John 16:7–11). Such conviction is not merely negative, just concerning sin, guilt, or shame. It includes conviction of what is righteous, thus giving God's Spirit a positive role, and this role can be found at times in human conscience.[1]

God's Spirit convicts people in conscience of righteousness, not coercively, but when they allow the fruit of the Spirit to challenge them to cooperate with righteousness as active moral goodness. This is a matter of letting the Spirit of God be the Spirit of God, and thus letting God be God, in one's own moral experience and life. We need to clarify this human response.

Intentional Human Response

We humans settle on the kinds of goodness we value and their relative priorities, such as economic, aesthetic, prudential, cognitive, and moral goods. We can go wrong, however, particularly relative to divine priorities. For instance, we can subject moral goods to economic goods or prudential goods. This would be a mistake relative to God's morally perfect character.

An important voluntary human role toward God includes letting the fruit of God's Spirit come to maturity or fruition in a human life. The result is typically a difficult challenge to our own priorities for moral goodness. This challenge involves letting the fruit as intentional moral values come to fruition in salience and constancy, whereby a positive formation of human moral character occurs. In such character formation, God emerges as powerful and faithful in interpersonal action toward humans. In thus letting God be God, humans let God become salient and morally powerful in their experience. As a result, they can let God be God in bringing them righteousness in cooperative relationships with God and others. They thus can allow God to self-vindicate divine righteousness in their lives as they manifest God's unique moral character.

Our obstructing or disallowing God (with God's allowance) takes two general forms: direct and indirect. Our direct obstructing arises when we contradict or deny some fruit of God's Spirit, such as love for other people. So, when I hate other people, intending their final destruction or severe harm, I directly obstruct God's moral intervention in my experience with divine love. I thereby block God from leading me into a righteous relationship with God and others. I then directly disallow God from being God in my moral experience and life.

Our indirect obstruction of divine love occurs when we ignore or disregard, without a direct denial, (the value of) such love in our experience and lives. For instance, I can be presented in conscience with the value of unselfish care of my annoying neighbor but divert my attention from this moral challenge. I can focus my attention instead on ways to exclude and ignore my neighbor. In that case, I indirectly would disregard the divine love challenging me to exercise unselfish care to other people, including my annoying neighbor. I then would indirectly disallow God from being God in relationship to me and my experience and life. This would be an individual and a social failure, from a moral point of view.

Divine love offers forgiveness to humans for their wrongdoing in order to lead them to reconciliation in righteous love between God and themselves (2 Cor 5:19, 21). Humans are voluntarily to receive this forgiveness through their acknowledging a need of it, given their moral failure and needed restoration before God. Such forgiveness, when received cooperatively, can be experienced as pardon that releases one from guilt, shame, and condemnation, at least in some areas of life. It thus can prepare a person for cooperative reconciliation with God, in attitudes and actions. It also can extend to social reconciliation among humans.

When humans cooperatively receive divine forgiveness, they can and should let go of assumed moral self-justification and self-righteousness before God. They can and should let God be God with a divine gift that credits them as acceptable or approved before God, courtesy of this gift, despite their moral unworthiness. Paul calls this a "gift of righteousness" in divine grace (Rom 5:15–17). It is unearned by humans, and they receive it by their voluntary trust in God (Rom 4:2–5). Whether a person can become worthy of such a gift, with God's power, will depend on how a person cooperates with the divine moral power on offer.

Paul thinks of God's manifested goodness, we noted, as intended to prompt people to turn to God in cooperatively receiving divine grace (Rom 2:4). Humans need, however, to let God be God in leading people to the kind of repentance that issues in reconciliation with God. This challenge prompts people to decide where they stand relative to divine righteousness as God's active effort to attract people to loyal cooperation with that righteousness, in relationship with God. Ignoring this challenge will not serve God's purpose of the moral renewal of humans.

Human responses to divine righteousness can be explicit or implicit regarding a person's understanding an experience of such righteousness. When understanding an experience is informationally explicit (*de dicto*), people are aware *that* the experienced righteousness is divine, *that* God is involved in manifesting the righteousness. In contrast, when a response is informationally implicit (merely *de re*), people respond without recognition that God is the promoter of the manifested righteousness. God still can be the source, and people still can experience the divine righteousness, but they lack recognition *that God* is at work in the experience.

Jesus gave an example of merely *de re* response to righteousness, without people recognizing that divine intervention is present (Matt 25:31–45). He indicated that an explicit response with recognition that God is involved was not required for his approval. An implicit response with cooperation toward righteousness, he suggested, can get divine approval. People thus can let God be God in promoting righteousness without their explicit response of recognition that God is involved. The needed "letting God be God" can be implicit and merely *de re* regarding human information about God. Jesus suggests as much in his example of his assessing humans in divine judgment. We turn to how the desired human response figures in the divine re-creation of people.

Letting God Re-Create

Kierkegaard remarks that an obedient response to God is "to let God command, to leave to God to ordain."[2] This is fitting advice if we are willing to let God be God as commanding Lord of our lives. A broader injunction, bearing on God as redeemer, is: Let God be God in saving us from ourselves and other deadly threats. We need more than obedience to be saved, given our prospect of moral failure and lasting death. We need power to counter what will kill, without recovery, our moral and bodily lives. Having been included in creation, without our being consulted, we must ask about the prospect of re-creation whereby we are saved from moral failure and lasting death.

We obscure our moral predicament if we confuse the original creation of humans with their needed re-creation. The efficient causation behind human existence in the original creation does not dominate the re-creation needed by humans with moral inadequacies. The basis for the asymmetry is that the re-creation is inherently moral, treating typical candidates for re-creation as morally responsible agents who respond voluntarily to God, for or against.

A voluntary response by humans needs freedom from dominating causation that blocks their responsible agency. We need to consider how this consideration fits with letting God be the savior who re-creates willing persons. As such a savior, God creates a context of needed salvation, if with pain and suffering, that can uncoercively attract people to cooperate with God in divine righteousness. In such a context, people can voluntarily share in divine self-vindication in manifested righteousness. Their own lives can become a manifestation of God's righteous character, in a cooperative relationship with God.

P. T. Forsyth has commented on the kind of re-creative salvation needed by wayward humans:

> The final moral conviction can . . . be brought about [not] by the conscience alone, but [only] by God's Spirit in the conscience. Salvation, if it means anything real, means a new heart; and the new heart is not simply a new affection, but a new relation[ship], a new [hu]man, the conscience forgiven, recreated, and reassured before God by the atoning, reconciling act of God. That is real religion, real faith. That is what gives the great accent of reality. It does not mean being true to our convictions; it means that our convictions be true to the conviction and conversion of the conscience by the Holy Spirit.[3]

The divine "reconciling act" in question lies at the center of the "new heart" and the new life on offer for humans. It also underwrites divine self-vindication in righteousness among and within humans, socially and individually.

Forsyth adds, "It is a divine reconciliation, but reconciliation of the conscience more even than of the affections (2 Cor 5:19, 21); it is a recall from guilt and not from mere coldness. And it is a reconciliation which means re-creation and not mere rehabilitation, as being the birth of a power in us and not merely the gift to us of a [psychological] state."[4] The relevant power is an intentional, personal power that seeks ever-deepening reconciliation of humans with God. It is, however, nonmechanical and uncoercive; if received, it is received voluntarily by humans. They can, and sometimes do, decline the divine offer.

Paul clarifies our challenge from divine power by a comparison between Adam from the original creation and the second Adam from the re-creation. He refers to the first "Adam who is a pattern of the one who was to come," namely, Jesus Christ (Rom 5:14). The pattern concerns a decisive role for each Adam in representing humans and relating to God as God in righteous obedience.

Paul writes about the contrast, "If, because of the one man's trespass, death reigned through that one, much more surely will those who receive the abundance of grace and the gift of righteousness reign in life through the one man, Jesus Christ. Therefore just as one man's trespass led to condemnation for all, so one man's act of righteousness leads to justification and life for all. For just as through the one man's disobedience the many were made sinners, so through the one man's obedience the many will be made righteous" (Rom 5:17–19). The righteous obedience of Jesus is at the center of Paul's account of divine re-creation for humans. This re-creation relies on Jesus as a human representative (of God and humans) who obeys God in order to manifest and circulate God's life-giving power of righteous love.

Paul says of Jesus that "the last Adam became a life-giving spirit" (1 Cor 15:45). In the same context, Paul commands the Corinthian Christians, "Sober up, as you rightly ought to, and sin no more, for some people have no knowledge of God" (1 Cor 15:34). He thus assumes a voluntary human response to the divine effort of re-creating humans through the risen Jesus as life-giving spirit. This re-creation, then, does not coerce or force human wills but preserves their responsible moral agency. It seeks their full willing cooperation with the re-creation launched by Jesus on behalf of God and wayward humans.

In his Gethsemane crisis, Jesus voluntarily lets God be God over all of his life and death. He yields fully to God with a prayer that lets God have full authority: "Abba, Father, for you all things are possible; remove this cup from me, yet not what I want but what you want" (Mark 14:36). He thereby was empowered by God to obey God with all he had. He committed his will and life to God's will, thereby showing and enacting what it is to be a blameless, righteous child of God. He thus vindicated God's righteousness in his own life. His life shows that his Father is worthy of human obedience, trust, and love, without qualification.

By cooperative identification with Jesus in his obedience of faith in Gethsemane, wayward humans can find the divine power to obey God in a way that enables their divine re-creation. Humans then can let God be God over all of their lives and deaths, after the pattern of Jesus. The last Adam thus leads to a family of people reflective of his righteous obedience, thereby enabling God to manifest and offer divine re-creative power to others. This life-giving power spreads as people voluntarily let God be God in their re-creation in righteousness. It builds a community based on socially shared letting God be God, even in death. Jesus inaugurated this community in his leading by example, from Gethsemane to Calvary and beyond. He thus promoted the self-vindication of God in righteous human lives. We thus see that God's purpose extends beyond individual salvation to a community of people conformed to Jesus in Gethsemane.

From Explanation to Rapport

We have identified our letting God be God, and letting God's Spirit be God's Spirit, as central to the divine renewal of people and thus the divine self-vindication in righteousness among humans. This identification is an explanatory position; it names what engages humans to cooperate with God's effort toward their renewal. By divine lights, however, it is not enough for humans to settle for an explanatory position. The divine aim, going beyond mere explanation, is to form without coercion human character, attitudes, and actions suited to righteousness in relationship with God. It aims to color and motivate all of human existence in relation to God and divine righteousness. By way of response, humans are to include all areas of their lives in the challenge to let God be their God in all areas of righteousness.

How are humans to proceed in letting God be God and letting God's Spirit be God's Spirit? Gethsemane is the model set by Jesus: It shows a moral rapport between Jesus and God in his prayer to let God's will be done in his life and death (cf. Matt 6:10). This model contrasts with mere moralism because it includes direct divine-human interpersonal interaction. In this interaction, God uses human conscience to manifest divine fruit of the Spirit, such as righteous love, to humans and thereby to seek their responsive cooperation with this fruit. Moral rapport of humans with God arises from their encountering the divine fruit of the Spirit in conscience and cooperating with it.

I am suggesting, along with P. T. Forsyth, that God has a moral conscience and aims to share it with humans as they voluntarily cooperate with its fruit of the Spirit as intentional spiritual values that can motivate humans. Such cooperation depends on their attending to the divine activity in moral conscience. In particular, it relies on their welcoming its values (or fruit of the Spirit) intended by God to lead to human moral renewal in righteousness. Such renewal is at the center of a cooperative relationship between God and humans.

Forsyth characterizes the role of conscience that can serve as a basis for moral rapport in righteousness:

> All comes back to the conscience, to a will in relation to a Will. The only universal religion is the religion of the conscience and its redemption. It is a religion of moral redemption. All its affectional power and beauty centres there, in holy love.... The new creation... is a matter of righteousness.... Its power

> is righteousness, its field is the conscience, and its warrant is in God's treatment of the conscience once for all in Christ's Cross. The root of conscience is in our sense of responsibility, our sense of being trustees and subjects—i.e., our sense of divine power and majesty over us.[5]

An important issue is whether we attend to our conscience in such a way that lets divine righteousness work through it with re-creative moral power for us. God, we have suggested, intends the process to be interpersonal and thus not mechanical or coercive. We thus have a voluntary response to make.

The focus of divine-human moral rapport is not our conscience itself but the self-manifestation of God in our conscience. Specifically, the focus is the fruit of God's Spirit as value-like personality traits intended by God to bring divine-human reconciliation in righteousness. Our conscience is the interactive area where we can directly apprehend God's moral personality traits that extend to us an opportunity for moral rapport with God. Gethsemane shows us the moral rapport of Jesus with God, whereby he directly faces his divine Father and shows his filial and faithful obedience toward God. The reality of this rapport is suggested by Luke's remark that "Jesus often withdrew to lonely places and prayed" (Luke 5:16, NIV). It enabled obedience in Gethsemane to be a preferred and well-grounded option for him.

Paul affirms the value of ongoing moral rapport with God, along with letting God's Spirit be God's Spirit in one's life: "Pray without ceasing, give thanks in all circumstances, for this is the will of God in Christ Jesus for you. Do not quench the Spirit" (1 Thess 5:17–19). He means "give thanks to God," thus indicating attentiveness to God at work in all things. This fits with, and receives support from, his remark that "we know that in all things God works for the good of those who love him, who have been called according to his purpose" (Rom 8:28, NIV).

Paul, we noted, follows the view of the book of Isaiah that God self-manifests to people, seeking to draw them into loyal cooperation

(Rom 10:21; Isa 65:1). He also suggests the view supported here that the challenge in human conscience from the divine fruit of the Spirit gives God's self-manifestation salience. As people respond cooperatively, without quenching God's Spirit, they enter moral rapport with God, moving toward a life in divine righteousness. Such a life contributes to the self-vindication of God as righteous among humans.

Paul thinks of the needed rapport as based in "the obedience of faith" (Rom 1:5, 16:26), the kind of "obedience which leads to righteousness" (Rom 6:16). He thinks of such obedience to be paradigmatic in Jesus, who was led to his death by it (Phil 2:7–8). This fact points us, again, to the defining crisis of Gethsemane for Jesus, and this crisis bears on his followers and on candidates for being his followers. If God works in all things, the "all things" calling for our response raise the Gethsemane option: My will or God's will as primary? In short, do we let God's will be primary in all of our decisions, whether for life or death? The relevant "letting God be God," in Paul's thought, includes active obedience as one's presenting oneself to God for righteousness, including as a living sacrifice to God (Rom 6:16, 19; Rom 12:1).[6]

Paul holds, we have observed, that we humans face a kind of ongoing Gethsemane challenge within, involving a conflict between "the flesh" and "the Spirit" (Gal 5:16–21). This is an inner conflict between "what the flesh desires" and "what the Spirit desires." We also face a choice whether to be "led by the Spirit" (cf. Gal 5:25) and thus whether to "live by the Spirit." Being thus led and living depend, then, on letting the "flesh"-opposing fruit of the Spirit form and motivate our moral characters and lives, after the moral character of Jesus and God.

Paul identifies the conflict in conscience in his following remark on the Gentiles: "They show that what the law requires is written on their hearts, as their own conscience also bears witness, and their conflicting thoughts will accuse or perhaps excuse them" (Rom 2:15). He sees the Spirit of God at work in this conflict for moral life with God over moral death in conflict with God. Paul adds that his conscience confirms the truth of his message by the Spirit of God (Rom 9:1). God's Spirit thus works in human conscience, and hence in moral experience, to present and confirm vital truth regarding God's reality and goodness.

Conscience is not automatically the voice of God or even a flawless witness to God. It represents God only when it presents, courtesy of divine manifestation, God's moral character of righteousness. In doing so, it offers a voluntary choice for a person between righteousness and unrighteousness, between God and anti-God. It thus maintains human accountability before God. So, a human response to God arises in a context of moral conflict, thus including a vital decision between God and opposition (or at least indifference) to God.

Paul affirms a human need of God in the moral domain. He affirms a need of divine moral power to empower humans against moral weakness and failure (Rom 7:22–25). He also recognizes a human need for God in preventing human moral efforts from collapsing into futility from final death (1 Cor 15:32, 54–57). The divine gift-giver is needed as the Lord, who is the intentional moral leader for humans in need of moral leading toward righteousness in relationships (Rom 8:14). This need brings a need of accountability for humans before the God of righteousness.

God cares about human accountability for letting God be God, and this caring has a good reason. God seeks human responsiveness in a divine-human relationship where God is Lord, and human accountability is central to the relationship. Personal accountability before God as Lord enlivens, with due motivation, interpersonal relationships by manifesting their moral importance before God and thus their importance for human life. Paul gives us a sense of its importance: "Now we know that, whatever the law says, it speaks to those who are under the law, so that every mouth may be silenced and the whole world may be held accountable to God" (Rom 3:19). He reiterates, with reference to all people, "Each one of us will be held accountable" (Rom 14:12).[7]

The divine aim is to show that "the whole world" is "accountable to God" in a context of divine self-vindication. A larger goal is that thereby people will voluntarily let God be their God as Lord and thus ultimately be formative and self-vindicating in their moral lives. This goal is central to the even larger divine aim to build a voluntary universal commonwealth or society under God as authoritative righteous benefactor toward all humans. Divine righteous love pursues this aim, unrelentingly, and it provides for the human accountability needed to motivate and achieve it. In realizing it, as humans let God be God, God finally will be Lord as "all in all" (1 Cor 15:28). In this eschatological fulfillment, humans finally will let God be God as morally victorious and self-vindicated over all things, courtesy of the triumphant Spirit of God and its unique fruit. God's desired commonwealth will then become reality, in a cooperative divine-human relationship of self-giving love, modeled on Jesus.

Conclusion

We now can see why some people have a salient experience of God and others do not. Our cooperative response to the manifested fruit of God's Spirit is pivotal for divine salience for us. Our failure to cooperate blocks God's moral-character traits from coming to fruition with power and salience in our lives. Divine power thus suffers from human obstruction. Human cooperation in response, in contrast, opens our lives to the coming to fruition of the divine fruit of the Spirit on offer. This powerful role for humans takes seriously their accountability before God and enables them to become victorious co-sustainers of lasting righteousness with God. It also enables them to become co-vindicators of divine righteousness in their lives and in a renewed community reflective of Jesus. A higher calling is hard to imagine, on earth or in heaven.

CHAPTER SEVEN

Higher Ways in Vindication

Beyond Divine Neglect

> *As the heavens are higher than the earth, so are my ways higher than your ways and my thoughts than your thoughts.*
>
> —Isaiah 55:9

A CHARGE OF DIVINE neglect often arises from humans when God puts God on trial before them. Many people feel neglected by God at some time; they thus think of themselves as victims of divine neglect. Jesus may have been one of them, with his cry of abandonment on the cross. In any case, we must start with the standard of neglect at work. The neglect in question typically includes a person's failure to help when this person readily could help another person. Is God guilty of such neglect? If so, how does this consideration bear on God's moral character?

This chapter identifies a role for lack of care or concern for good in neglect, and on this basis it contends that God has not been shown guilty of moral neglect. Even so, the chapter explains why many people assume that God is guilty of such neglect, owing to their unawareness of a crucial distinction between character-knowing and occurrence-knowing regarding God and the purposes for human suffering and evil. It offers them a viable alternative for God, identifying how God is, in the end, not proven guilty of divine neglect. It contends that God's moral character can be known by us without our knowing all of the divine purposes for allowing the occurrence of suffering and evil.

Time and Purpose in Neglect

Questions of neglect raise questions of time in a delayed response. One issue concerns how long inaction toward a person must extend to become neglect of that person. In other words, how much delay in intervention in a person's life makes for neglecting that person? Suppose that your young daughter is learning to ride her bike without training wheels in a large grassy field (much better than a concrete parking lot). You ask her to try to ride in large circles, and then you help her with an initial push. Her ride is wobbly, but you do not intervene. You allow her to maintain her circular course without interruption. She risks falling off of her bike, but you watch with vigilance while refraining from intervention.

Your inaction has a good purpose: to allow your daughter to form her own self-understanding and strategy of response in her challenge to learn to ride the bike. You aim to build her self-understanding in learning to ride, and you want her to gain hope in her learning to ride. You are vigilant nonetheless.

Your momentary vigilant inaction is not neglect, as you have your daughter under your careful watch. Suppose, however, that your inaction continues for a longer time, and during this time, she falls while you do nothing (when you could have intervened). Perhaps a question of your neglect then arises. Perhaps but perhaps not.

The reality of neglect is not inherently about the length of time in a delayed response. Instead, it is about what, if anything, is in the delay, regarding a purpose or the absence of a purpose for the temporary inaction. If there is no purpose in the delay, then there is no intentional action in it, and neglect is a live option. Similarly, if there is only indifference in the delay, then there is no adequate purpose or caring in the inaction, and neglect is a live option. A prospect of neglect can arise, then, owing to a lack of caring in the inaction, regardless of the length of the delay.[1]

You could have a purpose in your temporary inaction toward your daughter's bike-riding, while others do not know of your purpose. We could fail to recognize your having a good purpose in your temporary inaction and infer that you are guilty of neglecting your daughter. Our assumption of your neglecting her, however, would be wrong, a result of our failure to see that you have a good purpose in your delay in action. We could expect, in addition, a quick fix from you when your daughter is about to fall, but your failing to comply with our expectation would not entail neglect on your part. In the delayed response, your purpose in training your daughter to ride could exonerate you from a charge of neglect toward her.

God, it is arguable, has some things in common with you as you train your daughter to ride her bike:

1. God could have a purpose in temporary divine inaction toward some human suffering and evil, while we fail to recognize that God has a purpose. We could fail to recognize, in particular, that God has a good purpose in temporary divine inaction and thus infer that God is guilty of neglecting some people.
2. Our inferring that God neglects some people, however, would be wrong, given our failure to recognize that God has a good purpose in divine delay inaction.
3. We might expect an immediate fix from God for people faced with severe suffering and evil, but God's failing to comply with our expectation would not entail divine neglect. God could have a good purpose, perhaps unknown to us, for avoiding an immediate fix.
4. In our suffering, God could aim to clarify for us our need of God and our self-understanding of that need, and God thereby could seek to elicit our hope in God as a needed sustainer of good for us humans.

God's effort to elicit our hope in God, thereby replacing our contrary hopes, can be turbulent for us. Paul, as previously noted, writes, "The creation was subjected to futility, not of its own will, but by the will of the one who subjected it, in hope that the creation itself will be set free from its enslavement to decay and will obtain the freedom of the glory of the children of God" (Rom 8:20-21). Created things (real estate, money, etc.) attracting our hope can be contrary to our hope in God. When they are, God may subject them to futility, or failure, as an object of our hope, for the sake of making room for our hope in God. In addition, we can rely on the Spirit of God to enable us to put to death the unrighteous deeds of our body, to enhance our room for divine righteousness in our lives and for our hope in God (Rom 8:13). Sometimes God needs to make room in our lives for what we truly need.

God is neither a physical object nor a physically visible object; so, physical sight is not our means of access to God. Something else must serve here. Paul remarks, "In hope we were saved. Now hope that is seen is not hope, for who hopes for what one already sees? But if we hope for what we do not see, we wait for it with patience" (Rom 8:24–25). Hope here includes hope or expectation *in God*, and the latter hope includes hope in God's coming to us in divine goodness. So, we need to be able to apprehend or perceive divine goodness coming to us. This goodness need not be full divine goodness, but it can be a voucher or down payment for full or at least unchallenged divine goodness in the fullness of time (2 Cor 5:5; cf. Eph 1:13–14). We thus can face what we have called a "now (in part) but not (fully) yet" relation to divine goodness.

We often look in the wrong places for divine goodness, such as in places where our selfish desires will benefit. Instead, we should look for indicators of the reality and goodness of a God worthy of worship, in keeping with God's moral character. Such indicators are summed up in Paul's aforementioned list for the Galatian Christians of God's moral personality traits: "The fruit of the Spirit is love, joy, peace, patience, kindness, generosity, faithfulness, gentleness, and self-control" (Gal 5:22–23). These are qualities of God's moral personality, and God can manifest them in a person's moral experience, such as in conscience. When we find them presented to us, we should consider God to be seeking to engage us toward reconciliation and cooperation with God in divine righteousness. This divine effort can occur in a context of evil and human suffering.

Paul, we have noted, recognizes the primary fruit of the Spirit to be evidence for the reality and goodness of God and thus a basis for human hope in God. He states, "Hope [in God] does not put us to shame, because God's love has been poured into our hearts through the Holy Spirit that has been given to us" (Rom 5:5). His idea of our not being "put to shame," we have suggested, includes the notion of an evidentially responsible basis for hope and trust in God. This basis is the self-manifestation of God's love in a person's moral experience, including conscience (another word for "heart"). Paul would appeal to the same basis for faith in God, given his concern in the same context for such faith (Rom 5:1).

Two Kinds of Understanding and Knowing

Divine love manifested to us supplies interpersonal evidence in support of hope and faith in God. Nevertheless, it does so in a context of mixed evidence. As a result, Helmut Thielicke remarks, "[believers in God] do not just believe *in* God. They also believe *in spite of* what they may see and cannot understand."[2]

The writer of Psalm 73 expresses a believer's struggle in the moral conflict of human life:

> When my soul was embittered,
> when I was pricked in heart,
> I was stupid and ignorant;
> I was like a brute beast toward you.
> Nevertheless, I am continually with you;
> you hold my right hand. (Ps 73:21–23)

The psalmist acknowledges his being embittered toward God. Such embitterment is no surprise, given the frustrations of human life, along with their resulting pain and suffering. Even so, the psalmist expresses continued commitment to God and recognizes divine support of him: "Nevertheless, I am continually with you; you hold my right hand." He finds his embitterment toward God to be, on reflection, "stupid and ignorant." This expression sounds like repentance for a presumptuous attitude toward God. In any case, it supports his "nevertheless" commitment to God.

The author of Psalm 22 shares the "nevertheless" attitude of Psalm 73:

> My God, my God, why have you forsaken me?
> Why are you so far from helping me, from the words of my groaning?
> O my God, I cry by day, but you do not answer;
> and by night but find no rest.
> Yet you are holy,
> enthroned on the praises of Israel.
> In you our ancestors trusted;
> they trusted, and you delivered them.
> To you they cried and were saved;
> in you they trusted and were not put to shame. (Ps 22:1–5)

The psalmist anticipates Jesus's cry of abandonment on the cross (Mark 15:34; Matt 27:46). Even so, he follows up with an attitude-changing "yet" that points in a new direction of focus, equivalent to "nevertheless." He thus turns to God's moral character and praises God for being holy and a trustworthy deliverer and savior: "In you they trusted and were not put to shame." How can we reconcile the contrasting attitudes before us: the initial lament and the subsequent praise of "yet" or "nevertheless?"

We begin with a needed distinction between:

1. our currently unexplained suffering or evil with no indication of prompt rescue,
   and
2. a perfectly good divine moral character motivating delayed rescue from our unexplained suffering or evil.

This distinction helps us with the issue of what it takes to be willing to say "nevertheless" for trusting God in the face of unexplained suffering or evil. An approach to a person's value-ranking can figure in such willingness: particularly, ranking the value of God's moral character and delayed rescue higher than the value of our explaining the suffering or evil in question.

Corresponding to the distinction between the value of God's moral character and delayed rescue and the value of our explaining the relevant suffering or evil, we need a distinction between two kinds of understanding (or knowing):

> *Occurrence understanding (or knowing)*: understanding or knowing *why an instance of suffering or evil occurs,* and
> *Character understanding (or knowing):* understanding or knowing *God's moral character* that allows for our having unexplained suffering or evil.

I may not understand or know, for instance, why you allow your daughter to wobble toward falling while bike-riding, but my knowing your moral character could enable me to refrain from assuming neglect on your part toward her. The same often holds for a child's trusting her parent. Likewise for God, we may not understand why God delays rescue from an instance of suffering or evil, but our knowing God's moral character could lead us not to assume divine neglect toward the people facing that suffering or evil. Knowing God's moral character enables us to know the kinds of morally relevant things God would do or not do.

We might ask if the previous value-ranking supporting "nevertheless" is "right" in that it matches reality. This would raise the question of *which* reality is to be matched, and some will suggest the reality of God's value-ranking as the standard. Why, however, God's ranking? It is not enough to reply that it is God's universe because normative considerations of right and wrong about value rankings are relevant. If, however, God is worthy of worship and hence morally perfect, the matter changes. We then have a morally suitable value-ranking in God, even if we have a hard time identifying it.

Someone might argue that we all should share God's value ranking, given God's moral perfection. The pressing issue, however, is whether we all share adequate evidence for the success of such an argument, that is, evidence that will convince all people of the reality and goodness of God and of the value ranking in question. It is hard to identify such evidence for all concerned. It seems to be available to people only from God's moral character manifested to them. It is questionable, however, whether God has manifested the same relevant evidence of divine moral character to all people. Some people have reported, evidently with candor, that they have not received the evidence in question. So, it is doubtful that we can dislodge agnosticism or atheism here in one fell swoop for all people. (We shall return to this matter in the final section of this chapter.)

Evidence of God's moral character allows for God's having "ways higher than our ways," whereby we lack understanding or knowing why some suffering or evil is allowed by God. The book of Isaiah portrays God as saying:

> For my thoughts are not your thoughts,
> nor are your ways my ways, says the Lord.
> For as the heavens are higher than the earth,
> so are my ways higher than your ways
> and my thoughts than your thoughts. (Isa 55:8–9)

Paul concurs, given his following expression: "O the depth of the riches and wisdom and knowledge of God! How unsearchable are his judgments and how inscrutable his ways!" (Rom 11:33). He also has God's higher ways and thoughts in mind when he echoes Isaiah 40:13: "Who has known the mind of the Lord? Or who has been his counselor?" (Rom 11:34).

The factor of higher and inscrutable divine ways and thoughts should not surprise us if God is morally perfect and we are not. In that case, we should expect God to have ways and thoughts superior to ours, with the result that we are unable, in our inferior position, to explain all of God's ways and thoughts, including God's purposes in allowing some suffering or evil. So, our limitation in occurrence-knowing does not entail or otherwise undermine character-knowing of God. The two can coexist, and we should expect this result.

The superiority of some of God's ways and thoughts lies behind the following advice from the book of Proverbs:

> Trust in the Lord with all your heart
> and lean not on your own understanding;
> in all your ways submit to him,
> and he will make your paths straight. (Prov 3:5–6, NIV)

The important assumption here is that reliance on our own understanding can obstruct trust in God. Our trusting our own understanding of why some suffering or evil has occurred can be at odds with our trusting in God. In some cases, we are to trust God even though we lack understanding of why God has allowed some suffering or evil. We can express this lesson in terms of the priority for humans of character-understanding (or -knowing) over occurrence-understanding (or -knowing) regarding God's role in delayed rescue from suffering or evil.

The book of Jeremiah sums up our proposal for distinguishing and ranking two kinds of understanding or knowing: "Thus says the Lord: Do not let the wise boast in their wisdom; do not let the mighty boast in their might; do not let the wealthy boast in their wealth; but let those who boast boast in this, that they understand and know me, that I am the Lord" (Jer 9:23–24). Jeremiah prioritizes our "understanding and knowing" God (as Lord) over our being "the wise [who] boast in their wisdom," the latter including their wisdom that seeks understanding of various occurrences of human suffering or evil when it is at odds with God. I take his distinction to include our previous distinction between character-understanding and occurrence-understanding, with priority for humans given to the former.

We arguably will not know God's moral character firsthand if we do not, with due care, let it express itself firsthand. To avoid distorting it, we must welcome an experience of its goodness, thereby letting it express itself to us as it really is and, on that basis, knowing its unique quality. The biblical injunction to "taste and see" thus bears on the manifestation of God's moral character, as we are dealing with an interpersonal relation and not a coercive intervention. It would be a mistake, we have noted, to regard God's moral power as coercive of human wills. According to Isaiah and Paul, God holds out his hands to oppositional people (Isa 65:2; Rom 10:21). We should let these hands express themselves for their uncoercive moral quality in relating to humans.

What we do with our tasting and seeing matters. Either we extend it with our cooperating with God's moral character, or we curb it with our declining to cooperate. In order to know God in a robust sense, we need to cooperate, thereby allowing God's expressed moral character to become salient for us and to elicit and support what it intends: a cooperative, faithful human response that reflects the love expressed by God. This active character of God thus aims not just to self-present to us but also to draw us closer to God in cooperative moral likeness.

"Like knows like" best in relating to God, owing to the interpersonal attraction of moral likeness. As we humans become like God in moral character, then, we improve our opportunity for knowing God. We thus can move from tasting and seeing to embracing and sharing with love in the divine interpersonal goodness presented to us. In that case, we will be personally changed as we are willingly drawn, in our moral character, closer to God's moral character of perfectly righteous love. We thus come to know God and God's moral character firsthand, even while being ignorant of many divine purposes in allowing suffering and evil.

Important indicators of divine goodness in our experience, as previously suggested, come from what Paul calls "the fruit of the Spirit" and the "fruit of righteousness" (Phil 1:11). Such fruit can be an active, intentional basis for revealing God to us and for challenging us to conform to God's character. Knowing God on this basis prevents a chasm between the evidence for God, on the one hand, and who God is regarding God's moral character, on the other hand.

Many arguments of natural theology, we have noted, allow for a chasm in their appeal to alleged effects of God's actions apart from God's moral character (such as a first cause, order in nature, and human consciousness). Knowing the latter effects does not entail knowing God, the active moral agent behind them. We can know these effects without having evidence to resist a charge of divine neglect. Evidence for resisting such a charge involves knowing God and God's moral character is ultimately responsible for this world's existence and for allowing its suffering and evil. Such evidence underwrites the aforementioned kind of character-knowing that can be incomplete in occurrence-knowing but can nevertheless counter a charge of divine neglect.

Strikingly, Paul claims that "we know that all things work together for good for those who love God, who are called according to his purpose," the latter purpose including our being "conformed to the image of his Son" (Rom 8:28). Paul does not claim to have full occurrence-knowing of God's purposes in allowing suffering and evil. He thus remarks, "We are afflicted in every way but not crushed, perplexed but not driven to despair" (2 Cor 4:8). We can be "perplexed" about God's purposes in allowing some suffering and evil but still know God's character in a way that underwrites Paul's view that God guides all things for good. Character-knowing thus has priority over occurrence-knowing in this perspective. Our limitations in occurrence-knowing, even though real and extensive, do not block our character-knowing regarding God.

We have asked about what we prioritize in cases of apparent neglect. This issue suggested a ranking of priority between our understanding underlying purposes for suffering and evil and our understanding God's moral character. Such a ranking will seem sterile, however, if we are altogether lacking in our experience of God's moral character. We then will lack a needed benchmark in our experience for a ranking, and any mere concept of God offered instead will call for something in experience to recommend it over competing concepts of God. So, we need to ask what the benchmark looks like in our experience.

Perhaps, as suggested, we have a qualitative voucher in our present incomplete experience of God for a later experience of the fullness of God's moral character. The voucher can come from the fruit of God's active, intervening Spirit, such as divine love for us manifested in our experience. It could help us learn who we are as moral agents in relation to God and what to trust in patient, if painful, waiting for full divine rescue. We may need special discernment for the challenge at hand.

Discerning Higher Ways of Character

Many agnostics disavow having adequate evidence for what the moral character of God is. They also deny having adequate evidence of how God works in human experience with unique indications (such as in the fruit of the Spirit) of divine reality and goodness. Perhaps, however, God waits for them to value how he works in this troubled world, without coercion of their wills. This situation is no mere intellectual matter; we rarely can argue agnostics out of their agnosticism. Instead, it is a matter of what we, along with agnostics, discern and value at work in this puzzling world.

Paul reports, "Those who are unspiritual do not receive the gifts of God's Spirit, for they are foolishness to them, and they are unable to understand them because they are spiritually discerned" (1 Cor 2:14). His idea of being "spiritually discerned" gains some clarity from his talk of (1) what "God has revealed to us through the Spirit" (1 Cor 2:10), (2) "words not taught by human wisdom but taught by the Spirit" (1 Cor 2:13), and (3) our having "the mind of Christ" (1 Cor 2:16). He thus suggests that spiritual discernment relies on input from God's Spirit that coheres with the mind or character of Christ. Christ and God's Spirit, then, figure importantly in our discerning what God reveals to us.

A key factor for our spiritual discerning is the divine love found in "the grace of God that has been given you in Christ Jesus," including the crucified Christ of God's self-giving love (1 Cor 1:4, 18, 23–24, 2:2). Such divine love, we have noted, is the primary fruit of the Spirit, in Paul's understanding, and sets a constraint on the value of knowledge and faith (1 Cor 13:2). In willingly receiving this love (it comes first from God as a gift of grace), we share in "the mind of Christ," and his mind (= spirit), we have suggested, can be a divine standpoint for our discerning and knowing the unmatched character of God.

Paul claims that "the love from Christ moves us" (2 Cor 5:14, my translation), and he infers, "From now on, therefore, we know no one according to the flesh [a worldly point of view]; even though we once knew Christ according to the flesh, we no longer know him in that way" (2 Cor 5:16, my translation). Divine love from Christ is thus a standpoint for us to know reality, including God and Christ. We may consider it a focusing lens to view God's moral character, including the fruit of the Spirit, active in our experience and the world.

Paul sums up his aim in commenting on faith and wisdom to the Corinthian Christians: "so that your faith might rest not on human wisdom but on the power of God" (1 Cor 2:5). Such power lastingly endures because, according to Paul, it is found in Christ (1 Cor 1:24), and Christ lastingly endures courtesy of God and divine resurrection power. The power in question includes the divine moral power found in Christ and in the fruit of God's Spirit. It is intentional, active divine power that is irreducible to abstract moral principles or concepts. Its purpose is to attract people, without coercion, to join and support the family of God, in keeping with the image of God's Son.

God, according to Paul, aims to destroy the wisdom of "the wise" (1 Cor 1:19; cf. Isa 29:14), including "the wisdom of the world." He thus asks, "Where is the one who is wise? Where is the scholar? Where is the debater of this age? Has not God made foolish the wisdom of the world?" (1 Cor 1:20). The divine motive is, according to Paul, "in order that, as it is written, 'Let the one who boasts, boast in the Lord'" (1 Cor 1:31; cf. 1 Cor 1:29; Jer 9:24).[3] This boasting "in the Lord" includes boasting in the Lord's moral character, even when we do not know the Lord's purposes in allowing suffering or evil. So, we return to the aforementioned priority of knowing the character of God.

God has the option to put people, or allow people to be put, off balance morally in their lives. The divine aim would be for them to confront how God is needed to stabilize, at least morally, their vulnerable lives. An experience of divine love now, we have noted, can serve as a voucher for God's more complete provision or reparation in the future. We see a version of this option in the parable of the prodigal son, where the younger of two sons was allowed by his father to go away to a troubling place but eventually "came to his senses" and returned to his waiting (running) father. Thus: "The younger of [the two sons] said to his father, 'Father, give me the share of the wealth that will belong to me.' So he divided his assets between them. A few days later the younger son gathered all he had and traveled to a distant region, and there he squandered his wealth in dissolute living" (Luke 15:12–13). The lesson includes that God must intervene first, thus enabling people to find God. Even so, people must have enough "sense" to look for indications of God in their experience, that is, indications fitting for a God worthy of worship and hence morally perfect.

The indications of divine character, as noted, need not clarify all divine purposes in allowing suffering and evil. A result in knowing God's moral character thus can be frustration in explaining some of God's ways, and we should expect such a result given our extensive ignorance in the area of divine purposes. Another frustration can arise from the suffering involved in human experience of the self-giving love that characterizes God's compassionate character and underwrites our knowing God's moral character.

Suffering was linked to the ministry of Paul from its start. The book of Acts describes the calling of Saul of Tarsus with the following remark by the Lord: "I myself will show him how much he must suffer for the sake of my name" (Acts 9:16). Paul's own testimony on the role of suffering in Christian life is also clear. He holds that we as Christians are "heirs of God and joint heirs with Christ, if we in fact suffer with him so that we may also be glorified with him" (Rom

8:17). So, the self-giving love characteristic of God and God's people is compassionate, suffering love. It is love where God suffers with God's people for the benefit of all concerned. Jesus manifested this lesson with his life and death.

Suffering Love

As this book's Introduction suggested, God intends to show in human lives, as part of divine self-vindication, that the compassionate love characteristic of God is stronger, more enduring than any suffering, death, or evil that opposes it. God thus allows such suffering, death, and evil to exist in some forms for this general purpose at least. If this is a sketch of a general theodicy, it is not a full theodicy, given its shortcomings on the specific purposes of God in particular cases of allowing suffering, death, and evil. As suggested, I doubt that we have a full theodicy available to us now.[4]

The divine self-vindication through humans includes vindication of God as compassionately loving in being worthy of worship. God chooses to vindicate God through humans because humans, we observed, have tended to question God's goodness, ever since the opening chapters of Genesis. A fitting human response will agree with Dietrich Bonhoeffer's remark in July 1944 that "Christians stand with God to share God's pain."[5] By standing with God in sharing divine compassionate love, through cooperating with it, humans testify to the trustworthiness of God as compassionately loving. (See the related divine challenge to Job for loyalty to God.) The love in question is inseparable in reality from its dependence on God (if unknowingly by humans), and it is required by the perfectionist title *God*.

Standing with God in divine compassionate love is central to resilient faith in God, and this faith is subject to frequent testing in human life by suffering, death, and evil. We humans thus figure in the extent of divine self-vindication in human life. Our frequent decisions whether to support divine compassionate love with God, toward God and humans, matter in this regard. They reveal where we stand in relation to God, going beyond our claims about God. They show whether we are truly standing with God.

The divine call to know God's moral character of suffering love includes the call for us to participate in this love, thus exceeding mere recognition of it. The plot thickens here because it challenges our comfort and desire for full or at least consistent comfort. We understandably are tempted to turn away in an effort to avoid suffering. We thus can lose interest in knowing God's moral character of compassionate, suffering love. We might shift our focus instead to seeking to know the purposes God has in allowing human suffering and evil. This would be a mistake if we proceed in a way that hinders our opportunity to know God's moral character.

Perhaps all people, including agnostics, should constantly face a big question: Will we let God, in keeping with Romans 5:5, pour out divine suffering love in our hearts in a way that becomes our priority in life? Perhaps a common answer is: sometimes yes, other times no. In any case, a cooperative response would give us the evidence in our experience to know God's moral character, even if we do not know many of the particular divine purposes in allowing suffering and evil. Such a response would be participatory knowing of God's character, as we share in some of God's moral-character traits. God would value such knowing because it would entail righteous co-loving with God that shows such compassionate loving to be stronger than suffering, evil, and death. It thus would contribute to divine self-vindication through cooperative human lives. Our sharing in divine suffering love can attract us to God as we experience firsthand the kind of compassionate love God has shown for us in Christ.[6]

As anticipated by Jeremiah (chapter 31) and Ezekiel (chapter 36), the divine goal does not settle for a standard outside of us. It aims for us to have (the fruit of) the Spirit within ourselves, in our "heart," the center of our personhood. Paul thus tells the Roman Christians that "the Spirit of God dwells in you" (Rom 8:9), and he says the same of Christ (Rom 8:10). He sets a goal of Christ being "formed" in his disciples (Gal 4:19), adding that "it is Christ who lives in me" (Gal 2:20).

So, the people of God are to bear God's moral character from within themselves, in their deepest motives. With such help from within, we are to learn to love as God and Christ love, and the learning curve nevertheless can be steep. In such learning, we will deeply reflect God's moral character, including its righteous compassionate love for a world in need of such love. As a result, God's unique character of love will be known and vindicated by and among the people of God (cf. Isa 62:1–2).

Having internally appropriated divine love, the people of God will tend to dissent from the disciples' response to Jesus in the following situation: "A great windstorm arose, and the waves beat into the boat, so that the boat was already being swamped. But he [Jesus] was in the stern, asleep on the cushion, and they woke him up and said to him, 'Teacher, do you not care that we are perishing?'" (Mark 4:37–39). Instead, their fitting response will acknowledge God's character of suffering love and then move away from despair and toward conformity with that character. Their response will not depend on their knowing all of God's purposes in allowing suffering and evil but will depend on their character-knowing of God.

We get some confirmation of our approach from Jesus's cry of felt abandonment on the cross, "My God, my God, why have you forsaken me?" (Mark 15:34; Matt 27:46). The interpretive key here is Jesus's recognition of "my God, my God" in the second person, in his praying directly to his God. His question is not the abstract issue: Does God have a purpose in allowing me to feel this pain? Instead, his why-question arises in a context of prayer directly to "my God, my God," thus showing his commitment to God and God's moral character.

Jesus subjects his why-question to recognition of his God's being God and thus to recognition of God's divine moral character. This agrees with the aforementioned divine ranking of character-knowing over occurrence-knowing. Such character-knowing does not preclude occurrence-knowing, but it does subject the value of occurrence-knowing to the higher value of character-knowing regarding God. (I suspect we find an analogue in Jesus's reply in Luke 13:3, noted in chapter 6 above, to a question about evil, but we cannot digress now.)

Jesus, as far as we can tell, did not get a prompt answer to his why-question for his God. No divine purpose was immediately described in answer to his prayer to God. We have seen that Psalm 22 begins with a similar question anticipating Jesus's cry, but it turns immediately to an endorsement of God's holy character. It thus subjects our difficult questions regarding the occurrence of suffering and evil to the righteous character of God. Jesus follows suit, if with more subtlety, with the language of his prayer, "My God, my God." He thus confirms the priority of character-knowing of God over occurrence-knowing regarding God's purposes. This priority does not allow a limitation in occurrence-knowing to create despair about character-knowing of God. It thus lets God be God among God's people, even over human occurrence-knowing regarding divine purposes.

Our examples drawn from Mark 4 and Mark 15 are not tightly analogous, but there seems to be an underlying similarity. In both cases, people are feeling neglected (they want more help), whatever the source of their feelings. Jesus is not scolded by his God for raising his painful question, whatever Jesus's feelings and motives were. He seems to want more immediate help from his God, but the divine plan seems not to have allowed for this without some delay. Having him die may have been part of the planned help, and the resurrection definitely was part of the help according to subsequent reports. In addition, Jesus holds no grudge against his God after his resurrection by God. He assumes that the divine timing of "giving help" has priority over the timing of his "wanting help," in agreement with a biblical injunction to "wait upon the Lord" (Ps 27:14).

The Gospel of Luke agrees with our approach to the priority of character-knowing of God. It omits the cry of abandonment in the Gospels of Mark and Matthew and offers instead: "Jesus, crying out with a loud voice, said, 'Father, into your hands I commend my spirit.' Having said this, he breathed his last" (Luke 23:46). Luke puts the focus on God's character as the "Father" worthy of receiving Jesus's spirit. No further explanation is needed for the purpose of Luke's portrait. Jesus's character-knowing of his divine Father sees him through with suffering love in his encounter with evil on the cross. He endures in faithfulness, standing with God in compassion, as a result of his primary commitment to the character and will of his divine Father.

Jesus's character-knowing of his Father brings us to his aforementioned hallmark prayer of Gethsemane: "Abba, Father, for you all things are possible; remove this cup from me, yet not what I want but what you want" (Mark 14:36). Again he addresses God as "Father," thus focusing on God's unique character rather than on the purposes in God's plan of suffering for him. He opts for obedience to his Father even though his initial preference was to request a different plan ("remove this cup from me"). The Gethsemane prayer of Jesus thus confirms our case for the priority of character-knowing of God. Such knowledge can leave us with unanswered questions about alternative purposes and plans regarding suffering and evil. God's character, rather than our understanding of divine purposes, has top priority in this knowledge. This seems to be how things should be.

Our position on the priority of character-knowing of God fits with the first commandment, "You shall have no other gods before me" (Exod 20:3). Giving priority to God's character is to give priority to God, thus denying priority to "other gods." Failure here, with priority given to something else, is idolatry. In Gethsemane, Jesus shows us how to avoid idolatry by putting his Father first, and we see a similar option for relating character-knowing of God to occurrence-knowing. The bearing of the first commandment confirms our case for giving priority to character-knowing of God over occurrence-knowing. From God's perspective, this makes good sense.

The priority of character-knowing of God will not attract people who sincerely claim not to experience divine love at all. We need not impugn their candor, but we may ask what exactly they have looked for as divine love. While honoring the priority of God's timing for self-revelation to an individual, we can ask about the role of God in human conscience more generally. Bracketing psychopathy, people experience moral challenges in conscience, and many of these challenges are for their moral good. Many of them also seem intentional in a way that is purpose-directed. Conscience is thus a place to explore an experience of divine goodness, including divine love.[7]

When some people explore their moral experience, including conscience, they report experiencing unsurpassed goodness, including divine love, toward them. God can be self-authenticating for them in this way, bringing the fruit of the Spirit to them as the divine calling card representative of God's moral character in their experience. When they sense and value this fruit, they report encountering God in their experience, as their compassionate God in search of them. In that case, it is their challenge to value God as their top priority, given divine worthiness of worship, despite shortcomings in their understanding of many divine purposes.

Perhaps the best counter to a suspicion of divine neglect is to let God be God in pouring out divine love in our hearts. Perhaps in doing so we can encounter God's higher way, including God's higher character, of divine love. According to Paul, this is God's "still more excellent way" (1 Cor 12:31), beyond familiar gifts in the church: "Now faith, hope, and love remain, these three, but the greatest of these is love" (1 Cor 13:13).

Conclusion

We have seen that character-knowing of God allows for gaps in occurrence-knowing of God's purposes in allowing suffering and evil. We also have seen, on the basis of the first commandment, that God gives priority among humans to character-knowing of God over occurrence-knowing. The divine aim is to discourage human idolatry that values human understanding of various purposes for suffering and evil over knowing God and God's unique moral character of righteous love. Such idolatry unduly exalts human understanding in relation to God.

When God puts God on trial among humans, a familiar charge is that God is guilty of neglecting many humans as they face suffering and evil without a prompt rescue or explanation. We have questioned this charge on the ground of our vast ignorance of God's purposes in allowing suffering and evil in particular cases. We should expect such ignorance, given our typical inability to discover God's purposes on our own and given God's not revealing many of these purposes to us. The situation is different regarding God's moral character and our prospect for knowing that character. We can know God's moral character firsthand, on the basis of the manifested fruit of God's Spirit, without knowing divine purposes for unexplained suffering and evil. Knowing God's character thus can save us from a misplaced charge of divine neglect. It also can make room for our seeing how God self-vindicates in the cooperative renewal of God's people, individually and socially.

CHAPTER EIGHT

Concluding Postscript

Vindication Through Divine Cooperative Prayer

Pray without ceasing.

—1 Thessalonians 5:17

THIS BOOK HAS argued that a God worthy of worship uses the voluntary transformation of cooperative humans to self-vindicate divine righteousness among them. This vindication, like the transformation, is cooperative between God and some humans, but its initiative and contours are God's. God sets the standards for humans to follow in receiving divine approval. We have noted the standard of divine grace through faith, whereby God credits righteousness to people of faith in God, after the model of Abraham. We need to clarify how prayer fits with this standard and the divine pursuit of self-vindication through righteousness in human lives.

From Faith to Divine Cooperative Prayer

The faith sought by God is interpersonal between God and humans. It includes faith *in* God relating a human directly to God, *de re*, and not just to informational content, *de dicto*, about God. Part of the direct relating desired, and even commanded, by God is human prayer toward God. There is, however, a wrinkle: God seeks to be a guide for prayer through cooperative humans, and we may call such prayer *divine cooperative prayer*. This co-prayer is not exactly God praying to God, but it is God influencing and guiding human prayer to God. Much discussion of prayer focuses solely on a human contribution and thus neglects divine cooperative prayer in the sense indicated. In restoring attention to divine cooperative prayer, we shall see a crucial role for prayer in divine self-vindication in righteousness among humans.

Paul remarks to the Roman Christians, "The Spirit helps us in our weakness, for we do not know how to pray as we ought, but that very Spirit intercedes with groanings too deep for words. And God, who searches hearts, knows what is the mind of the Spirit, because the Spirit intercedes for the saints according to the will of God" (Rom 8:26–27; cf. Rom 8:15–16). God's Spirit thus has an active role in the relevant kind of human prayer that we have called *divine cooperative prayer.*

Two considerations are important. First, God's Spirit can guide human prayer with nudges and other interventions deeper than words. Second, this guiding is "according to the will of God." There are thus real contours or boundaries, set by God, on divine cooperative prayer.

Paul adds, on the heels of his previous comment on the Spirit in prayer, "We know that all things work together for good for those who love God, who are called according to his purpose. For those whom he foreknew he also predestined to be conformed to the image of his Son, in order that he might be the firstborn within a large family" (Rom 8:28–29). Since the "good" in question includes righteousness, we have confirmation of this book's main thesis. God seeks righteousness among the people of God, as they are conformed, by voluntary character transformation through God's Spirit, to the image of Jesus Christ, the perfect image of God (2 Cor 4:4). A broader divine goal is "a large family" that voluntarily reflects divine righteousness and thereby contributes to God's self-vindication among humans in their transformation.

The idea of human co-praying with God captures what Paul has in mind with his acknowledgment of the Spirit's role in human prayer. This role aims for re-creative change of human character, with human cooperation, toward the moral and spiritual image of God and Christ. Paul's mention of divine influence "deeper than words" merits attention in our understanding of God's contribution to human co-prayer with God. This influence is not purely intellectual or discursive, given that neither God's Spirit nor its work here is purely intellectual or discursive.

Divine influence in prayer includes the uncoercive nudging from a divine personal will toward humans. It can come with "groanings" that express God's will without words to humans. We humans sometimes express a similar influence in relating to children needing some felt direction in life. The felt expression of influence behind the term *ugh* comes to mind as an example. We may think of the "pathos of divine cooperative prayer" as the felt uncoerced nudging of our will by God's will. This nudging expresses without words the direction of God's will in order to woo or attract us toward cooperation with God in a righteous relationship.

We humans can, and sometimes do, refuse the offered gracious gift of divine cooperative prayer and its pathos. This is the opposite of a response of faith or trust in God. We are then self-alienating toward God, obstructing our being reconciled to God. As a result, our sense of God's presence and goodness wanes and can even disappear; likewise for our faith or trust in God for goodness. God, in addition, can withdraw divine presence to us in such a case to allow us to learn firsthand the tragedy of a life alienated from God (see Rom 1:21–25).

A refusal of divine cooperative prayer will have observable consequences in a human life, and those consequences will not be upbuilding toward righteousness in that life. Such a refusal typically stems from a human concern to retain self-control over a life, and it is often joined with a fear of losing this control to something or someone else threatening our own benefit. We often want to do things our own way, and this can lead to our rejecting divine influence, including divine cooperative prayer, in our lives. Such a quest for human control does not favor trust in God; it actually promotes distrust in God.

Sometimes a quest for human control aims for a kind of human autonomy that excludes divine influence. It can result in observable indifference toward divine righteousness in a human life or at least toward love of one's enemies. Such indifference can obscure for indifferent people the genuine goodness present in their lives. It can contribute, for instance, to inattentiveness toward the actual divine goodness aiming to transform their lives, in a voluntary manner, toward righteousness. In that case, the people in question would be self-excluding, if unknowingly, toward relevant available evidence of God's presence and goodness. We humans thus can bring ourselves to fail to receive available evidence and knowledge of God. We can position ourselves to be unreceptive and uncooperative toward such evidence and knowledge. In that case, God would not be blameworthy for our evidence deficit regarding God's reality and goodness.

Epistemology of Prayer

Inquirers about God rarely attend to the epistemology of prayer, that is, the assessment of the origin, nature, and limits of evidence and knowledge of God acquired through prayer. This is a discipline in need of careful workers, as it promises to illuminate a kind of interpersonal volitional knowledge of God neglected by many inquirers. The interpersonal knowledge in question requires humans to settle on an attitude of their will: a volitional attitude of willingness, with intention, to cooperate agreeably with any settled evidence given to them by God in prayer. Such settled evidence represents God's expressed final will in contrast with a preliminary expressed will. As a result, sincere human participants in divine prayer will not be volitionally hostile to God, even if they struggle to have God change some perceived initial expectations from God.

Our willingness to cooperate with settled evidence from God figures centrally in our agreeably receiving available evidence of God in divine cooperative prayer. It fits with God's intention in giving divine evidence in prayer: to attract people to agreeable cooperation with God toward righteous love for God and all humans. This willingness responds positively to the divine pathos in prayer: God's nudging, without coercion, a human will to cooperate with God in righteous love. Even so, humans can dissent from God's pathos, thus frustrating God's goodwill for them. A familiar divine response to such dissent is for God to withdraw and to hide divine presence while waiting for a more opportune attitude among dissenters.

Significant factors in human dissent from God are anticipated human suffering and actual human suffering. These factors can discourage people from pursuing evidence of God that will add to their suffering. Humans are correct if they anticipate their own resulting suffering when they cooperate with God's will indicated in divine pathos. They typically should expect to suffer in that case, given the nature of God's compassionate love. This lesson is confirmed throughout the biblical writings, and chapter 7 above noted this in relation to the calling and ministry of the apostle Paul (see Acts 9:15–16; Rom 8:17). Paul's letters confirm his repeatedly suffering for his mission from God.

Paul, as suggested, relates suffering to prayer (Rom 8:15–17). John Koenig has put Paul's lesson concisely: "To call God 'Abba' [in prayer], as Jesus did, to be led by the Spirit in prayer, means to share in the sufferings of Christ for the sake of the world's healing and ultimate glorification."[1] Crying "Abba! Father!" is a form of prayer, and it assumes the filial relation to God presented by God's Son, Jesus. As a result, it calls for human participation, including through prayer, in his suffering for the benefit of other people. We noted, in chapter 7, that this participation also figures in the self-vindication of God in cooperative human lives that show God's righteousness and God's worthiness to be obeyed, trusted, and loved. It includes, as indicated, humans "standing with God" in sharing divine suffering love, to echo Bonhoeffer.

Paul remarks on a benefit of his own suffering in relation to trusting God, "We do not want you to be ignorant, brothers and sisters, of the affliction we experienced in Asia, for we were so utterly, unbearably crushed that we despaired of life itself. Indeed, we felt that we had received the sentence of death so that we would rely not on ourselves but on God, who raises the dead. He who rescued us from so deadly a peril will continue to rescue us; on him we have set our hope that he will rescue us again" (2 Cor 1:8–10). Paul has in mind a divine goal for human suffering, namely, "so that we would rely not on ourselves but on God, who raises the dead." Suffering, in this perspective, can contribute to our trusting God rather than ourselves. This lesson is not a full theodicy, by any means, but it can make some sense of a divine goal for some human suffering. In divine cooperative prayer, humans show their reliance on the righteous God who raises the dead and hears those who pray.

Paul relates his weakness in suffering to his receiving "the power of Christ." He begins with a statement from God: "'My grace is sufficient for you, for power is made perfect in weakness.' So I will boast all the more gladly of my weaknesses, so that the power of Christ may dwell in me. Therefore I am content with weaknesses, insults, hardships, persecutions, and calamities for the sake of Christ, for whenever I am weak, then I am strong" (2 Cor 12:9–10). The divine power in grace, according to Paul, is to empower followers of Christ as they conform to the compassionate life of Christ in relationship with his divine Father.

Paul states that his afflictions have a distinctive goal: "always carrying around in the body the death of Jesus, so that the life of Jesus may also be made visible in our bodies" (2 Cor 4:10). Our bearing the compassionate, suffering love of Jesus thus can make the compassionate life of Jesus visible to others, according to Paul. The author of the Epistle to the Colossians, representing Paul, adds, "I am now rejoicing in my sufferings for your sake, and in my flesh I am completing what is lacking in Christ's afflictions for the sake of his body, that is, the church" (Col 1:24). Again, our sharing in the suffering love of Christ can extend this love to benefit followers of Christ, among others. This benefit depends on our voluntary commitment to cooperate with this love even in the face of opposition from suffering, death, and evil. We are thus tested for our faithful endurance and sharing in compassionate divine love for us. Our challenge is to endure to show God's worthiness of being obeyed, trusted, and loved.

The compassionate life of Jesus is manifested in human weakness, including in divine cooperative prayer as humans yield their wills to God in prayer as Jesus did. In such yielding, "the power of Christ" takes priority over human power, and God's moral character influences human moral characters toward righteousness. These factors are central to divine self-vindication through humans as they manifest God's unique reality and goodness.

Paul identifies, in connection with divine character-building, a role for suffering that involves an important feature for prayer—faithful endurance: "We rejoice in our sufferings, knowing that suffering produces endurance, and endurance produces character, and character produces hope" (Rom 5:3–4). In a related vein, regarding the suffering from persecution, Jesus remarks, "The one who endures to the end will be saved" (Mark 13:13). God thus values faithful human endurance in suffering that builds moral character in relationship with God and manifests God's righteous character. When ongoing suffering manifests our ongoing need of God, we typically can recognize our need to endure faithfully toward God in divine cooperative prayer. In such endurance, we are helped to recognize God's goodness as a needed ongoing reality and power in our lives. Our endurance brings a maturity to us that enables the fruit of the Spirit to come to maturity in our lives and to be seen by others in need of God. This is a path to divine self-vindication in cooperative human lives.

The best model for faithful endurance toward God, in suffering and in divine cooperative prayer, is Jesus. Gethsemane offers his exemplary response to God in his suffering and prayer. Luke indicates his intense suffering by noting that he sweat blood in Gethsemane (Luke 22:44). Jesus nonetheless prays to God, as we have noted, "Abba, Father, for you all things are possible; remove this cup from me, yet not what I want but what you want" (Mark 14:36). We thus may capture Jesus's attitude toward God in prayer as: You, Father, are perfectly good, and I will comply.

Jesus initially struggles with God in asking God to "remove this cup" from him, and this indicates his willingness to challenge God in prayer. His challenge to God, however, yields to his considered commitment to obey God's settled will: "Not what I want but what you want." The latter commitment fits with the image of Jesus, in various New Testament contexts, as the obedient Son of God. The focus is less on his physical suffering than on his suffering volitional struggle to obey God fully, come what may.

The pathos of divine cooperative prayer undergoes a test to vindicate God as righteous among humans. It tests their endurance in sharing this pathos in its nudging a human life toward divine righteousness. This sharing requires that humans conform to the divine nudging of them toward God's righteous character. Jesus models such volitional sharing in Gethsemane as he yields his life to his Father. Before him, Job anticipated the importance of sharing the divine pathos toward righteousness under suffering. Jesus, however, is the ultimate human model for cooperative prayer. He is God's perfect representative for divine self-vindication among humans.

The epistemology of prayer should attend to the human volitional suffering in the pathos of prayer. In doing so, it can illuminate difficulties humans face in receiving available evidence from God in prayer. When "Deep calls to deep" in prayer, humans can turn away owing to their fear of anticipated difficulty resulting from the call. They thus can suppress available evidence of God's presence and goodness. In doing so, they will hinder available knowledge of God for themselves. God offers divine self-evidence in the volitional pathos of prayer in order to attract people to cooperative fellowship with God in divine righteousness. Indifference or opposition to the latter fellowship undermines the divine purpose in offering such evidence. So, God can postpone such evidence for an opportune time. An epistemology of prayer should accommodate this lesson.

Divine Prayer as Gift

Divine cooperative prayer, we have suggested, includes a needed human response to the divine pathos of uncoercively nudging humans toward righteousness. In the Lord's Prayer, Jesus presents the following requests, among others, to God:

> Our Father who art in heaven,
> Hallowed be thy name.

> Thy kingdom come,
> Thy will be done,
> On earth as it is in heaven. (Matt 6:9–10, RSV)

These three requests raise the question about a response: By whom? That is, by God or by humans? We should be doubtful of an exclusive disjunction here, as if God and humans could not work together to satisfy Jesus's requests. A cooperative approach between God and humans makes good sense, given God's effort toward reconciliation with humans in thought, volition, action, and emotion.

Jesus directs his prayer to his Father, but he also has in mind a role for humans in satisfying his requests. He considers God to empower cooperative humans to hallow God's name, to advance God's kingdom, and to do God's will on earth. God is not expected, in this prayer, to meet the requests without co-work by humans to the same ends.

P. T. Forsyth remarks,

> In prayer we do not so much work as interwork. We are fellow workers with God in a reciprocity. And as God is the freest Being in existence, such co-operant prayer is the freest things that man can do. It we were free in sinning, how much more free in the praying which undoes sin! If we were free to break God's will, how much more free to turn it or to accept it! Petitionary prayer is man's cooperation in kind with God amidst a world He freely made for freedom.[2]

The teachings of Jesus on obeying God recommend such interactive co-work between God and humans, and they extend to obedience in human prayer. We thus can illuminate the Lord's Prayer by understanding it to ask for divine power through the co-work of human cooperation with God.

We should not infer that all of God's work in prayer includes human co-work. God extends benefits to us, inside prayer and outside, that do not depend on our co-work. For instance, God can extend to us a feeling of being cared for even when we do not cooperate with God. We can disregard or ignore this feeling, and we can even interpret it to be illusory regarding reality. This is one way to exclude God from recognition in our lives. It is a definite alternative to cooperating with hallowing God's name.

An epistemology of prayer must accommodate the directedness of much prayer to the benefit of other people. In particular, it should recognize a role for needed power in prayer for bringing benefit to other people. Charles Elliott remarks, "If we see prayer as a mean of releasing God's power into the world, of enabling [God] to pour his transforming love into the critical centres of decision-making and activity, we begin to see that we are not powerless at all. Our power to transform the world is God's power."[3] The proposal here is that through prayer, we receive God's power to offer to the world and, with cooperation, thereby transform it. This power counters any human tendency to selfishness in divine prayer.

A remaining question is: How can our power be God's power? The answer is in the previous suggestion of human sharing in divine power and glory, courtesy of God's generosity in grace. The source of the needed power is divine, but God generously shares this power with us to make it our power, too, as long as we resolve to cooperate with God. Divine love is like that in its self-giving grace—likewise for divine glory, as we have seen. So, the vindication of divine righteous love can emerge in us humans, as we share in it. We thus become co-vindicators of God with God as divine vindication is shared with us in righteousness. The divine sharing, in particular, of the fruit of the Spirit with us enables our co-vindication of God, for the good of all concerned.

When our praying shares in divine righteousness, it serves to vindicate God as righteous among us. It enables this righteousness to enter into and to be reflected in our lives, including our actions. Prayer thus can lead to an observable change for better in our lives. In that case, prayer serves as evidence for the reality and goodness of God, thereby contributing to divine self-vindication in righteousness among humans.

An obstacle to prayer in yielding evidence of God is human lack of enduring in divine cooperative prayer and its pathos. In giving up on attending to this pathos, we turn away from available evidence of divine activity in human experience. We then exclude ourselves, by our own will, from receiving significant evidence of God's presence and goodness. We then block ourselves from apprehending God's moral character in action. God thus becomes morally inert or absent in our recognized experience. The options of atheism, agnosticism, and deism become viable from the perspective of such restricted experience. Even so, they represent a missed opportunity from an evidential point of view. They suffer from insufficient attention to available evidence discerned by humans who have a willingness to cooperate with divine pathos in prayer.

The divine directness in divine prayer adds a special epistemological value to such prayer. In self-presenting the divine will through nudging toward righteousness, God presents God to humans, including in divine prayer. So, there is no need for human speculation, argument, or research to ground the relevant evidence in experience. In that case, a human is confronted directly in experience with God, with an I-Thou meeting of God, in the second person.

Some of the Jewish psalms assume an I-Thou meeting of God. Psalm 23 begins with reference to God in the third person: "The Lord is my shepherd, I shall not want. . . . He restores my soul. He leads me in paths of righteousness for his name's sake" (Ps 23:1, 3, RSV). The psalmist then turns to praying to God in the second person: "Even though I walk through the valley of the shadow of death, I fear no evil; for thou art with me; thy rod and thy staff, they comfort me. Thou preparest a table before me in the presence of my enemies; thou anointest my head with oil, my cup overflows. Surely goodness and mercy shall follow me all the days of my life" (Ps 23:4–6, RSV). The psalmist is thus no longer simply informational about God by merely affirming truths about God. Instead, the psalmist is calling on *God* directly as "thou," *de re*. This is prayer in its most direct form, representing a direct meeting between a human and God, courtesy of divine pathos expressed toward an attentive human.

What a person does with an I-Thou meeting with God is up to that person; the same holds for how a person interprets this meeting. A person could misinterpret this meeting and even fail to recognize God in it. Fallibility in human interpretation applies here, as it does pretty much everywhere else. Even so, direct divine self-presentation can occur and challenge people who are cooperative in prayer. Is also can give to humans, as suggested, divine self-evidence of God's reality and goodness. In that case, God self-authenticates divine reality and goodness, thereby vindicating divine righteousness, for some receptive humans.

Philosophers of religion have had relatively little to say about the epistemology of prayer, and this deficit is regrettable. A result is undue neglect of a vital avenue of direct evidence and knowledge of God. Perhaps this result stems from a certain deficiency among many inquirers about God: a lack of firsthand experience of divine pathos in divine cooperative prayer. Without the firsthand experience, a person will tend to be inattentive to firsthand evidence in an I-Thou meeting with God. An epistemology of prayer can suffer as a result.

The author of Psalm 23 suggests an important factor in divine cooperative prayer, as follows: "Goodness and mercy shall follow me all the days of my life" (23:6, RSV). The psalmist is referring to *God* following him with goodness and mercy; he has no place for abstract or impersonal goodness or mercy, whatever that might be. The purposive God is the one who tracks his troubled life with divine goodness and mercy. The significance is that the psalmist has experienced God's intentional goodness and mercy and, as a result, is familiar with God's distinctive moral character. So, the psalmist is not praying to an unknown god or a morally indeterminate god. He is praying to the God worthy of his trust for goodness and mercy. His ongoing experience confirms this lesson for him.

A problem emerges from a contrast with the psalmist. Some people do not recognize that "goodness and mercy shall follow" them. They thus lack the psalmist's confidence in God and in prayer to God. Three questions arise for such people. First, do they want or allow divine goodness and mercy to arise in their experience? Second, do they explore whether such goodness and mercy occur in their experience? Third, if they do explore this, how do they explore it? We shall consider these questions in turn.

Some people report that they do not want God's goodness and mercy, if they exist, to arise in their experience. They do not want their lives to be constrained by such goodness and mercy. They prefer independence from such divine influence, as they desire more self-control or autonomy than would be allowed by such influence. If this is their settled preference, they raise a serious problem for God's aim to attract all people without coercion. If God cannot attract them, God may find it pointless to self-reveal in their experience. If they rule out reconciliation with God, they block God's main purpose in self-revelation. We thus see that human preferences can frustrate God's plan for self-revelation and human redemption.

Some people choose not to explore whether divine goodness and mercy occur in their experience. Complete indifference and confident doubt are often motives behind such a choice. These people, however, are not in a good position to assess available evidence of God because God desires human willingness to seek God and corresponding evidence. God merits being sought by humans, given God's value for them, and human seeking of God helps to focus the value of God for humans. So, we should not expect God to encourage human indifference about seeking God and corresponding evidence. On the contrary, we should expect God to challenge it when a good, worthwhile opportunity arises.

If some people explore the prospective reality of divine goodness and mercy in their experience, we should ask how they explore this. A big issue is whether their exploration of such reality is non-distorting in allowing it to be what it actually is: an unearned gift of lasting good with a serious moral challenge for all humans, including all inquirers of God. We easily distort the reality and its evidence in a way that obscures their morally powerful aim to have people morally transformed toward the gift of life with God in divine righteousness.

A typical distortion recasts the reality in question and its evidence as our creation or achievement, our human accomplishment. Many people thus regard the fruit of the Spirit as simply a human moral achievement, whether for an individual or for a group. In this perspective, some humans work hard on their moral character and thereby achieve love, joy, peace, and so on. They thus take self-credit for this "achievement" and see no need for divine involvement or credit.

Human self-credit for the fruit of the Spirit, from God's perspective of grace, amounts to misguided moral pride, a misplaced moral badge of honor. It also undermines the purpose of the divine gift of the fruit of the Spirit: to attract grateful human cooperation with the gift giver while displacing harmful and misleading moral pride among humans. God's gift of grace in the fruit of the Spirit is a needed human equalizer before God. It thus counters the self-exaltation of human pride and the resulting human abuse of divine moral power, given such power as a needed gift on offer to all.

Paul sums up the divine strategy behind righteousness by grace offered to all humans: "God has consigned all to disobedience, that he may have mercy upon all" (Rom 11:32, RSV). In other words, the moral standard for righteousness set by God leaves all humans in need of divine grace and mercy. Paul thus remarks, "Then what becomes of our boasting? It is excluded" (Rom 3:27, RSV). Human self-credit is thus not a live option (Rom 10:3). Divine "choice by grace" (Rom 11:5) through human trust for divine approval, rather than through human self-credit or earning, has seen to that, for the good of all concerned.

Distortions of the divine gift of grace in the fruit of the Spirit are many and varied. A common distortion weaponizes the gift by using it in an exclusive way against some people. History is riddled with invoking God's moral character to demean or condemn perceived enemies or challengers. For instance, some psalmists report that God "hates" evil people (Ps 5:4–6, 11:5–7). These psalmists might have benefited from reflection on their own falling short of God's exalted standards of righteousness. Perhaps consideration of the divine demand for love of one's enemies (Matt 5:43–48) can challenge weaponizing the gift of divine grace.

A serious problem in distorting divine grace among us is that it blocks or hinders the intended inner renewal of us by God. Paul remarks, "We do not lose heart. Even though our outer nature is wasting away, our inner nature is being renewed day by day. For our slight, momentary affliction is producing for us an eternal weight of glory beyond all measure" (2 Cor 4:16–17). If we resort either to taking self-credit for what is a gift of grace or to using it as an exclusive weapon, we are in conflict with renewal by grateful trust in response to this gift.

The gift in question is not a commodity or a wage. Instead, it is the active, guiding presence of God's Spirit, including the fruit of the Spirit as God's personality traits. This fits with the following remark from Jesus: "If you, then, who are evil, know how to give good gifts to your children, how much more will the heavenly Father give the Holy Spirit to those who ask him!" (Luke 11:13). Paul strikes a similar note about receiving the Spirit without human earning: "Did you receive the Spirit by doing the works of the law or by believing what you heard? Are you so foolish? Having started with the Spirit, are you now ending with the flesh?" (Gal 3:2–3). The divine gift is thus a divine personal agent who intentionally guides the people of God (Rom 8:14). In this regard, the gift is a gift like no other.

What has this gift to do with what Paul calls "the Spirit of Christ" (Rom 8:9)? Paul notes that Jesus as "the last Adam became a life-giving spirit" (1 Cor 15:45). Some commentators, as suggested, have noted the similarity between the fruit of the Spirit and the personality traits of Jesus. We can benefit by recognizing a moral similarity between the Spirit in question and the moral character of Jesus. This effort does not require us to digress to speculative metaphysics about the relation between Jesus and the Spirit of God.

Charles Elliott has identified a lesson hard to dispute: "If the essence of prayer for the Kingdom of God is to stand naked before God and withstand the power of evil, it is good to know what kind of God we stand before." Knowing "what kind of God we stand before" includes knowing what God expected of Jesus at his cross of torture. Elliott identifies a noteworthy feature of the cross of Jesus: "Because love [in Jesus] has yielded every last vestige of self-protection—even the assurance of Yahweh's deliverance—the Kingdom of God, with its message of hope for the poor and judgement for the rich, can be offered afresh. This is mystery; many say it is nonsense."[4] Jesus did yield self-protection, and he felt abandoned by God. The latter abandonment is indeed a mystery, but Jesus still cried, "My God, my God."

Elliott notes that many people have identified with suffering related to the cross of Jesus. He observes, "There are thousands of 'ordinary' people taking part in the same drama. Their role is not representational, in the sense that Christian doctrine sees Christ's death as representing the whole of humanity, but it is re-presentational in the sense that it brings to life the capacity of suffering love to overthrow and transform the forces of evil."[5] He adds that even experience of the absence of God can be "a privileged glimpse into the heart of Christ at the moment of dereliction."[6] Perhaps the latter is true, but it is not clear what the actual privilege as a benefit that glimpse would be. A person might come to see the tragedy of life without God's presence, but it is unclear that the extreme crisis of the cross is needed for that result.

Renewal from Death to Life

Jesus's death on the cross does not stop with death; it moves ahead to a gift of life that lasts. Elliott comments, "The quality of love that the cross demonstrates . . . makes the resurrection the natural sequel."[7] This emphasis on divine love fits with Paul's remark that "God proves his love for us in that while we still were sinners Christ died for us" (Rom 5:8, RSV). He adds that this love comes as a gift of grace through righteousness: "As sin reigned in death, grace also might reign through righteousness to eternal life through Jesus Christ our Lord" (Rom 5:21, RSV). Such grace and righteousness lead to "eternal life through Jesus Christ." Paul thus comments, "The free gift of God is eternal life in Christ Jesus our Lord" (Rom 6:23, RSV). How does this gift of life relate to the death of Jesus?

Paul regards the death and resurrection of Jesus Christ as a pattern for his followers. He remarks, "Do you not know that all of us who have been baptized into Christ Jesus were baptized into his death? We were buried therefore with him by baptism into death, so that as Christ was raised from the dead by the glory of the Father, we too might walk in newness of life" (Rom 6:3–4). Christ's death, then, leads to his being raised by God to new life, and the same pattern applies to his disciples "so that . . . we too might walk in newness of life."

Paul adds, following the pattern of Christ, "You also must consider yourselves dead to sin and alive to God in Christ Jesus" (Rom 6:11). He has in mind "walking in newness of life" now and being "alive to God in Christ Jesus" now, not just in the future. In this regard, the resurrection of Christ is shared by his followers now and not just in the future. Bodily resurrection awaits the future, but life's resurrection for Christ's followers now alive begins and continues now, extending later to the survival of bodily death. Dying and rising with Christ is thus a present reality for his disciples, in Paul's perspective. The rising calls for human cooperation with God's Spirit as represented by the distinctive fruit of this Spirit.

Paul states, with regard to the new life now, "Just as you once yielded your members to impurity and to greater and greater iniquity, so now yield your members to righteousness" (Rom 6:19, RSV). The voluntary human cooperation in receiving the new life from God is "yielding your members to righteousness." This is a matter of yielding oneself to divine righteousness, particularly as God presents the fruit of the Spirit in one's experience. So, dying to the old life of unrighteousness is to be joined with rising into the new life of righteousness in the Spirit of God with its life-giving fruit.

Our response to the presented fruit of the Spirit indicates our response to the renewing resurrection life on offer. If we ignore or reject the fruit, we fail to receive cooperatively the new life offered to us. If, in contrast, we cooperate with the fruit, we enter and grow into the resurrection life with Christ. Divine prayer, as suggested above, is part of receiving and growing into this renewed life. It brings one into fellowship with God that enables the fruit to mature in righteousness, in relationship with God and divine righteousness.

Divine victory in righteousness, according to Paul, is God's goal in our dying and rising with Christ: "The sting of death is sin, and the power of sin is the law. But thanks be to God, who gives us the victory through our Lord Jesus Christ" (1 Cor 15:56–57).[8] Paul has in mind God's conquering sin and death through Christ, for the sake of all God's people. We can elaborate as follows: The power of the fruit of the Spirit, representative of God in Christ, withstands and conquers the power of sin and death, as God in Christ did in the cross and resurrection. This expressed power of the Spirit is a moral theophany that vindicates God as righteous among humans who cooperate with this Spirit. God's Spirit self-manifests to conquer, as it moves intentionally and actively against evil and death. It shows directedness in its conquering and therefore is not static or abstract. This battle, then, is not inert or merely intellectual. It is ongoing and active, and it involves people with a divine priority for their decision.

The people of God must show their directedness in being willing to stand with God against sin and death, without retreating in distrust toward God. The pressing question for them is: Can you look evil and death in the eye without blinking in distrust for God? They still can lament, grieve, and even protest the obstacles they face. They are called, nevertheless, to represent God's conquering of sin and death, and this requires maintaining trust in God in the often gruesome presence of sin and death.

In his cry of dereliction, Jesus called, "My God, my God," thus showing that he had not lapsed into distrust for God. Jesus himself held that nothing this world throws at him is beyond redemption by his Father. (As suggested, Job also comes to mind as a faithful witness to God in the presence of sin and death.) The disciples of Jesus are to follow Jesus here in responding to sin and death, for the sake of divine vindication and outreach to others for reconciliation in divine righteousness. The divine expectation for God's people is high indeed, but the divine power is equally effective. They are offered the power to stand with God in divine compassion, righteousness, and vindication.

Paul reports that "in Christ God was reconciling the world to himself, not counting their trespasses against them, and entrusting the message of reconciliation to us" (2 Cor 5:19). This divine "reconciling the world" to God includes forgiveness for trespasses but not just that. It includes the additional divine action in God's beloved Son, Jesus Christ, and in the Spirit of God. This action is not exhausted by forgiveness or even justification. Forgiveness and justification are a means to reconciliation with God, and such reconciliation includes this: "While we were enemies we were reconciled to God through the death of his Son" (Rom 5:10). This is the "objective" side of divine reconciliation, involving just divine activity. It also has a "subjective" side including a cooperative human response.

The subjective side of reconciliation emerges from the following question: Are we willing to appropriate the fruit of the Spirit as a top priority in responding to God's activity in our experience? A metaphor from Paul is: "Put on the Lord Jesus Christ, and make no provision for the flesh, to gratify its desires" (Rom 13:14).[9] Putting on the Lord Jesus Christ, as the image of God, includes putting on the fruit of his Spirit. Fruit thus appropriated by us for maturation is God presented in us and vindicated as righteous in the character formation of our lives. We then value what God values and thereby reflect God's unmatched goodness as vindicated in us. We thus become a witness of God to a world in need of God.

Our own priorities matter to divine self-vindication because they matter to our character formation, particularly in situations of a Gethsemane challenge: God's will or our will first? Such a challenge arises with prayer: Do we ultimately promote God's will first or, instead, our will (when they are not in agreement)? If the latter, our prayer is out of order. It then uses God as a means to our inferior ends. This is idolatry, if without a golden calf. So, our prayers reveal where we stand in relation to God: for or against cooperation with God's will. They thus reveal whether we are in a position to represent

God and divine vindication. We thus might say: By their prayers you shall know them.

Finale

We have seen that God seeks self-vindication among humans in righteousness. This effort promotes their character transformation represented in the presented fruit of the Spirit as a moral theophany. God self-authenticates divine reality and goodness to receptive humans in this manner. As we have noted, Paul identifies faith in God as having its proper basis in "the power of God" (1 Cor 2:4–5). Faith in God thus has its supporting evidence that humans cannot supply; its support comes courtesy of God with divine power. The heart of this power is the offered fruit of God's Spirit, the expressed Christlike personality traits of God.

We have explained the importance of recognizing God's powerful fruit of the Spirit as an unearned gift of divine grace. It is not a human earning or wage. As a result, it resists humans taking self-credit for it or self-boasting in it. Instead, it invites human gratitude to God and willingness to include other people, even enemies, in the gift. It also is at odds with what Paul calls "the wisdom of the world," the kind of wisdom that has no place for God's righteous power. Some wisdom from philosophy and religion qualifies as what Paul has in mind. Divine wisdom, in Paul's perspective, depends on God's righteous character and thus comes with moral power. We have found the center of this power in the fruit of the Spirit as represented by the moral character of God in Christ.

Humans have a crucial role to play regarding their reception of the divine gift of grace on offer. They do not constitute or control this grace, but they must voluntarily receive and cooperate with it for its efficacy in their lives. It is thus interpersonal, and not mechanical or coercive, in its effectiveness. So, humans must not "frustrate the grace of God" (Gal 2:21) with their lack of cooperation with it.

What is the cooperation in question? Jesus in Gethsemane shows the basis of the best answer, with his aforementioned filial prayer: "Abba,

Father, for you all things are possible; remove this cup from me, yet not what I want but what you want" (Mark 14:36). The people of God live their lives in the context of Gethsemane, being cooperatively led by the Spirit of God, through its fruit, to be conformed to the image of God's Son. This leading is at the center of character transformation by God toward divine righteousness and divine vindication among humans. Such transformation includes human sharing of the glory of God in a way that exceeds mere morality.

The prayer of Gethsemane, although foundational for relating to God, is not the full story. It must be joined with faithful and loving obedience, the kind of "obedience leading to righteousness" (Rom 6:16). Such obedience is what Paul calls "walking in newness of life" (Rom 6:4), after the newness of the resurrection of Jesus. He also calls it "continuing in God's kindness" (Rom 11:22). Such walking and continuing require "putting to death the [evil] deeds of the body," but Paul adds a qualification: "by the Spirit" (Rom 8:13). This is the Spirit whose leading motivates being a child of God (Rom 8:14) and whose fruit represents God's own personality traits. So, the relevant "putting to death" depends on the resurrection life of the Spirit and is for the sake of character transformation toward divine righteousness and its Christlike love.

Paul sums things up as "Christ formed in you" (Gal 4:19). We thus may think of theophany incarnate as Christ and his Spirit abiding in a cooperative person. Divine self-vindication among humans thus arises from "Christ formed in you" by the fruit of his Spirit and divine cooperative prayer as a response. Humans share, then, in moral theophany as part of God's vindication among us. This is the high calling at the center of the good news of God in Christ. This news draws humans into its divine goodness, for the benefit of all concerned.

If the Messiah's arrival must renew the whole world now, it is undeniable that the cross and the resurrection of Jesus are a messianic failure. Even so, God is not bound by renewal on the spot but can work a gradual renewal to accommodate the slowness of humans. Divine mercy toward all is at work and thus is slow in its enduring renewal of humans. Patience is therefore advised.

We await full renewal in bodily resurrection, and thus we await full self-vindication by God. Even so, the divine renewal is underway now, with the remarkable beginning of divine self-vindication in moral theophany among us. We need, however, eyes to see and ears to hear. We also must want to have such eyes and ears. Our response will reveal who we truly are and will be. So, when Jesus asks us who we take him to be, we will reveal who we really are. This inquiry is unsurpassed in importance for us. It will reveal whether we allow God to be self-vindicated among us with our cooperation in the divine renewal of humans.

SELECT BIBLIOGRAPHY

Alston, William P. *Perceiving God.* Cornell University Press, 1993.

Aulén, Gustaf. *Christus Victor.* Translated by A. G. Hebert. Macmillan, 1961 (German original, 1930).

Baillie, John. *Our Knowledge of God.* Oxford University Press, 1939.

Baillie, John. *The Idea of Revelation in Recent Thought.* Columbia University Press, 1965.

Barclay, J. M. G. *Paul and the Gift.* Eerdmans, 2017.

Bushnell, Horace. *Nature and the Supernatural.* Scribner's Sons, 1895.

Dunn, J. D. G. *Jesus, Paul, and the Gospels.* Eerdmans, 2011.

Dunn, J. D. G. *The Theology of Paul the Apostle.* Eerdmans, 1998.

Farley, Edward. *Divine Empathy.* Fortress Press, 1996.

Farmer, H. H. *The World and God.* Nisbet, 1935.

Fiddes, Paul S. *The Creative Suffering of God.* Clarendon Press, 1988.

Forsyth, P. T. *The Justification of God.* Duckworth, 1916.

Forsyth, P. T. *The Principle of Authority.* Hodder and Stoughton, 1913.

Hays, Richard B. "A Hermeneutic of Trust." In *Reading with the Grain of Scripture.* Eerdmans, 2020.

Jones, Rufus. *Pathways to the Reality of God.* Macmillan, 1931.

Keck, Leander. *Christ's First Theologian.* Baylor University Press, 2015.

Kelly, Anthony J. *The Resurrection Effect.* Orbis Books, 2008.

Kirk, J. R. Daniel. *Unlocking Romans: Resurrection and the Justification of God.* Eerdmans, 2008.

Koenig, John. *Rediscovering New Testament Prayer.* Harper, 1992.

Mackintosh, H. R. *The Christian Experience of Forgiveness.* Harper, 1927.

Mavrodes, George. *Revelation in Religious Belief.* Temple University Press, 1988.

Moberly, R. W. L. *Prophecy and Discernment.* Cambridge University Press, 2006.

Moltmann, Jürgen. *The Way of Jesus Christ.* HarperCollins, 1990.

Moltmann, Jürgen. *The Spirit of Life.* Fortress Press, 2001.

Oman, John. *Grace and Personality.* Cambridge University Press, 1917.

Oman, John. *Honest Religion.* Cambridge University Press, 1941.

Robinson, H. Wheeler. *Suffering, Human and Divine.* Macmillan, 1939.
Thielicke, Helmut. *The Evangelical Faith.* 3 vols. Translated by G. W. Bromiley. Eerdmans, 1974.
Watson, Philip S. *The Concept of Grace.* Epworth, 1959.
Wolterstorff, Nicholas. *Divine Discourse.* Cambridge University Press, 1995.
Yandell, Keith. *The Epistemology of Religious Experience.* Cambridge University Press, 1994.

NOTES

INTRODUCTION: GOD'S SELF-VINDICATION IN VOLUNTARY HUMAN RENEWAL

1. James D. G. Dunn, *Commentary on Galatians* (A&C Black, 1993), 295–96; cf. James D. G. Dunn, *Jesus and the Spirit* (Westminster Press, 1975), 222–25.
2. Anthony J. Kelly, *The Resurrection Effect* (Orbis Books, 2008), 64.

CHAPTER 1: VINDICATION THROUGH REVEALING AND HIDING

1. Richard B. Hays, "A Hermeneutic of Trust," in *Reading with the Grain of Scripture* (Eerdmans, 2020), 392–402; hereafter "HT." He acknowledges influence from Peter Stuhlmacher's notion of a "hermeneutics of consent (*Einverständnis*)" in Paul. For Stuhlmacher's hermeneutics of consent, see his *Historical Criticism and Theological Interpretation of Scripture*, trans. R. A. Harrisville (Fortress Press, 1977).
2. Hays, "A Hermeneutic of Trust," 397.
3. Hays, "A Hermeneutic of Trust," 399.
4. Hays, "A Hermeneutic of Trust," 399.
5. Hays, "A Hermeneutic of Trust," 400.
6. Hays gives credit for this idea to N. T. Wright (Hays, "A Hermeneutic of Trust," 396, n. 5).
7. Hays, "A Hermeneutic of Trust," 398.
8. Hays, "Reading Scripture in Light of the Resurrection," in Hays, *Reading with the Grain of Scripture*, 57.
9. For reasoning that "the Lord" is God (and not just Christ), see Victor Paul Furnish, *II Corinthians*, AB (Doubleday, 1984), 211–13, 234–36. For

reasoning that it is Christ as exalted Lord from God, see Rob A. Fringer, *Paul's Corporate Christophany* (Pickwick Publications, 2019), 167–69.

10. Hays, "A Hermeneutic of Trust," 396.
11. On human sharing of divine glory, in Paul's thought, see chap. 5.
12. For further discussion, see Paul K. Moser, *God in Moral Experience* (Cambridge University Press, 2024), chap. 7.
13. For discussion of the role of a partial theodicy, see Moser, *God in Moral Experience*, chap. 7. See also chapter 7 in this book.
14. For discussion of Paul on being led, see André Munzinger, *Discerning the Spirits: Theological and Ethical Hermeneutics in Paul*, SNTSMS (Cambridge University Press, 2007), 157–62. His discussion, however, gives inadequate attention to the role of theophany in Paul's understanding of being led by God.
15. Paul's injunctions assume that God has given humans power to make voluntary decisions for or against divine commands for humans. For elaboration, see Robby J. Kagarise, *Paul's Charismatic Imperatives*, JPTSS (Brill, 2014). See also Munzinger, *Discerning the Spirits*, 155. (Chapter 6 returns to this topic.)
16. On Paul's use of "I" here, see Will N. Timmins, *Romans 7 and Christian Identity*, SNTSMS (Cambridge University Press, 2017), 156–65.
17. For discussion of resurrection and glory in Paul's perspective, see Carey C. Newman, "Resurrection as Glory," in *The Resurrection*, ed. Stephen Davis et al. (Oxford University Press, 1997), 59–89, and Anthony J. Kelly, *The Resurrection Effect* (Orbis Books, 2008), 79–100.
18. For elaboration of this position, see Paul K. Moser, *Understanding Religious Experience* (Cambridge University Press, 2020), chaps. 7–8. See also Paul K. Moser, *The God Relationship* (Cambridge University Press, 2017), chap. 5.
19. Rufus Jones, *Pathways to the Reality of God* (Macmillan, 1931), 217.
20. On the historical background and integrity of this passage, see John Meier, *A Marginal Jew, vol. 4: Law and Love*, AYBRL (Yale University Press, 2009), 499–527. See also Victor Paul Furnish, *The Love Command in the New Testament* (Abingdon Press, 1972), 62–69.
21. For discussion of the role of divine love in the self-understanding and mission of Jesus, see Paul K. Moser, *The Divine Goodness of Jesus* (Cambridge University Press, 2021), chap. 3, and Paul Moser, "The Modus Operandi of Jesus," forthcoming. Cf. John Piper, *Love Your Enemies*, SNTSMS (Cambridge University Press, 1979), 76–99.
22. On the historical integrity of this verse, see W. D. Davies and Dale C. Allison Jr., *A Critical and Exegetical Commentary on the Gospel According*

to Saint Matthew, vol. 2, ICC (T&T Clark, 1991), 275–76. See page 278 for their comment in favor of the historical authenticity of Matthew 11:25–26, with their conclusion that "the arguments could hardly be stronger." See also A. M. Hunter, "Crux Criticorum—Matt 11:25–30—A Re-Appraisal," *New Testament Studies* 8 (1962): 241–49. On the parallel passage in Luke and its authenticity, see Joseph A. Fitzmyer, *The Gospel According to Luke*, vol. 2, AB (Doubleday, 1985), 864–76.

CHAPTER 2: VINDICATION FROM A GOD'S-EYE STANDPOINT

1. On the role of righteousness in the Jewish scriptures, see Abraham Heschel, *The Prophets* (Harper, 1962), 202–20, and Walter Brueggemann, *Theology of the Old Testament* (Fortress Press, 1997), 187–201.
2. On the treatment of the aforementioned passage from Isaiah by the writers of the synoptic Gospels, see Arland J. Hultgren, *The Parables of Jesus* (Eerdmans, 2000), 453–67.
3. For discussion of various biblical claims about the human heart, in relation to idolatry, see Edward P. Meadors, *Idolatry and the Hardening of the Heart* (T&T Clark, 2006). *The Oxford English Dictionary* offers a definition of *affect*: "a feeling or subjective experience accompanying a thought or action or occurring in response to a stimulus; an emotion, a mood."
4. Walther Eichrodt speaks of the focus on "inward transformation" in this connection; see his *Ezekiel: A Commentary* (SCM Press, 1970), 144.
5. For relevant discussion, see Victor Paul Furnish, *II Corinthians* (New York: Doubleday, 1984, 329–33, and J. Louis Martyn, "Epistemology at the Turn of the Ages: 2 Corinthians 5:16," in *Theological Issues in the Letters of Paul* (T&T Clark, 1997), 89–110. On new creation in Paul's thought, in relation to 2 Corinthians 5, see Moyer V. Hubbard, *New Creation in Paul's Letters and Thought*, SNTSMS (Cambridge University Press, 2002), chap. 10.
6. H. R. Mackintosh, *The Christian Experience of Forgiveness* (Harper, 1927), 35.
7. For a distinctively Christian approach to conscience, see P. T. Forsyth, *The Principle of Authority* (Hodder and Stoughton, 1913). Joseph A. Fitzmyer recognizes the relation between Paul's talk of "the mind of Christ" and a role for the Spirit of God; see his *First Corinthians*, AYB (Yale University Press, 2008), 185–86.
8. For discussion, see Paul K. Moser, *Paul's Gospel of Divine Self-Sacrifice* (Cambridge University Press, 2022).

9. See Timothy B. Savage, *Power Through Weakness: Paul's Understanding of the Christian Ministry in 2 Corinthians*, SNTSMS (Cambridge University Press, 1996), chaps. 5–6. Savage recognizes the importance in Paul's thought of knowing Jesus as Lord, in the light of 2 Corinthians 4:5–6. This fits well with my previous suggestion about the significant role of lordship knowledge in Paul's thought, beyond mere factual knowledge that God exists.
10. I thus dissent from the suggestion of Raymond E. Brown that John has in mind only conviction against sin (that is, being found guilty of it) "in that [the world] has not acknowledged" divine righteousness. See Raymond E. Brown, *The Gospel According to John*, vol. 2, AB (Doubleday, 1970), 705. This narrow reading, adopted by many commentators, misses the positive role of the Spirit in nudging people toward divine righteousness, particularly through conscience. Less narrow readings are offered by C. K. Barrett, *The Gospel According to St. John*, 2nd ed. (Westminster Press, 1978), and George R. Beasley-Murray, *John*, WBC (Word, 1987).
11. For discussion, see Raymond E. Brown, *The Epistles of John*, AB (Doubleday, 1982), 368–77.
12. See Plato, *Republic*, trans. Benjamin Jowett (Oxford University Press, 1953), Book VI, 511a–e. Neglect of a cooperative volitional role, in relation to God's Spirit, is found in Volker Rabens, *The Holy Spirit and Ethics in Paul*, 2nd ed.(Fortress Press, 2014), 190; Grant Macaskill, *Union with Christ in the New Testament* (Oxford University Press, 2013), 219–50; and Craig S. Keener, *The Mind of the Spirit: Paul's Approach to Transformed Thinking* (Baker Academic, 2016), 210–16. The influence of Plato's primarily contemplative approach to ultimate reality obscures Paul's cooperative volitional approach among many inquirers.
13. For discussion, see Paul S. Minear, *Eyes of Faith: A Study in the Biblical Point of View* (Westminster Press, 1946), 45–62. For further elaboration on the role of volitional transformation in response to evidence of God's reality and goodness, see Paul K. Moser, *The God Relationship* (Cambridge University Press, 2018), and Paul K. Moser, *God in Moral Experience* (Cambridge University Press, 2024). Cf. William J. Wainwright, *Reason, Revelation, and Devotion* (Cambridge University Press, 2015).
14. For discussion, see Moser, *Paul's Gospel of Divine Self-Sacrifice*, chap. 1.
15. On the importance of such turning and the corresponding transformation of humans, in Paul's thought, see Savage, *Power Through Weakness*, 135, 145–54.
16. James D. G. Dunn notes the importance of character formation here, after the standard of God's moral character manifested in the fruit of the Spirit.

See his *The Epistle to the Galatians*, BNTC (A&C Black, 1993), 221, 308. Dunn emphasizes that the character of Christ is Paul's standard: "The Son as attesting the character of God, the Spirit as expressing the character of God's Son," and "Christ-like character is the principal product of the Spirit." This fits with our proposed role for the mind of Christ. On Paul's understanding of the relation of the cross of Christ to the Spirit of God, see Charles H. Cosgrove, *The Cross and the Spirit* (Mercer University Press, 1988), 169–94.

17. We arguably have such a distinction assumed in Matthew 25:31–45, but we cannot digress now. See Paul K. Moser, "God De Re et De Dicto: Kierkegaard, Faith, and Religious Diversity," *Scottish Journal of Theology* 74 (2021): 135–46.
18. For discussion, see Paul K. Moser, "A Deflationary View," in *Natural Theology: Five Views*, ed. James K. Dew and R. P. Campbell (Baker Academic, 2024), 153–74. See also Paul Moser, "Moderating Natural Theology: A Heuristic Interrogative Approach," *Religions* 15 (2024): 1–13.
19. On the relevance of abduction, with a recognition of potential underminers and divine hiding on occasion, see Paul K. Moser, *Understanding Religious Experience* (Cambridge University Press, 2020), chaps 7–8. The relativity of evidence should not be confused with the (more dubious) relativity of truth.

CHAPTER 3: VINDICATION THROUGH INTERPERSONAL SHOWING

1. Walther Eichrodt, *Ezekiel: A Commentary*, trans. Cosslett Quin (SCM Press, 1970), 496–97.
2. Eichrodt, *Ezekiel*, 500.
3. On the bearing of a theodicy, see Paul K. Moser, *God in Moral Experience* (Cambridge University Press, 2024), chap. 7. See also chapter 7 below.

CHAPTER 4: VINDICATION WITH MORAL DIRECTION

1. Gerhard Von Rad, *Old Testament Theology*, vol. 1, trans. D. M. G. Stalker (Harper and Row, 1962), 370.
2. Alan Richardson, *An Introduction to the Theology of the New Testament* (SCM Press, 1958), 79.
3. P. T. Forsyth, *The Church, the Gospel, and Society* (Independent Press, 1905), 19.
4. On the guidance in question, see Paul K. Moser, *Divine Guidance* (Cambridge University Press, 2022).

5. For relevant discussion, see Paul K. Moser, *Paul's Gospel of Divine Self-Sacrifice* (Cambridge University Press, 2022).
6. I use the translation of the *Qur'an* by Talal Itani, http://www.clearquran.com/.
7. H. R. Mackintosh, *The Christian Experience of Forgiveness* (Harper, 1927), 94.
8. Mackintosh, *The Christian Experience of Forgiveness*, 35.

CHAPTER 5: VINDICATION FOR RIGHTEOUS SPLENDOR

1. Israel Abrahams rightly suggests the importance of not confusing the glory of God with the context of that glory. See his *The Glory of God* (Oxford University Press, 1925), 25.
2. Gerhard von Rad comments, "It was an utter oversimplification to speak of Jahweh as a 'thunderstorm god.'" *Old Testament Theology*, vol. 1, trans. D. M. G. Stalker (Harper and Row, 1962), 240.
3. Terence E. Fretheim, *Exodus*, Interp (John Knox Press, 1991), 299.
4. For a plausible approach to the relation between Isaiah and Deutero-Isaiah, see Otto Kaiser, *Isaiah 1–12*, 2nd ed., trans. John Bowden (Westminster Press, 1983).
5. Abraham Heschel, *God in Search of Man* (Harper and Row, 1955), 82. Heschel characterizes divine glory as "a living presence or the effulgence of a living presence" (83), but this falls short in omitting the centrality of divine moral grandeur. Abrahams is more accurate: "All the great theophanies, with their storm scenery and visible manifestations, are also revelations of the Divine essence—the Glory of God, witnessed in storm phenomena, is a moral and spiritual Glory. Its most prominent feature is power, but a power directed to righteousness." Abrahams, *The Glory of God*, 24.
6. Victor Paul Furnish, *II Corinthians*, AB (Doubleday, 1984), 242. Similarly, see Ralph P. Martin, *2 Corinthians*, WBC (Word Books, 1986), 71–72.
7. For some support, see Martin, *2 Corinthians*, 46–47.
8. For considerations against a restriction to a christological sense of "Lord" here, see Furnish, *II Corinthians*, 211–213, and Margaret E. Thrall, *A Critical and Exegetical Commentary on the Second Epistle to the Corinthians*, vol. 1, ICC (T&T Clark, 1994), 271–73, 278–82.
9. Furnish, *II Corinthians*, 241. Similarly, see Martin, *2 Corinthians*, 72.
10. Furnish, *II Corinthians*, 235.

11. On the role of repentance in Paul's thought, see Eckhard J. Schnabel, "Repentance in Paul's Letters," *Novum Testamentum* 57 (2015): 159–86. I suggest that Paul's talk of reconciliation typically includes a notion of repentance as turning to the Lord.
12. Ernst Käsemann, *Perspectives on Paul* (Fortress Press, 1971), 40.
13. See Leander Keck, ed., "The Accountable Self," in *Christ's First Theologian* (Baylor University Press, 2015), 133–45.
14. For such a worry, see C. E. B. Cranfield, *A Critical and Exegetical Commentary on the Epistle to the Romans*, vol. 1, ICC (T&T Clark, 1975), 90. See also Ernst Käsemann, *Commentary on Romans*, trans. G. W. Bromiley (Eerdmans, 1980), 226.
15. See Rudolf Bultmann, *Theology of the New Testament*, vol. 1, trans. Kendrick Grobel (Charles Scribner's Sons, 1955), 284, 316–17. Herman Ridderbos seeks to avoid the problem by proposing that faith is "absolutely receptive" in Paul's perspective and not a productive "work." See Ridderbos, *Paul: An Outline of His Theology*, trans. J. R. De Witt (Eerdmans, 1975), 172. For discussion of Bultmann's position on faith and obedience, see John M.G. Barclay, *Paul and the Gift* (Eerdmans, 2015), 135–40, taking exception to the interpretation of E. P. Sanders, *Paul and Palestinian Judaism* (Fortress Press, 1977), 474. For further discussion, see Paul Moser, *Paul's Gospel of Divine Self-Sacrifice* (Cambridge University Press, 2022), chap. 5.
16. We need not digress here to the status, subjective or objective, of the genitive used by Paul. For discussion, see Arland J. Hultgren, "*Pistis Christou:* Faith in or of Christ?," in *Paul's Letter to the Romans* (Eerdmans, 2011), 623–61. However the interpretation goes, Paul promotes human faith in Christ (see Gal 2:16).
17. Käsemann, *Perspectives on Paul*, 51.
18. Käsemann, *Perspectives on Paul*, 50–51, 54.
19. On "the fruit of the Spirit" as divine personality traits self-manifested to receptive humans, see Paul Moser, *God in Moral Experience* (Cambridge University Press, 2024), chap. 1. See also James D. G. Dunn, *The Epistle to the Galatians*, BNTC (A&C Black, 1993), 220–21, 308–10.
20. Käsemann, *Perspectives on Paul*, 55.
21. Käsemann, *Perspectives on Paul*, 58.
22. For discussion, see A. M. Ramsey, *The Glory of God and the Transfiguration of Christ* (Longmans, Green, 1949), chaps. 6–7.
23. John's Gospel relates Jesus's obedience in Gethsemane to bringing glory to God; see John 12:27–28.

24. Richard Bauckham, ed., "God Crucified," in *Jesus and the God of Israel* (Eerdmans, 2008), 49–50.

CHAPTER 6: FRUSTRATING DIVINE VINDICATION

1. I thus dissent from the view of Dietrich Bonhoeffer that "conscience is always a prohibition, Thou shalt not." See Bonhoeffer, *Ethics*, trans. N. H. Smith (Macmillan, 1962), 148.
2. Søren Kierkegaard, *The Gospel of Our Sufferings*, trans. A. S. Aldworth and W. S. Ferrie (James Clarke, 1955 [original, 1847]), 55.
3. P. T. Forsyth, *Missions in State and Church* (Hodder and Stoughton, 1908), 64–65.
4. P. T. Forsyth, *The Justification of God* (Duckworth, 1916), 14.
5. Forsyth, *The Justification of God*, 12.
6. On Romans 12:1, see Paul Moser, *Paul's Gospel of Divine Self-Sacrifice* (Cambridge University Press, 2022), chap. 1.
7. For discussion, see Victor Paul Furnish, *Theology and Ethics in Paul* (Abingdon Press, 1968), 120, and Leander Keck, *Christ's First Theologian* (Baylor University Press, 2015), 133–46.

CHAPTER 7: HIGHER WAYS IN VINDICATION: BEYOND DIVINE NEGLECT

1. On the relation between caring and loving, see Nicholas Wolterstorff, *Justice in Love* (Eerdmans, 2011), 101–109.
2. Helmut Thielicke, *The Evangelical Faith*, vol. 3, trans. G. W. Bromiley (Eerdmans, 1982), 152.
3. For a discussion of Paul on boasting, see J. D. G. Dunn, *The Theology of Paul the Apostle* (Eerdmans, 1998), 363–65.
4. For a wide-ranging discussion of divine suffering love, see Paul S. Fiddes, *The Creative Suffering of God* (Clarendon Press, 1988). See also Jürgen Moltmann, *The Trinity and the Kingdom* (SCM Press, 1981), 21–60.
5. Dietrich Bonhoeffer, "Christians and Pagans," in *A Testament to Freedom*, ed. G. B. Kelly and F. B. Nelson (HarperSanFrancisco, 1990), 541.
6. For discussion, see Philip L. Quinn, "Tragic Dilemmas, Suffering Love, and Christian Life," *Journal of Religious Ethics* 17 (1989): 151–83. See also Nicholas Wolterstorff, "Suffering Love," in *Philosophy and the Christian Faith*, ed. T. V. Morris (University of Notre Dame Press, 1988), 196–237. On the role of human perplexity in suffering, see Karl Rahner, "Christian

Pessimism," in *Theological Investigations,* vol. 22, trans. Joseph Donceels (London: Darton, 1991), Pt. 2, 155–62.

7. For discussion, see Paul K. Moser, *God in Moral Experience* (Cambridge University Press, 2024), chap. 1.

CHAPTER 8: CONCLUDING POSTSCRIPT: VINDICATION THROUGH DIVINE COOPERATIVE PRAYER

1. John Koenig, *Rediscovering New Testament Prayer* (HarperSanFrancisco, 1992), 60.
2. P. T. Forsyth, *The Soul of Prayer* (Independent Press, 1951 [1916]), 52.
3. Charles Elliott, *Praying the Kingdom* (Darton, Longman, and Todd, 1985), 20.
4. Elliott, *Praying the Kingdom*, 116.
5. Elliott, *Praying the Kingdom*, 116.
6. Elliott, *Praying the Kingdom*, 117.
7. Elliott, *Praying the Kingdom*, 118.
8. For a classic attempt to clarify this theme, see Gustaf Aulén, *Christus Victor*, trans. A. G. Hebert (Macmillan, 1961 [German original, 1930]).
9. For discussion, see Michael B. Thompson, *Clothed with Christ* (JSOT Press, 1991).

INDEX